TED TURNER
The Man Behind The Mouth

TED TURNER
The Man Behind The Mouth

by Roger Vaughan

Sail Books, Inc.
BOSTON

For Norman, by air
Molly, by land
Possum, by sea

The downtown bus . . . was driven by a mustached man in a leather jacket, whose swashbuckling motions recalled the devil-may-care bomber pilots of the motion picture screen. His cap, its wire frame removed, clung rakishly to the back of his oily head, as he guided his huge machine down the runway for another take off. . . . The phantasies of the passengers were suspended, as they tore through clouds, shuddered at air pockets, dove low over landmarks. From their empty faces, none of the passengers resented the driver's incursion into their own phantastical domains: watching his weaving back they appeared to respect his right to perform in allegory, to redeem, as best his numb imagination would permit him, the absurdity of reality.

—The Recognitions *by William Gaddis*

CONTENTS

ACKNOWLEDGMENTS

It was a pleasure working with Russ Hoyle, who edited this book, and with Bob Mamis, who had the perception.

Richie Boyd compiled the chart of Ted Turner's sailing record which appears on pages 178 through 183.

The following have provided various indispensable goods and services with uncommon style: Jackie Taylor, Winnie Bell, John Leventhal, Jerry Russo, Joe Rocchio, Wedad Stephan, Ray Souza, Crow Balzano, Ruben Gorewitz, John Perkins, Ben Wilke, Paul Borges, Kitty and George Barnett, Dee Woods, Phyllis Collins, Paul Larsen, H. N. Wilcox Co., Carlo Porfini, The Commons Lunch, Amore Pizza, Concept Builders, and the All-Girl Bank.

Rhoda Weyr, Doug Stewart, Jon Sallet, Kim Vancil, Norah Van Fliess, F. Ivan and Pearl Vaughan, Jeff Hammond, Barry Feinstein, Roger Vaughan Jr., Jay Sisson, Coll and Juanita Walker, Johanne Killeen, George Germon, Bill and Carole Watman, Roger Davis, Stephen Wilson, Jack LaFond, Steve Westheimer, Barry and Marcia Farrell, Irene Kubota Neves, Tom Kelly and Judy O'Sullivan, Chuck and Mary Rapoport, Jim Gaffney, Dick and Dory Bradley, Roger Adler, Mike Ryan and Denise Dunn-Ryan, Bob Derecktor, Manny Cavacas, Commodore Tompkins, Mike Drew, and Anne Madden have contributed general life sustenance by their very presence.

PROLOGUE

THE LIGHTS WENT OUT just before dessert. Newport, Rhode Island, was definitely being taxed beyond its capacity. A few evenings earlier another restaurant farther up Thames Street on the waterfront had suffered a sewage overflow which sent patrons scurrying. Now Newport's power had failed for the second time since the America's Cup trials began in June.

At Christie's sprawling seafood restaurant on the docks one dines by candlelight and the kitchen is gas-fired, so power wasn't critical. Waitresses scurried around with more candles for each table, brass uprights supporting a red glass globe inside which the candle burned. Ted Turner began tapping the red globe with his finger the minute the waitress set it down. It made a dull clunk each time his finger hit it. From Turner, it was an unmistakable sign of boredom.

Robert E. "Ted" Turner is a multimillionaire sportsman and businessman from Atlanta, Georgia. At the age of 24, when his father shot himself, Ted chose to put his back firmly against the wall by retaining the overextended outdoor advertising business his father was negotiating to sell when he took his life. He could have liquidated the business and indulged his passion—sailing—but he wondered what he would *do* with his life if he let the business get away. Just sailing, he knew, would not be enough. So he went deeply in debt to buy the business back. Then, while beginning to pile up one of the most impressive ocean racing records ever, Turner formed a second company, Turner Communications, which, through an astounding series of mergers and acquisitions, grew to include radio and television stations, and most recently two professional sports teams, the Atlanta Hawks and the Atlanta Braves.

Born in 1938, Ted Turner is handsome, loud, opinionated, arrogant; a self-styled Rhett Butler. His head is large, his features well sculpted and angular. His face is tremendously expressive, a touch sullen in repose, with a great, beaming childlike smile in delight. He is 6′ 2″, and stays lean by excluding bread and potatoes from his diet. His dark hair, which sets off light blue eyes, has been dusted with gray since college days. Women love him. Women want to meet him like they want to meet movie stars—and many have.

After a heavy lobster dinner preceded by drinks and accompanied by wine, Turner looked weary. It had already been a long summer. Skippering *Courageous,* Turner had won the June trials with a 7–1 record. With the July trials almost over, his record was now 14–5. There had been a lot of sailing, a lot of socializing, a lot of conjecture over Turner's supposed popularity with the New York Yacht Club Selection Committee, and a lot of politicking—in short, a lot of candlelit dinners.

"This is a real pressure cooker," Turner said, losing interest in the candle and staring at the ceiling. "It was almost easier last time. This time the grind of competition is fierce, it wears you down." He looked back into the table and his features were drawn.

"Last time" was 1974, the previous America's Cup defense trials in Newport. Trials are held for U.S. hopefuls in June, July, and August. Each set of trials lasts a week to ten days.

During the August trials, one boat is selected to defend the Cup. Also in August, the foreign contenders race off against one another, with the winner of that series becoming the September challenger.

The America's Cup business—and it is a business—is always a long, draining, taxing experience. It has to be the true sport of kings. No other non-commercially-funded effort costs so much and returns so little. A racehorse at least can win a purse now and then and maybe a stud fee later on. A new, state-of-the-art 12-meter yacht is often slow, and even a winning one breeds nothing but storage and maintenance fees.

The America's Cup defense is a team effort. A small syndicate of wealthy backers first selects a manager, designer, builder, and skipper. Counting sailmakers, the staff at the huge, rented syndicate mansion, the land-based project engineers, tender-drivers and mates, crew, wives, and (most recently) security guards, at full strength the support group for an individual boat numbers close to a hundred people.

The principals involved must not only suspend jobs, educational pursuits, or other career projects for six months, but must abandon life styles to become part of a homogeneous, genteel group with military-academy bearing. They eat together at appointed hours in the house mess hall, dress according to the syndicate manager's dictum, and hope to make a favorable impression on the God-like New York Yacht Club Selection Committee on land as well as on the race course.

Those who submit to the dictatorial social rigors of a Newport mansion turned into America's Cup syndicate prep-school dormitory, one should remember, are not only adults often with family and professional responsibilities, but people who have usually achieved a large measure of success in life as sailors, businessmen, or both. They are used to *being* the authority, not conforming to it.

Winning, one can shrug off the often forced, inevitably awkward, sometimes intimidating social restrictions of the defense effort. Losing, one tends to choke on them. And last time, Turner lost big. It was a disaster, in fact. Step one was putting a brand new boat together, *Mariner* by name. Step two was the sailing of the boat, the development of a precision crew, and the evolution of fast sails. *Mariner*, a radical design that turned out to be slow, never got beyond step one. All summer the crew played catch up. Sailing and racing never really began. During the July trials, *Mariner* was in the boat yard being cut apart, redesigned, and put back together. In August the boat kept losing, and Turner was fired from the helm, something that often happens to losing skippers in August. His replacement, his tactician Dennis Conner, lost the last four races the boat sailed.

This time Turner was running in front. The two new boats, *Independence,* designed and skippered by Marblehead sailmaker Ted Hood, and the Olin Stephens–designed *Enterprise,* skippered by San Diego sailmaker Lowell North, were winning occasionally, but mostly they were doing well just to keep up with Turner's four-year-old *Courageous.*

This was a surprising turn of events. Amid the hope that the state of the art is advancing, the new boats are always slight favorites at the outset, and Hood and North had been receiving the lion's share of pre-race attention. The confrontation between these two very accomplished helmsmen—who also run neck and neck for number one in sailmaking—was being billed as the match-up of the century. Turner's entry into the competition was considered makeshift at best.

But while North seemed preoccupied experimenting with breakthrough sail design, and Hood was continuing to make unsettling crew changes day after day, Turner came out with an old sail inventory and a solid crew on a proven boat (*Courageous* won the Cup in 1974) and went sailboat racing. It wasn't easier last time. He was winning, and he was loving it.

"You know," Turner said, "getting axed last time was the best thing that could have happened to me. Because it was an opportunity to show I could function under adverse circumstances." (Turner had urged his crew to keep sailing with Conner for the good of the effort, then he had taken the helm of the even slower trial horse *Valiant* and put his heart into it.) "It was a chance to show the boat was slow."

Someone at the table wondered why, after the painful ordeal of 1974, Turner would want to do the America's Cup again.

"Because," he said, and he wasn't joking, "for years I have had to prove myself in increasing circles of competition. The reason I have to do this is my latent inferiority complex, and frankly I am beginning to think the whole deal is full of crap." Turner's frequent cryptic self-appraisals always shock with their unmistakable ring of truth and casual, matter-of-fact delivery.

Two men carrying drinks came into the dining room from the direction of the bar. They peered around the room, spotted Turner, and made their way to the table. They were middle-aged workingmen, prompted by several beers to shake Turner's hand. Baseball fans, they talked about the Braves and told Turner they rooted for him every day of the week. Turner quickly shifted gears and thanked them in a folksy, down-home way, and they left flushed with their good fortune.

Owning a baseball team was such a boy's dream. Did Turner appreciate that?

"Sort of," he said, pumped up a bit by the recognition. "But you know what I do dig? Being a folk hero. Because I am just one of the folk." The pronouncement was spoken in slow, delicious Atlanta tones. His smile was large and pasted on, revealing the space between his front teeth, a design detail that fits nicely there in the center right below the neatly clipped mustache, visually leading the observer straight down to the deep, perfectly centered chin dimple. He chuckled in his throat with contagious amusement at the notion of Ted Turner, folk hero.

Turner picked up the spring-loaded metal cracker he had used to dismember the two boiled lobsters he had just eaten and began fooling with it. He held one leg of the tool steady, drew the other leg to it, and snapped at the salt shaker, knocking it over. Then he drew a bead on his empty wine glass (clink).

"People like me, they really do. (Clink.) How about Jimmy Carter for two terms, then me for two? (Clink.) I could do it if I wanted to."

Turner misjudged the swing of the cracker arm. The wine glass shattered with a marvelous and surprising sound. Pieces of glass were arranged around the base like petals fallen from a flower. The waitress arrived as Turner was taking aim at the red globe of the candle. She scolded him.

"Hey," he said, spreading his hands, appealing to us for support and understanding, "it's not my fault we had a blackout."

TED TURNER
The Man Behind The Mouth

The Fray

THE MORNING OF THE FIRST RACE of the June observation trials in Newport, Ted Turner threw up three times walking from the house to the dock. Athletes who participate in dangerous, hair-raising events—downhill skiers, hockey goalies, luge racers, etc.—have been known to vomit before every race or game as a response to the adrenal excess produced to carry them past physical fear to successful performance. The fact that racing sailboats—even the 12-meters of America's Cup competition with their big gear and awesome stress loads—is not particularly dangerous to life and limb indicates the extreme degree to which Turner was psyched for winning the Cup. By his own hand he had created, over the years, an operating environment for himself in Newport that contained enough adversity, controversy, hostility, hero worship, and pure confusion even for Ted Turner. Like a mad scientist in a science fiction late show, he gleefully fastened the electrodes to his temples and threw the switch. This was the moment he had been waiting for.

3

Coaches who understand desire would have been pleased to send Turner into the fray. He was ready. He wanted it bad.

Perhaps the primary stimulus was that Turner had lost in 1974. It wasn't just a loss. It was nearly a disgrace. Turner in any situation is so visible that his losses, as well as his wins, are momentous. And from the outside, the whole *Mariner* caper in 1974 was a *McHale's Navy* laugher. From inside it was painful. Dissension within the syndicate was obvious, and it was difficult to single out any of the principals who were performing well. Turner carried on in his usual loud, brash way, hiring an airplane during the July trials when *Mariner* was being rebuilt to tow a banner announcing that the boat would be back, satisfying the press with memorable quotes comparing *Mariner's* troubles to various stages of German infantry campaigns, and climbing aboard the slow trial horse *Valiant* after his dismissal from *Mariner's* helm with a smile and a song and his best cigar forward. But his grace in defeat couldn't hide the pain.

The sailing slump Turner entered after *Mariner* was short-lived. Within four months he was winning his class in the Southern Ocean Racing Circuit (SORC) in a chartered boat, and doing well in the spring races on Long Island Sound. But for once he was keeping a low profile, perhaps to conceal the psychological damage he was working to repair. The criticism that he did well in the ocean, where stamina and endurance count heavily, but not on the closed course, where cooler heads prevail, brought on a crisis of self-doubt about his leadership ability and his sailing talent that nagged at him like an abscessed tooth. It was a crisis severe enough to stagger many men permanently. For Turner, it bore the seeds of resolution.

Controversy rides shotgun with Turner no matter what the situation. His voice has no soft pedal. His forthright, often startling behavior is impossible to ignore. Like a skunk at a lawn party, it forces one's attention, first of all, and creates anxiety by eliminating any neutral position. Those who are brushed by

Turner's presence—even long distance, via the mass media—are either for him or against him, with feeling.

Hence the element of hero worship this time. Never has the man in the street been as captivated by the usually mundane America's Cup races as he was in 1977. People whose interests are normally consumed by pennant races, softball leagues, and bowling scores began following Turner, rooting for Turner, in fact. They could finally relate to somebody out there on the horizon. "Hey, he's the guy who told [Baseball Commissioner] Bowie Kuhn's lawyer he'd give him a knuckle sandwich. Right on—go get 'em, Teddy baby." One afternoon in June the girlfriend of a local fisherman spotted Turner standing alone for a moment not far from Bannister's Wharf, where *Courageous* was berthed. She ran up to him: "Hey, aren't you Teddy Tucker, the captain of the *Outrageous*?"

When one attempts to defend the America's Cup, one does so with the blessing of the New York Yacht Club or not at all. The skipper of the defender, for instance, should be a member of the New York Yacht Club. That isn't a hard and fast rule—in the old days the Cup boats were often skippered by professionals—but since competition in the smaller 12-meter sloops began in 1958, every skipper has been a member. And make no mistake: the club is still an exclusive, venerable, powerful, and traditionally bigoted organization. Its sole clubhouse is a grand building on West 44th Street in Manhattan.

Turner had entered the world of big-boat racing with the same fervor with which he attacks any new project. He won the Southern Ocean Racing Circuit his second year out. Then he got roaring drunk. Then he crowed about it in *Sports Illustrated*: "I don't think my boat is that much better than the others. We're just a bunch of dumb Georgians who don't know nothing about this ocean racing business, but look what we did."

In 1975, when he was named skipper of *Mariner,* it was necessary Turner be admitted to the club. Necessary because admission would constitute a blessing—acceptability—without which it would be very difficult to raise money, for one thing. The first time around, Turner didn't make it. His name was put up again. Letters against his acceptance were written (one member says more than 20 letters were written, but officials at the yacht club deny this), and inside the club there was a political pull-haul which has been publicly smoothed over. "Too much has been made of Turner's difficulty getting in," Commodore Robert McCullough said when asked. "Other people who made it have had a tougher time than he did." Turner made it on the second try. He responded by pinning his new NYYC burgee to the rise of the blue and white striped engineer's cap he wears sailing.

In the spring of 1977 when it was too early to judge accurately the relative merits of the three American boats (*Enterprise* was still on the coast), it was possible to conclude after a dozen or so serious races off Marblehead that Turner and *Courageous* were more than holding their own against Ted Hood's *Independence*. Don MacNamara, a former America's Cup helmsman and one of the anti-Turner letter writers, was convinced there was no way Turner would be selected to defend. "If he *is* selected," MacNamara said, "he will be the first skipper in the history of the Cup to appear on the starting line wearing a muzzle."

As the trials began, even with George Hinman as chairman of the selection committee—a dignified gentleman of the old school who had previously stuck his neck out for Turner, and who openly admired the courage and loyalty Turner had displayed during the deluge of 1974—it was damn near impossible to find knowledgeable people willing to express confidence in Turner's chances.

The yachting press was having a field day with rumors that the selection committee would appear on the race course wearing motorcycle boots and skinny-leg blue jeans before they would select Turner. "We chuckled over that," Bob McCullough says. "If we did have a problem with Turner, we would have told his syndicate to get another man. We couldn't have members putting up a lot of money to sponsor a boat that was the object of prejudice or ill-feeling from the start."

Hostility was also coming from within the Kings Point Syndicate, which was sponsoring Ted Hood's *Independence* and *Courageous.* This was perhaps something Turner hadn't bargained for. It was low-key hostility at first, but it would build throughout the summer in direct proportion to the degree of success Ted Turner enjoyed on the race course. The hostility was present in the ominous, hulking form of Alfred Lee Loomis Jr., syndicate manager.

Loomis stands 6′ 4″, weighs around 230, and appears even larger because of the mass of his shoulders and large head. His hair is clipped Marine-Corps short, and he has a drill sergeant's demeanor to match. He has the unnerving, steely-eyed smile of a James Bond villain. As an old sailing acquaintance says, Loomis is a tough customer, he has a mind of his own. He is so big he can literally swing his weight around and rarely hesitates to do so. For all his success in the business and sailing worlds, Loomis hasn't exactly left a glowing wake astern. A younger relative characterizes him as "something of a drunk, something more (when in the former condition, at least) of a bully, and altogether no favorite of mine."

At first glance, it appeared the heavy-handed Loomis might steamroller Turner. But it became clear quickly that Loomis was the kind of brick-wall adversary Turner relishes.

In the 1974 defense effort, Turner's boss was George Hinman, who ran the syndicate like a benevolent grandfather. Turner's reaction to Hinman's soft-spoken, elder-statesman approach was a reversion to military school manners and almost total deferral. He addressed Hinman exclusively by his title—commodore—never George, and spent the summer inventing rationales to support Hinman's often shaky game plan. Turner remarked at the outset of that campaign that everything was working great. "We may have chains on," he said at the time, "but they are chains of gold."

It didn't work, in fact. Turner was out of step from the very beginning. Golden chains don't suit folk heroes.

This time, Turner lined up his ducks carefully. He had the boat he wanted, the crew he wanted, and with meticulous attention to detail, Turner was stirring the big pot himself, stirring and tasting, spicing it *au piquant,* cackling mischievously as he added logs to the fire, until the mix was to his exclusive specifications. He didn't care who else liked it. This one was for him.

Loomis was going to work out just fine: here was an openly combative, aggressive authority figure with whom it would be a pleasure to lock horns.

Turner is a man who always keeps a weather eye open for sturdy, overly confident antagonists. Such people provide essential foils for his favorite, back-against-the-wall position, targets for the psychological warfare at which he is so adept. They are critical to his overall game plan. Complementing his other qualifications for the role, Lee Loomis's background and station in life were in almost perfect discordance with Turner's Southern Rebel.

Lee Loomis was born to the purple. His great-grandfather was a nineteenth-century tuberculosis specialist. His grandfather was a prominent New York City physician. His father attained prominence in three fields: law, banking, and science. His father's work in the precise measurement of time and in the analysis of brain waves and sound waves brought him into collaboration with the leading scientific figures of the day, Vannevar Bush, Enrico Fermi, and others. He was a motivating force in the development of radar and held the basic patents for loran. He was involved in the Manhattan project and was an original member of the Rand Corporation think tank. He was elected to the National Academy of Science.

Alfred Lee Loomis Sr. was a compassionate elitist whose closest associates were high-ranking government officials and Nobel Prize winners, a brilliant dilettante who played by rules he had written, who insisted on privacy, and who moved the nation during crises.

While sailing was something that interested his father only in terms of scientific experimentation, Lee Jr. took up the sport with passion. The financial independence which came to Lee at age 18 (his father divided his estate early, figuring the boys would make smaller mistakes at 18 than at 30 or 40) allowed him to indulge in boats. In his twenties, he was winning in 8-meters, and while sailing in England when he was 23 he was to steer *Endeavor I,* the huge J-boat which had challenged unsuccessfully for the America's Cup in 1934, against the new *Endeavor II* in a trial regatta. He won.

It is difficult to imagine a comparable thrill for a 23-year-old today. With the passage of time the breathtaking J-boats have attained mythical status with their 180-foot masts, 130-foot hulls, 7500 square feet of sail, displacement of 160 tons, and their born-to-the-manor afterguards. The real thing had to be a boy's dream of unattainable proportions, even for one born to the manor.

A few years later (1938—Lee was then 25), after Lee had finished Harvard and Harvard Law School, his father presented him with a new 12-meter sloop, *Northern Light,* which he successfully campaigned as the youngest skipper in a fleet of seven on Long Island Sound. "The 12-meter came about," Loomis recalls, "because both father and I felt there was a war coming. He said one day he had the feeling he might never see me again. What was there to do, he wondered. I had been sailing a 12-

meter that year and getting beaten, so I said to him, why not build a 12-meter, give it to me, and I'll invite you to be my navigator."

In 1948, Loomis was a member of the 6-meter crew out of the cloistered Seawanaka Yacht Club that won the Olympic Gold Medal. In the fifties and sixties he began to concentrate on ocean racing.

Loomis interrupted his law practice in the 1940s by writing a letter to the Navy Department asking for a commission. He was convinced by the Battle of Dunkirk that the United States was going to enter the war, and he wanted in. "I told them I was a successful lawyer, that I had skippered three Bermuda Races and cruised extensively offshore. I said I thought they would need men who could handle small boats." Loomis was accepted. After a tour on an old World War I destroyer as junior officer, his legal experience moved him into the job of flag lieutenant to an admiral.

After the service, Loomis went to the investment banking firm of Smith-Barney, where he was head of the venture capital department until 1949. "I quit in 1949 and became a customer," Loomis says. "You could borrow money at $2\frac{3}{4}$ percent, and you could earn 7 percent with it. But everyone was waiting for a repeat of the Depression. I sailed in the 1950 Bermuda Race, and when I got to the Royal Bermuda Yacht Club there was a telegram waiting for me. My first oil well had come in. I started looking for a boat, and bought *Good News* with that first well."

Loomis began a lasting friendship with Ted Hood in 1956. One of Loomis's sailing rivals had suddenly begun improving his showing against *Good News,* so Loomis started asking questions. It turned out the guy had been using Hood sails.

"I went to see Hood," Loomis says. "I told him we did pretty well in the A-minus, B-plus league, and that if we made a quantum jump with his sails, a lot of business would come his way. I told him I wanted a complete set at half price."

The sails performed well for Loomis, who became one of the first big-league ocean racers to buy Hood sails. Hood gained visibility and went on to become one of the top sailmakers in the country, and the premiere builder of America's Cup sails.

Hood, who had taken over the helm of *Courageous* for the last few races in 1974 and won the Cup, was asked by the New York Yacht Club to enter the competition again in 1977. Hood said he would if he could find someone of his choice to manage the effort. He asked Loomis.

"I vowed after the summer of 1938 that I would never do the 12-meter thing again," Loomis said. We were sitting in the den of his elegant apartment on East 52nd Street, which overlooks the East River, and as he spoke his glance drifted to a huge black and white photograph of two 12-meters under spinnaker, running bow to stern in a breeze.

"The America's Cup is business, and I didn't want to dedicate that much of my life to it. It's too much of a commitment. I had been asked before and I had always said no. But Ted Hood is a friend, and said if I would help he would do it. He spoke of a new boat, and the idea was congenial to me. He's a wonderful guy to do things with. Plus the America's Cup was in danger. Here we were a year into it with a strange foreign challenge [the Swedes, an unknown quantity, were mounting a heavily sponsored effort] and nothing happening. So I agreed to do it."

Courageous was made available to Hood through the Kings Point Fund Syndicate, but Hood was set on designing a new boat. Someone had to be enlisted to skipper *Courageous,* preferably someone who would also be a large financial contributor. Loomis called Turner.

Loomis says Turner was his first choice. Others involved were advocating Dennis Conner, but, as Loomis says, "I made up my mind after all the protesting Conner did at the 1976 Congressional Cup that I didn't want him. I let people know I wasn't selecting Turner over Conner. I was simply selecting Turner. He's obviously a good sailor. He has a hell of a record; forget about *Mariner*. Next, he's a good organizer. I wanted someone to do it top to bottom, not to use Hood castoffs, and when you buy Turner, you get a crew. I wanted someone to put together an independent organization that would force Hood to do his very best. And I wanted a non-experimenter, a doer. Turner has built only a few new boats. He usually buys a proven boat. He was someone I thought could take an old boat and do his best with it. Fundamentally I like him . . . but he's a peculiar guy."

Turner had wanted *Courageous* since the day *Mariner* was eliminated in 1974. He had approached Bob McCullough, who managed the *Courageous* effort in 1974, about buying the boat well before the last Cup races were over. He had told Hood that he would be willing to sail *Courageous* against his new boat and help raise money to campaign her.

At their meeting, Loomis told Turner he wanted to talk with him about sailing one of the twelves. Turner told Loomis he was listening. "I had only met Loomis once or twice," Turner says. "I didn't know him well. But he can be a nice guy—almost charming—when he wants something.

"He said he was looking for someone to work with Ted Hood, get him geared up, and then come June, they would decide which boat Ted Hood was going to sail. Hood would have his choice. I would get the second fastest boat."

Turner told him it sounded like a nice deal. But not for him. He told Loomis he couldn't even get his crew interested if they knew they were going to be second best from the start. "I was the wrong guy. There were plenty of guys he could get who were eager to break in, eager to make it. I told him I had a baseball team I paid ten million dollars for. If I was that hot to be sailing a 12-meter I could have built one.

"He was hinting around that I was going to have to make some kind of financial commitment. So I told him what I *would* do." Turner agreed to raise the basic campaign expenses for racing, and to pay for converting *Courageous,* which weighed less than she officially should have during her victory in 1974. Assuming conversion cost $100,000 and campaigning another $250,000, Turner said he would either raise or put in $350,000. But the boat would become his to sail on June 1 no matter how Hood's boat was doing.

Loomis went back and talked to Hood, then called Turner and said the deal was acceptable. Turner made one other point. He told Loomis he didn't want to get fired, like last time. "If I was putting up the dough and sailing the trial horse, the old boat," Turner says, "I wanted to be there at the end, win, lose, or draw. So we agreed I couldn't be fired without Perry Bass's assent." Perry Bass is a wealthy Texan, something of a father figure to Turner, and well regarded by Loomis.

Loomis says involving Perry Bass was his idea. "I got a lot of advice before I signed Turner on," Loomis says, "and all of it concluded I should keep him on a tight leash. He had a strong father, a military school background, and I was told he reacted well to discipline.

"I told him I would have the right to fire him at any time, for any malfeasance on or off the boat. But I also knew that Ted irritates me from time to time, just like I irritate him. I wanted a safeguard so I wouldn't just get angry and fire him one day. Using Perry Bass as a safety valve, not a veto, was my idea. In fact I wrote an agreement, an aide memoire, just so we both knew where we stood. Turner and I signed it.

"If Turner says that isn't so," Loomis says, "tell him I'll put up $10,000 against his $10,000. If I'm wrong, it's all his."

Turner asked Loomis if there were any other little things. Loomis said there was. He said this was Ted Hood's effort, and he was doing it because he liked Hood, and that Turner had to use Hood sails.

"I told him to count me out," Turner says. "I didn't think Ted Hood would want me to be forced to buy his sails and no one else's. This was already being billed as an event between two professionals, and I was going to buy some North sails and some Hood sails. He said any North sails would have to be paid for outside the syndicate."

Loomis: "I told him he could buy North sails, but I didn't think it was a sensible way to spend money, and that we couldn't allow a man from North in our camp."

Turner: "I said okay, but that it would be nice to have one amateur out there who wasn't part of the factory team, who was doing it like it had always been done.

"So it was a deal. Loomis said he put the whole thing in writing, but I never got a copy. I told him, 'Lee, when this summer is over, you're going to like me as much as you like Ted Hood.'"

That was either wishful thinking on Turner's part, a clouding of vision caused by his desire to get his hands on the wheel of *Courageous,* or a simple lapse in judgment. Because on paper, Turner and Loomis match up as classic antagonists.

Lee Loomis epitomizes the eastern establishment ruling class Yankee, from the khaki-clad paid hands on his personal yacht who keep the varnish like mirrors and the teak the color of raw gold, to his back room, heavy-muscle way of conducting business. He speaks with some yearning of sailing 12-meters in the thirties when half the crew were paid professionals. "It made it easier with fewer personalities interfering," Loomis says. Lee Loomis is at home in large chauffeured automobiles, obscure private clubs, Long Island estates surrounded by heavy iron gates. Loomis is snobbery and elitism, arrogance and condescension. Upstart, new-money Southerners like Ted Turner would not automatically be Loomis's favorite people.

And, of course, men like Loomis are what make Turner live. If Turner is the pirate, they are his Spanish galleons. For Turner the rebel, they are the authority figures. He would enjoy eating them for breakfast. It is because of classic match-ups like Lee Loomis and Ted Turner that the United States fought a civil war.

At Newport, the Turner-Loomis conflict ran according to the script. With Turner providing the focus for more press coverage than the Cup had ever attracted, Loomis played tough guy, rousting the press from both the house and the dock, often with all the grace of a bouncer in a saloon. "If the press did what they were told and didn't try to cheat and sneak onto the dock, okay," Loomis said. "Otherwise, they were out. No second chances. If they wanted war, we could beat them."

In an earlier conversation at the Wall Street offices of Loomis's St. Vincent's Island Company, where a photograph of his old 12-meter hangs on the wall of the reception area, Loomis had said that he simply didn't want people around during the summer. He asserted his "right to privacy," and said he didn't want to catch anyone "sniffing around the edges." He said the press would be handled with a "polite minimums" in the form of releases when and if he saw fit to issue them. He likened the America's Cup competition to war: "We aren't going to tell you how we're going to win the Battle of Midway before we win it, are we? Or when we're going to bring our carriers up?" Loomis had reminded me, that day, of early John Wayne movies.

It wasn't just the press that was given a hard time in Newport. Relatives of crew members were made uncomfortable by Loomis at the house ("Who are *they* with?" he loudly inquired about nervous visiting parents one evening) and on the dock. Loomis controlled the scheduling of personnel aboard the tenders, and wives and relatives often found themselves waiting until the last minute, then running to catch a belatedly assigned boat. "He treated us like cattle," one irate *Courageous* parent said. "I guess we were supposed to kiss his feet every morning."

And there was the day Loomis raised hell about a large blue Mercedes parked in a syndicate space just outside the dock. When the puzzled owner was located, he turned out to be a syndicate contributor Loomis had told to park there the day before.

Much later, after the races were over, Loomis expanded on his right to privacy. "If the game was for profit," he said, "we would perhaps owe it to the public to be more open. But the America's Cup isn't for profit. We owe nothing to anybody. We were entitled to privacy. It was hard to do, pulling together a project of 50 people or so. You don't make good decisions in the glare of publicity."

One lazy afternoon off Newport, *Courageous* was flopping around in a calm, waiting for breeze enough to get sailing. The crew was lying about, soaking up sun, eating lunch, and listening to the bull session in the stern. "Loomis had come aboard," *Courageous* tactician Gary Jobson related, "and we had begun talking about commuting. Loomis said he used to commute, but after the Long Island Railroad cut out the club car, it was no fun. He said with the club car it had been like going to your private club for an hour on the way home, but when they took the car off he had gotten an apartment in the city because he couldn't take riding with everybody else.

"After Loomis went back to the tender, Turner couldn't get over it. He was really annoyed. He kept saying, 'Imagine that guy, too good to ride with everybody else!' "

In Newport, Loomis didn't live in Conley Hall, the Salve Regina College dormitory that had been rented to house and feed the crews of *Independence* and *Courageous*. He rented a smaller house nearby for himself and Ted Hood and their wives. But he presided over dinner each evening at Conley Hall, and exercised his authority early on by demanding jackets *and* ties for meals, personally reprimanding those who forgot.

Turner didn't pass up the chance to nail him when it came. Prior to the June trials, Loomis went aboard *Courageous* to see how things were going. He placed himself on the stern, aft of the wheel, with his feet dangling into the cockpit. It was light air, and after several diplomatic attempts were made to persuade Loomis to move his weight toward the middle of the boat, where it would have less of an effect, Turner said in his bullhorn voice, "Hey! Now I know why you named your boat *Northern Light*."

Loomis: "Why?"

Turner: "Because you're the Big Loom!"

The crew quickly faced forward, stifling laughter. The battle lines were drawn. The nickname, needless to say, stuck.

According to Turner, Loomis mounted a continuing series of threats to fire him from the helm, coupled with full-time harassment. Turner says it got to the point where he would try to eat dinner quickly and retire to his room before Loomis started in. More than one night Loomis carried the attack to Turner's room, asking Turner's wife, Jane, to excuse herself. One evening, according to Jane Turner, Loomis barged in and woke Turner up to have words with him.

When an interview given by Gary Jobson to the *New York Times* upset Loomis because of the credit for *Courageous*'s sails that Jobson gave to sailmaker and Hood vice president Robbie Doyle (they were "Hood" sails, after all), Loomis threatened Turner, saying he was responsible for what his crew said to the press.

The infighting became so severe that one syndicate contributor with good access to all parties was organized to report regularly to Turner on how the *Independence* side was faring, and mainly to learn about whatever schemes might be afoot to get him fired.

Loomis says he threatened to fire Turner just once, at Marblehead, after the third time Turner, on port tack, came dangerously close to hitting Hood, who was on starboard with right of way. Loomis didn't want to be specific about the incident, saying it would make Turner look bad. I told him I had already heard about the situation from Turner. "He likes to steer from the weather side," Loomis said, "so in crossing situations he was trusting someone else to tell him if he could make it or not. Twice Hood had to bear away to avoid collision. I told him he *had* to be to leeward in those situations and look for himself. I told him if it occurred once more he was out."

Tactician Jobson, who had been making the judgment calls, agrees it was something Loomis had a right to get angry about. But Turner took issue: "Of course, it didn't matter when Hood ran smack into a buoy while sailing out of Newport Harbor and put a big dent in the bow of his boat. If I had done that I would have been finished."

As Loomis said, "Turner was nothing but the designated skipper. Hood was technical director of the effort from the beginning."

The fact that *Courageous* was being treated second best of the two boats was obvious to the entire crew from the days she spent at Hood's Little Harbor Boatyard in Marblehead to the belated delivery of her first new sail in June. But then the new boat is always the star at first, and rightfully so. And it was easy to forget that over the long winter of 1976–77 Ted Hood had masterminded the design modification of *Courageous,* after a consultation with her original designer, Olin Stephens, that made her not only a legal 12-meter but, by general consensus, a faster one.

"It was Hood who discovered *Courageous* was a 12½-meter," Loomis said. "He was taking lines off *Courageous* and thought something was wrong. So we weighed the boats, and they weighed within 150 pounds of Hood's estimate. *Courageous* was too light. We weighed them again, as publicly as possible, of course." Loomis smiled. "Olin called and agreed to help make changes if we wanted. I said no. We didn't think that would be in our best interest. Olin obviously wanted his new boat [*Enterprise*] to be the faster. But we did discuss the possibilities with Olin.

"I won't listen to talk from Turner that he was treated inequitably," Loomis said. "During the redesign of *Courageous,* I told Turner to meet me at the Atlanta airport and I would fly to Miami with him to explain what we were doing. I told Hood we could do whatever we wanted, but I didn't want to ride roughshod over Turner. I wanted him to be happy. Then I sailed the Ocean Triangle Race on *Tenacious* [Turner's own boat]. He couldn't make the race. He had to fly back for a meeting with Bowie Kuhn." Loomis relished the memory.

"At first I was spending equal time on both boats," Loomis said. "Then after Turner did so well in June, he told me he was all set, that I should concentrate my time on *Independence.* So I took him at his word and did that. It was obvious he didn't want me on the boat. He may say I was partisan toward Hood, but after June he never invited me on *Courageous.* I could always ask and go, but the invitations stopped. Don't let Ted sell you the story he was a poor boy being plotted against. Part of his act is to be the underdog."

What ultimately rankled Loomis was Turner's visit to the Maritime Academy at Kings Point, New York, the day after he was selected to defend the Cup. The purpose of his visit was to work on securing *Courageous* for himself for the Cup defense in 1980. "I was never really disappointed in Turner until that happened," Loomis said. "For him to go to Kings Point on the sly and try to undercut me was complete disloyalty. If he wanted to be his own boss, okay. But he could have waited until it was over."

Rumors abounded that Loomis made at least one serious effort to fire Turner from the helm of *Courageous.* But the New York Yacht Club is a private, protective place where the word "classified" is freely used to cover a multitude of technical, political, and personal information. That and the international power politics of the America's Cup make such rumors impossible to confirm. No one, in other words, will speak for attribution. But why, one wonders, if Loomis had the written, if arbitrated, power to fire Turner, didn't he simply exercise it—if indeed that had become his wish?

For one thing, Turner is a well-established figure in the press. Like it or not, Loomis would have been forced to operate in public, and against a proven manipulator of the media. Turner had kept 'em smilin' with his threat of a "knuckle sandwich" to Baseball Commissioner Bowie Kuhn's lawyer during hearings in April. And he stunned 'em just prior to that with his widely reported foot-in-mouth breakfast speech to the eighteenth awards meeting of the National Sportscasters and Sportswriters Association in Salisbury, N.C., when he prefaced his explanation of why he didn't like baseball agent Jerry Kapstein by saying, "After all, you should have some reason to dislike a guy besides the fact he wears a full length fur coat and is a Jew." The New York Yacht Club was reportedly up in arms over the remark. Members wrote letters demanding Turner's removal from the club, which is a marvelous irony: Jewish membership in the club is less than two dozen, yet it could be suggested that a member be thrown out for maligning that group. Ahh, righteous indignation.

Then Turner gave 'em all a fine story when he launched the Atlanta Braves ball club—including Hank "Old Salt" Aaron— on the choppy race course to watch the action, with room on the boat for press. It wasn't all good public relations, but he was keeping everyone's attention. If Turner was removed from the helm of *Courageous,* he would leave like an atom bomb.

And of course Turner began winning big from the outset. It would be neither popular nor politic to fire the frontrunning skipper.

If indeed Loomis did want to get rid of Turner, he had to have an issue, something more flagrant than the port-starboard incidents, and disgraceful enough to turn the heads of the selection committee. But Turner was on pretty good behavior. Despite a few scurrilous attempts by the press to cash in on Turner's flamboyant image and a local weekly advertiser headline calling Turner "America's Bad Boy," he wasn't appearing in public much, and when he did, with a few minor exceptions, it was a low-profile scene. Then came the incident at Bailey's Beach just after the June trials.

The Spouting Rock Beach Association, better known as Bailey's Beach, is a private beach club in Newport with facilities for drinking, dining, and dancing as well as bathing. It is one of the remaining vestiges of old-school Newport society. Because of a mix-up between Dee Woods, Turner's secretary in Atlanta, and Jane Turner, who together were screening the scores of social invitations coming in, the Turners found they had inadvertently accepted the invitation of a couple from Atlanta who were summering in Newport. The invitation was for cocktails at their house, then on to a dinner at Bailey's Beach. The Turners didn't know the people, but by the time the misunderstanding was uncovered, it was too late to back out. Ted had vaguely recalled them. They had called previously, asking if they might watch a race. Turner obliged the fellow Atlantans by putting them on board an observation craft with the Braves.

The evening became a memorable one, mainly because of the excessive conjecture lavished upon the events by opportunistic news reporters, none of whom were present. But, it's really Turner's story to tell:

"First of all, I planned to leave early anyway. I normally went to bed at ten, and as I recall, the Braves were playing in Houston, starting about 8:30, and I wanted to see that game.

"When we got to their house, they pulled out 10 or 15 copies of *Sports Illustrated* with me on the cover and wanted me to sign them, which I did. And they were obviously people that—well, they showed me pictures of other famous people they had been photographed with. I mean, they were celebrity hounds. We got to Bailey's Beach around 7:30, and I'd already had about three or four vodka and tonics by then. Another cocktail party was just starting up, and dinner was slated for 9:00 or 9:30, which was bad news to me, so I had another drink or two.

"This couple took us around and introduced us to people as though we were lifelong friends, 'my friend from Atlanta,' 'the owner of the Atlanta Braves,' and I think I may have said after the fourth or fifth time that I wished they would tell the truth and say 'an acquaintance,' because I didn't know them at all.

"We'd already spent almost two hours amusing and entertaining our hosts before the cocktail party, and they'd taken two rolls of film of me with each of them, all this just because they were going to take us to dinner, and because I wanted to be polite. But then, when I started talking to Bruno Bich, the woman dragged me away to go meet some other people. They sort of wanted me to stand at the door with them and greet people as they came in.

"I began to get a little pissed off, okay, after about 25 forced introductions by this couple who wouldn't leave me alone. I didn't know if the other people wanted to meet me or not, and I don't like being shown off like a prize bull. At the time, I'd been in the limelight a lot, and I thought I was going to be able to get away from people down on the docks grabbing at me. Bailey's is a sophisticated group. I had been there before, and believe it or not, I was looking forward to a low-profile evening. This was turning into the highest-profile deal around."

Turner allows that he might have been just a little rude to his hosts in front of other people as a way to discourage them.

"There was an element of truth in one thing. I was introduced by these people to a highly painted lady who was sort of attractive, in her twenties or thirties. Her escort had to be in his mid-sixties. And it was 'miss' and 'mister,' so I assumed they were dating. I've always been amused by couples like that. It's usually a goofy old guy, who often has money, and some chick who's looking for more than romance and companionship. It just doesn't make much sense for somebody to marry a guy who's going to be dead in ten years when she's hitting her prime.

"Anyway, while he was talking to someone else, I was talking to her, and I didn't feel anyone was overhearing the conversation. And she wasn't his wife, she was a date, she was open; you can say anything you want to a date. And because I like to conduct surveys on this subject, I said, 'What are you doing with somebody so much older than you?' She said she enjoyed spending his money. And I said, 'Do you get enough lovin'?' And she said, 'From that old prune? I'm horny as hell.' And I said, 'Well, maybe we could arrange to have something done about that.' Or words to that effect. That was as far as it went. And I was thinking as much about lining her up for my younger crewmen, who were single, my virile young crewmen who were having trouble, as anything else.

"That is as far as the conversation went, except for one thing. Of all the people in the room other than Bruno Bich, who I had been dragged away from a couple times, I had finally met someone I was at least having an amusing conversation with. So I asked the Atlanta woman, since Janie and I were going to be split up at the dinner seating anyway, if I could sit at the same table with whoever this woman was. She said no, it wasn't planned that way. So now we get into the interesting part. I hadn't had a thing to eat, it was now 9:30, and after a bunch of drinks I was kind of P.O.'ed.

"Naturally I was seated next to the Atlanta woman, and as dinner began she said something about the woman I had been talking to, 'Aren't they a lovely couple' or words to that effect. And I said, 'What do you mean by that? I've always thought it was kind of silly to go out with someone that distant in age.' And she said, 'Well, not in this particular instance—they love each other so much, and they're planning to be married.' And I said, 'Well, she loves him for his money, I can tell you that.' And she said, 'Oh, you don't say, how do you know that?' And I said, 'Because she told me so!' Well, she was really in a huff after that."

Turner then left the table. He had to go to the bathroom. While there he decided rather than go back and risk saying any more things that might irk his hostess, the best thing to do was just leave. "The ball game was on, we were just sitting down to a dinner that would take an hour and a half, four courses, with people I didn't know, and I had drunk too much, and I realized at that point I shouldn't have said anything. I didn't go back in, that would have been worse. I didn't say anything to Janie, knowing she would find her way home. I just left.

"And that is the story. Oh, I might have said the younger woman was looking for a man to service her. Maybe I said that in front of eight people. But they were all adults. Apparently when the hostess found out I had left, she threw a fit and left the dinner. Now there is the other part of the story. Her husband stayed at the party, took Janie home, and made a pass at her. How about that?

"I am always unhappy to make someone unhappy, but they had made *me* unhappy. I mean, if I had committed murder don't you think it would have been judged justifiable homicide after three and a half hours? Maybe, *maybe* I said the younger woman was looking to get fucked, but all those people were married with children, after all.

"One of the most popular stories that came out was that I had said something about being willing to fix up some old broads who needed to get drilled. Now does that sound like me? I don't like drilling old broads!" Turner was indignant.

There are but a few additions and notations to the story. One: it should be pointed out that for all his other capacities—tenacity, energy, endurance—Ted Turner is a cheap drunk. Two beers or a couple of drinks is enough to cast him off. A few more and he sinks fast. Two: the dinner was in fact causing him to miss a pleasurable appointment that evening, and chances are he would have ended up in bed, watching the ball game. For all his posturing about being truthful, and for all his amazing ability to face up to the truth, Turner has his lapses. But his lies tend to be white ones, more omissions and colorations than blatant rearrangements. As he is fond of saying about his honesty, "In the world of the blind, the one-eyed man is king."

The last notation concerns the couple from Atlanta. Turner couldn't remember their name, but as he described them I knew I had met them during the course of the summer. A bit of checking sharpened the recollection. I met them before the June trials at the *Enterprise* syndicate house. The majority of *Enterprise* personnel were Californians, and quiet evenings at home in June for the crew were wonderfully comfortable and informal. A few pre-dinner drinks in shirt sleeves one evening were interrupted by the entrance of a matronly woman in her fifties, dressed in a floor-length, vivid blue caftan with trimmings. Conversation stopped and people were speechless for a moment as this creation flowed across the marble floor of the spacious imitation–Italian Renaissance ballroom of the rented mansion, past larger-than-life statues and lush fruit trees—the place was tailor-made for dramatic entrances. (A tenant once used it as the setting for a feature-length pornographic movie, much to the owner's dismay.) The woman beamed at us and began to speak. I wondered if a local amateur thespian group had arrived to rehearse a Lawrence Welk skit.

In gushing tones, she introduced herself, and then with sweeping hand gestures, her husband and son, who were trailing a number of paces behind her, single file. The younger crew members suddenly remembered appointments at the pool table. Syndicate stalwarts quickly regained their composure as hosts. The visitors were potential *Enterprise* contributors (their potential was never realized). They were from Atlanta. They belonged to Bailey's Beach. Turner recognized their name in a flash. They were the same couple.

Loomis, who was not at the party, was outraged by reports of Turner's behavior. There were threats. He told Turner he wished he were a dog, so he could beat him. He demanded Turner write a letter to Bailey's Beach. Turner did:

Dear Mr. Winslow:

It has come to my attention that my conduct at the party, July 2nd, at the Spouting Rock Beach Association may have been bothersome to some of your fine members. If this is the case, I wish to apologize profusely because I certainly did have a couple of drinks too many that Saturday night.

I, as all of the America's Cup competitors, am tremendously appreciative and respectful of the wonderful hospitality of your fine club.

Please accept my sincere apologies.

> Very truly yours,
> Ted Turner

John Winslow, head of Bailey's Beach, returned the letter:

Dear Ted:

Thank you very much for your friendly letter of August 12th. We do enjoy having all the *Independence* and *Courageous* syndicate at the Beach, and it is our hope that the Beach is a place to relax on a lay day. We all appreciate what an exhaustive schedule you have.

Each year the Association holds a small informal dance on the Saturday nearest to July 4th. This is a private party and has no official status in any way. A review of those attending the party on July 2nd, reveals that my friend Vice Commodore Harry Anderson was present as a member rather than in his official capacity. You and your wife were not here as a member of the Syndicate but as the personal guests of ———, who wanted to entertain you, being fellow residents of Atlanta.

Under the rules any complaints must be made in writing to either the President, Chairman of the Executive Committee, or the Board of Governors. A search of the records does not indicate any complaints were made about the July 2nd party. A meeting of the Board of Governors was held on July 16, 1977, at which I presided. No complaints were brought up, verbally or written. The matter referred to in your letter was not even mentioned.

Your letter reminds me of the story of President Lincoln and his cabinet. Several cabinet members complained that General Grant drank too much. After thinking a few minutes President Lincoln replied, "Find out the brand of whiskey he drinks and give it to the other Generals."

We do hope that you realize that you and your lovely wife and children are always welcome at the Beach.

Good luck to you in the days ahead and may you have clear sailing with a fair wind at your back.

With warmest personal regards,

Sincerely,
John G. Winslow
President

Turner knew he had come close to jeopardizing his job at the helm of *Courageous* by creating a rather large scene, regardless of extenuating circumstances. He took it to heart and curtailed his social life even more. He didn't even attend the America's Cup Ball. He was keeping his head down.

Loomis and Hood were using intimidation and fear to whip the crew of *Independence* into shape. As late as July, whenever *Independence* left the dock she would carry two more than her allotted crew of 11. When it came time to go sailing, after being towed to the practice area, two men would then be asked to leave the boat. Perhaps Loomis simply thought the same techniques would work on the *Courageous* skipper, who was admittedly a tough guy to control. Loomis protests as much: "I spent a hell of a lot of time taking care of Turner. Until the end he was conscious of it." And maybe Loomis was right.

Turner arrived in Newport with strong sailing momentum. The previous fall he had done well the few times he had gone to Marblehead to race against Ted Hood. *Courageous* had yet to be converted at that point, and the crew was makeshift, but Turner had obviously regained some of his old confidence. And just to make sure the folks at Ted Hood's Little Harbor Boat Yard knew he was around, just to make sure they didn't forget him in between racing weekends, he rented and had trucked from Florida a large, kidney-shaped fiberglass object that took up five precious parking spaces in the small, extremely crowded yard. It was an earth receiving station for Turner's Channel 17, WTCG/Atlanta, which enabled him to keep track of his ball team's misfortunes.

Turner had purchased a gorgeous five-year-old Sparkman and Stephens 60-foot sloop in the fall. Turner changed her name to *Tenacious* (she became his second boat with that name) and had "USA" plastered across the stern. She is a powerful, sleek-hulled beauty with amenities as well as good speed. When Turner bought her, she came with a couple of Chicago–Mackinac wins under her belt and a decent showing in several Bermuda Races. He bought the boat for a number of reasons. First, she was a proven winner. The boat is the exhaustive work of Lee Williams, a Chicago engineering genius, who spent six years fussing with computers to come up with a boat that would not be hurt by changes in the fickle racing rules.

Tenacious is approximately the same size and weight as a 12-meter, which is another reason Turner wanted her. If he was going to campaign a twelve, he wanted to get used to maneuvering and steering a boat with comparable characteristics, gear, and sails. *Tenacious* is also a yacht. She is nicely finished below, and she sleeps ten. There is a private cabin aft for captain and navigator, a comfortable eating salon, and two heads.

She would make an acceptable summer home in Newport for Jimmy Brown, a rotund, sharp-tongued black man who had worked for Turner's father before him, and Ted's children, and an adequate spectator craft for visiting firemen.

In January, 1977, Turner took the boat south for the SORC. *Tenacious* and *Running Tide,* a slightly older dame of comparable grandeur, proceeded to have one of the greatest head-to-head duels in anyone's memory. When it was all over, *Tide* had won by half a point.

Next was the Congressional Cup, the annual primo match-racing event held in Long Beach, California, sailed in Cal 40 boats loaned by Long Beach Yacht Club members and assigned by lottery. The boats are as identical as possible, and sails and gear are standardized. It is like racing big dinghies, *mano a mano.*

The Congressional Cup is always an important sailing event. Eliminations are tough, and to fill out the list of ten skippers, invitations are extended with care. The 1977 Congressional Cup was an international who's who of 12-meter skippers. Hood, North, and Turner would be there; so would Pelle Petterson, the Swedish skipper, and Noel Robbins of Australia. It was to be a good Cup preview.

But Turner beat all four rival 12-meter skippers, and lost only two races of the nine he sailed. Tony Parker, an Annapolis sailor who finished a frustrating second in the Congressional Cup for the third straight year, said he saw a noticeable difference in Turner's behavior on the race course. "A few years ago," Parker said, "if a couple things went wrong, Ted would turn into a nervous wreck. You could hear him yelling all over the race course. Then he would start this hacking cough. It was a trademark. He has been known to cough up blood. In our race this year I beat him at the start. We were ahead and to weather, and I was listening for the cough to start. But I took a look back and his boat was quiet. He was just sitting there steering, he was cool. He had a little boat speed on us, we made a mistake or two, and he got us."

In his seventh try, he had won the Congressional Cup, and it couldn't have come at a better time. Momentum! I was working on a magazine piece about Ted Hood and Lowell North at the time, and when Turner came walking down the dock, soaking wet, having been ceremoniously dunked by his crew, puffing on a big cigar, he raised his beer with a big grin and pronounced, "Vaughan, they sent you out here to cover the wrong guys."

Old Home Week

THE SECOND DAY after the July trials concluded, Turner left for Atlanta to spend a week getting reacquainted with his business, and to reflect on his suspension from baseball, which had been levied upon him by the commissioner for tampering with another team's player. July had been a little shakier than June on the race course. *Courageous* still had by far the best record, but she had lost five straight to *Enterprise,* an uncomfortable portent that North was getting it together. And June and July are really just warm-ups for August. When it comes to selecting the boat to defend the Cup, August means everything.

As he waited for Eastern flight 727 to finish boarding and depart for Atlanta, Ted Turner feasted his eyes on the sports page of the *Providence Journal* spread out on his lap. The headline was large, "Turner Switches from 12's to Dinghies, Keeps Winning," and the photograph of Ted's lanky frame squeezed into the little boat used for a good-will regatta was given good space. The story began, "When you're hot you're hot, so the saying goes, and Ted Turner continues to be the hottest sailor in Newport."

"Awright!" Turner exclaimed. "I was the only skipper who raced in that Demi-Tasse Regatta," Turner said. "But hell, the competition was good. My tactician Gary Jobson is one of the best small-boat sailors in the country. And Lowell North's son Danny is national Sabot champion. Hey—"

The chance mention of North's name launched Turner on his favorite sustained tirade of the summer: the vilification of Lowell North. Ever since Lowell North had informed Turner he would not (could not) sell him sails, Turner had been furious. Always ready to pounce into gaps in the psychological battle lines, Turner had seized the issue by the throat and, like a terrier, shaken it ferociously. He had, in fact, become obsessed by it.

"—Yeah, where were those professional sailmakers? How come they didn't race in the Demi-Tasse? North went cruising, I hear. You know, it was stupid of him not to sell me a few jibs. He would have gotten some feedback from me about them, an old and good custom. I'm not going to forget it. I'll never buy another sail from him, and I was a good customer.

"Did you know that John Marshall, who manages the North loft in Connecticut, tried to hire Jobson after he had agreed to become my tactician? He offered him a lot more money than he was making coaching sailing at Kings Point. There was one hitch: he couldn't have the summer off to sail with me.

"Their syndicate manager Ed du Moulin asked me if I had it in writing that North would sell me sails. Have it in writing? No. Since when do you need it in writing to purchase a sail? What we have here is a professional using his product to unfair advantage, and it is going to hurt him. What if Ted Hood said he wouldn't sell us sails? Then what would we do? North wants an unfair edge. Whatever happened to decency and good sportsmanship and fair play and honesty? North makes a half-million a year and what does he do for sailing? Nothing. I am overseas commodore of the Royal Ocean Racing Club, I serve on a bunch of committees. I give a lot of time. I don't know what to do with the rest of my life. Sailing has gotten so professional I don't even like it anymore."

Tom Jobson, Gary's father, compared Turner to a radio. You don't talk to him, Tom Jobson had said. You just listen to the stuff pour out as the stations flip past. It was evident, on the plane, that the tubes were warming up. Having won the June and July trials, capped by his Demi-Tasse victory, Turner's god was in his heaven. The plane's headlong rush down the runway and the exhilarating pressures of lift-off as we were tossed into the sky toward Atlanta (home!) crammed the stations with an amazing stream of babble. Listen:

"I could manage the Braves. The game isn't that hard. I could learn it quickly enough. I could make them winners. Hypnotize them: *you . . . are . . . winners!* Maybe I'll hire Billy Martin, then I'll manage the team when I'm home, and let him do it the rest of the time. We can't let morale rot. It isn't fair to the fans. Plus it would break my heart. If the guys are trying you can't fault them. The manager doesn't do anything to pump them up.

"It's too bad the team had to break camp after spring training and go north. They all looked so nice before the uniforms got dirty. They're the handsomest team in the locker room.

"The next time we do this America's Cup I'm going to be my own boss. I'm not going to worry about hanging around Newport having to be intimidated all the time by Loomis. Now I'm up at seven A.M., and I sneak off to my room after dinner at night so Loomis won't get me. I think we'll win, but not by much. It's going to be close.

"One reason the Braves are losing is that I've taken my psychic energy and concentrated it on the America's Cup. There's none left for the team.

"All I know is that I get what I want. Maybe because I want things more than others do. I wanted my TV station on the satellite, and there it is. I wanted to win the America's Cup, and that's getting close. I wanted to be worth 50 million dollars, and in a few years it might be double that. People love me, all over the place, they really do. I can communicate on all levels.

"You know, baseball isn't complicated like football," Turner went on. "One guy throws the ball, another guy catches it. Then you got squeeze plays, bunts, and all that stuff, but it isn't hard. And if I didn't know what to do, I would ask the players. Isn't that what happens on the sand lot? That's what I told Commissioner Kuhn when he told me I shouldn't manage. Nine-year-olds play this game, I told him. But he didn't agree. God, what am I going to run on Channel 17 at 11 o'clock. I'm supposed to solve *that* problem when we get home. Other stations run the news. I've got to come up with something to beat the news.

"*The Honeymooners* is too sophisticated for Atlanta. They like *Andy Griffith,* and *Gomer Pyle.* We run *Hogan's Heroes* at seven against the news. Maybe *Love American Style, Father Knows Best,* I don't know. . . .

"I want my baseball team to be like my boat crew. I want them to be my friends. If they're bad ballplayers then they have to go, sure. I don't want to be buddy-buddy with them, but I want them to respect me, and me them, you know, no back-stabbing, everybody pulling together. They don't have to be alike. Any race, creed, color, as long as they're good people. Take first baseman Tom Paciorek, who isn't playing regularly. If he can't play ball, I'll make him a TV salesman. I told him he had a long career with our company.

"There is another guy who puts the make on everyone. I do, too, only with more finesse. I don't bullshit them. I tell them to look at me like I'm a nice restaurant. You wouldn't want to be there all the time. You just enjoy it, then leave. I don't mislead them. When I was 17 I had written a suicide note, and I was standing on the fifth-floor ledge of the Read House in Chattanooga, ready to jump. It was over a girl. Then I thought, if I jump now, it's all over. Maybe I should jump tomorrow. After that I decided that women are like streetcars. If you miss one, another one comes along. Men are polygamists; it's the survival of the fit. I don't restrain myself. I take it the way I find it.

"For a while there, before I met Janie, I was killing myself. I was trying to be the world's greatest businessman, sailor, and lover. F. Scott Fitzturner. I was real low on sleep, and down to 140 pounds. I was burned out from taking the girls home at five A.M. I don't like sleeping alone. I like the patter of little bare feet in the morning. I like people too much."

Finishing with *Playboy,* Turner picked up *Sports Illustrated.* "Listen to this: 'At this point, any three of the boats could be named to defend.' Argh, say it ain't so.

"Come on, plane, I want to get there. There are too many decisions to make. What to run at 11. What to do about my manager. Of course, he won't talk to me because I'm suspended. That's what I might do. Play next year. Before I got suspended I was going to sign myself to a four-year contract and then go on the disabled list so I could get a pension. If they say I'm no good, I'll tell them I'm no worse than some of the guys we've got. The owners aren't eligible for pensions. Ha. I'll drive 'em all Q.Q.

"I think I'll tell Gary Matthews he has to play basketball this winter because he didn't earn his money playing baseball. How do you suppose he would like that?

"The team is a little weak all over. But we're bringing more kids up all the time. If you throw enough shit against the wall, some of it will stick. My *old man* said that. We don't have any Marv Throneberries on the Braves. Every player is equally capable of blowing it.

"We've got the worst record in baseball. Worse than the Mets used to be. Worse than Montreal last year. Last year there were only two teams with a worse attendance record than ours. This year we are next to last in attendance, and we have the fourth highest payroll of any team in baseball. Am I a dummy? Oh well, if I get hit by a truck at least I've had fun. God help me make the right decisions. I don't want to hurt anybody.

"The billboard business is good, but they don't write about that in the newspaper.

"We lead the league in errors, and our combined earned run average is over five. We're fourth from the bottom in batting. The owner has to take the blame. Steinbrenner of the Yankees blames Martin, which isn't right. The owner is responsible. I bet Gary Matthews *would* play basketball. But he's only 6' 4". Not big enough.

"You know that movie with Burt Reynolds? *W. W. and the Dixie Dance Kings*? I've been thinking of renaming the team the Dixie Dance Kings. Don't you think that's a great name for the worst team in baseball? When they get better we'll call them the Braves again. There's nothing brave about being 60 games out. They aren't actually 60 games out, but they're playing that way. We must be hopeful for the best, but we have to be prepared for the worst.

"The trouble with me is I say what I think. That's really why Kuhn suspended me. It didn't have anything to do with Gary Matthews. I don't need baseball anyway. I've got a better idea of a great evening than going to the ball park. My idea of a great evening is to have dinner at a nice restaurant, then go to a hotel or an apartment and get into it, then cuddle up and watch the late movie and go to sleep. It's a nice activity, and I could certainly do it more than once a week.

"So if Kuhn says I'm out, to hell with it. I've got 12 more years left, and I'm going to have a good time. I was going to shoot myself on the roof of the dugout. Tell me that wouldn't be colorful. I'm more colorful than North and Hood. I'm the most colorful guy around. My father taught me how to do it. He was colorful. Got in fights all the time. Then he killed himself. Bang. I wish he'd pushed me into Little League baseball. If I was a player I could sit in the dugout. Oh God, what am I going to run at 11 against the news?" Turner rested his head in his hands.

The Atlanta airport was jammed with people, as usual, and all of them seemed to recognize Ted Turner as we walked briskly toward the baggage claim. "Well, how'd you do?" asked one older woman, her hands on her hips, a smile on her face. And there were countless hey Teds, way to go Teds, atta baby Teds. Turner had a wave or a fast word for all of them.

A Braves official who met us remarked that Ted was better known in Georgia than Jimmy Carter. It is true that when Bowie Kuhn suspended Turner from baseball, nearly 40,000 people signed a petition in his behalf which was sent to Kuhn's office. And there were Ted Turner bumper stickers all over town.

"And I try to keep a low profile," Turner said with a grin.

At noon Turner drove his tan Chevrolet sedan into the tunnel under Atlanta–Fulton County Stadium, a round, three-tiered sports palace with a seating capacity of 52,807, and pulled into what he calls his ten-million-dollar parking space. During his suspension, his parking space was all that was left of his Braves purchase. The windows were down and Turner was yelling at everyone as we rolled in—security people, maintenance crews, stadium police, ticket takers, players, members of the press—and everyone was yelling back. Old home week. On the way to the elevator that would take us to the Stadium Club, Turner stopped.

"I'm not supposed to do this, being suspended, but have a look here," he said, and flung open the big door marked "clubhouse." The carpet was bright green, the walls light blue. Twenty-five freshly laundered white uniforms with red pinstripes and the word "Braves" across the front in script were hanging in front of twenty-five lockers. The players' names were hand-lettered on tape across the top of each locker. The chromium pipes and fixtures of the whirlpool bath glistened. There wasn't a towel's worth of clutter. Not a soul was in the clean, well-lighted place. The major leagues. It was a sight to make even a big kid's heart jump.

Turner stood at the door like a sergeant-at-arms who had just revealed the secret treasure room of King Solomon. He walked in a few illegal steps and soaked up the feel of the room, lifting his nose like a bear to inhale lingering vapors of liniment and sweat. His hand rested on the stainless rim of the whirlpool bath.

"Is this great? I'll tell you, it's great if you can stand the pressure of trying to hit a baseball moving at 90 miles an hour with 20,000 people watching."

On the elevator, a food concession lady told Ted she had seen him on TV (Walter Cronkite had done a *60 Minutes* piece on the Cup) and that he had looked wonderful.

"Thank you, sweetheart," Turner said as he left the car and ran into Hank Aaron, who Turner had hired to be the Braves' director of player development, giving some people a tour of the ball park. Hank Aaron? Hank Aaron! Jesus. Seven hundred and fifty-five career home runs. When a big sports magazine recently sought to determine the most significant sports accomplishment of the century, Hank Aaron's homers topped the list.

Will Sanders joined us for lunch at the Stadium Club. Sanders is financial vice president for Turner Communications, which includes two television stations, the Braves, and the Hawks. Everything but the billboard company. He is 40, under six feet and spare, an immaculate man impeccably suited in the three-piece, Eastern conservative manner he perfected at Yale. His shiny black hair was dressed and combed back in a little wave, and behind the gold-rimmed aviator glasses his active dark eyes missed nothing. His brows have a slight, habitual furrow, as though he has just been asked a difficult question. His quick laugh and abundant humor would be concealed until our second meeting.

Will Sanders knew Turner when they were both teenagers in Savannah, and later in college. They sailed against each other in Lightnings and Y-Fliers. Sanders's family had a billboard business, as did Turner's. Sanders's mother ran the business after his father died. After Yale, Sanders joined the accounting firm of Price Waterhouse. In the 1960s it was evident that Will had to run the family business or sell it. He mentioned it to Turner. Within 30 days, Turner had bought the business. Sanders stayed with Price Waterhouse until 1970, then went to work for Turner.

It was the first day in two months that Turner had been at work, so to speak, and Sanders's briefcase was full. Turner had been keeping up with business events by telephone from Newport each day, but, as Sanders explained, "On the phone, Ted's inclination is to say no to everything." Sanders didn't seem overjoyed that Turner had brought along a visitor to intrude upon his concentration, and to be party to a private business discussion. But privacy, as Sanders knew too well, is not one of Turner's strong suits. And the only way to get Turner's attention fully is to be totally alone with him. Secluded. Strangers, passersby, or marginally attractive waitresses are all sufficient diversions.

"You must be pretty hard up to take such a low-paying job," Turner told the waitress.

"I am," she laughed, "but I like the Braves."

"Well, I'm losing 1.5 million dollars a year on them, so you're doing better than me." Turner reminded me of the former Baltimore Colts tackle, Big Daddy Lipscomb. Lipscomb once said that he picked over the opposing backfield until he came to the one with the ball. Turner does the same thing, and not just with women.

With a sideways glance at me, Sanders started on his list.

One subject was an opportunity to sponsor a tennis tournament. "No way," Turner said. "Look, the guy who runs the Omni is no dummy. If there was any money in it, he'd be sponsoring it himself."

George, the manager of the Stadium Club, came over. Turner introduced him. "I've always wanted a restaurant. Now I own this place with George. Pretty strong, huh? George, you're my man."

Sanders wanted to talk about Mike Marshall's deferred payments. The Braves sent Lee Lacey and Elias Sosa to the Dodgers for relief pitcher Marshall, who didn't get along any better in Atlanta than he had with a variety of other teams. Marshall didn't like the way manager Dave Bristol was using him, so he left. The Braves still owed him contract money.

But Turner wanted to talk about his TV hook-up throughout the stadium. A big-screen Advent was at each end of the Stadium Club, and standard TV sets were mounted here and there on columns. Those who preferred could go out to the ball park and watch the game on closed circuit from the restaurant. "I was thinking of putting in Pong games on all the sets in case the ball game was no good," Turner said.

Sanders persisted. Okay, Turner told him, pay Marshall.

Ted Turner purchased the Atlanta Braves baseball team on January 14, 1976, from the Atlanta-LaSalle Corporation. Turner paid a reported ten million dollars for the team. The terms: one million down, and a million a year for nine years.

Phyllis Collins, who had been secretary to the team's previous owners for seven years, and who worked for Turner until 1978, when she left the Braves to become secretary to the president of the National League, recalls Turner's first appearance at the Braves offices. "We weren't really sure just what we had on our hands," Phyllis says, smiling at her own understatement.

Phyllis Collins is an attractive blonde who has more than her share of executive presence. "He is very dynamic, but he does startle you."

Bill Lucas, the Braves general manager, who was running the organization during Turner's absence, also recalls that first staff meeting. "He came in walkin' and talkin'," Lucas says. "He told everyone assembled that we had to work harder in order to be better. He said the business day would begin at 8:30 instead of 9:00. He told some story about a big guy and a little guy in a fight, how the little guy wouldn't quit, how he was bound to win even if he had to kick the big guy in the balls. Well, there were some secretaries present, you know, but a tempo was being set. Some people couldn't believe him. He does have a different way. Me, I thought he was something else. I dug his style." A pattern is noticeable: perhaps in counterpoint to Turner's loudness, the people close to him in business tend to be quiet, subdued.

Phyllis Collins recalls another moment from Turner's opening remarks. "He said he wasn't going to make us any promises," Phyllis says. "He said when he got married the first time he made a lot of promises he didn't live up to, and his wife got mad at him. In his second marriage he made no promises, and now he gets applause when he comes through. That's the way it would be with the Braves."

Turner approached baseball the way he approaches everything. He gets a good hold on the paintbrush, then confidently has the ladder removed. The results are always catastrophic at first, but he has a history of being able to pull up inches short of a complete crash and burn. From that point on he often goes on to master the project that nearly did him in. It's like those old movies of Esther Williams tossing six-month-old infants into a swimming pool.

Turner keeps making it through for the same reasons those little babies do: a strong sense of survival, to be sure, and innocence. There isn't all that much of the latter, but in the adult world *any* amount puts one in a special category. As a lady with an astrological interest once said of Ted, "If he didn't have Libra rising to counter his main sign, which is Scorpio, he would be pure awful. But the Libra gives him that childlike, innocent quality. The little-boy aspect makes people want to protect him. They can understand his game, and relate their fantasy to his."

Turner's trial-and-error method can be perilous at times. Like in 1964 when he decided he would charter a big boat and race in the SORC. Having never sailed or crewed on big boats, he left in October aboard a 40-footer with a pick-up crew to make the passage from New York to Miami. A fire in the galley almost got out of control. The boat was battered by storms and nearly sunk when the pumps malfunctioned. They ran aground. They got lost. Food and water supplies were insufficient. When they finally made a port, there was wholesale desertion among the crew. But a scant two years later, Turner *won* the SORC, an ocean racing plum that has escaped many a smart, devoted yachtsman who has spent a lifetime pursuing it.

As Lucas said, Turner's approach to baseball was "different." On April 10, 1976, Turner singlehandedly cracked open baseball's free agent situation by signing pitcher Andy Messersmith for a million-dollar, three-year package. A few days later, just in case there was anyone around who hadn't gotten the word about the Braves' new owner, Turner leaped out of the stands to congratulate a home run hitter as he crossed the plate.

"The Atlanta sports scene was dreary, low-visibility. I had to do something," Turner says.

When the Braves won eight of their first thirteen games, Turner offered each player a 500-dollar bonus for every game they won over 81; as further incentive, he offered each player an additional five percent of his salary for every 100,000 paid admissions over 900,000 at the end of the season. While National League President Chub Feeney was pondering that situation,

Turner decided to nickname Andy Messersmith "Channel" and assign him uniform number 17. Feeney's frown deepened when he heard that Turner was showering with the players after games and playing poker with them in the clubhouse.

The Braves began a long losing streak. During the tenth loss, Turner stood in for one of the buxom girls in pinstriped hot-pants who sweep the bases during the seventh inning, and brought in a minister to pray for the team. During the twelfth loss he lay in state on the top of the dugout with his hands folded on his chest. When the Braves beat the Mets to end the losing streak at 13, Turner leaped onto the field again.

Then Feeney told him to cancel his player bonus plans based on attendance and games won (as it turned out, Turner wouldn't have had to pay out a cent), to remove "Channel 17" from Messersmith's uniform, to stop playing poker with the players, and to quit yelling at free agents from the stands and telling them not to sign with other clubs.

A few games later Turner picked up the field announcer's mike and told a small, startled audience, "Nobody leaves here a loser tonight. If the Braves don't win, you are all my personal guests at tomorrow night's game." The Braves didn't let the fans down. They lost.

That season Turner participated in a number of Braves promotions. He drove a motorized bathtub around the field before a game. He put on jockey silks and raced an ostrich (he lost after whipping the bird into a catatonic fit of fear). He bloodied his nose while beating Philadelphia Phillies reliever Tug McGraw in a contest that involved rolling a baseball around the basepaths with one's nose. Accounts of the Nose Roll and other such moments were compiled by Channel 17 account executive Rob Fields in a book called *Take Me Out to the Crowd*. A picture of Turner with his nose scraped and bleeding adorns the cover.

Turner was slated to have more than his nose bloodied. His interest in San Francisco Giants slugger Gary Matthews was no secret. But Matthews wouldn't become a free agent until the end of the 1976 season, and the guidelines about making even second-hand contact with the player, or even "public comments indicating interest," were precise. At a cocktail party in New York hosted by the Yankees, Turner and Giants co-owner Robert Lurie had an exchange about the subject after several drinks. Turner told Lurie, "No matter what you offer Matthews, I'll offer more."

Lurie filed a complaint with Baseball Commissioner Bowie Kuhn, who considered the matter. Kuhn concluded that Turner's statements were "in clear violation of the prohibitions of the directives . . . clearly had the effect of subverting the Collective Bargaining Agreement . . . and were not in the best interest of Baseball." On January 18, 1977, Kuhn announced he was suspending Turner from baseball for one year, and also ruled that the Braves would be denied their first-round draft choice for the June draft of that year.

If Turner hadn't exactly made a hit with the baseball establishment, he was doing fine with the Atlanta press. Furman Bisher, a sports columnist for the *Atlanta Constitution* who had been at the cocktail party in question, capped off an amazing outpouring of support for Turner with a column headlined: "Turner, Atlanta Together in a Common Love."

Turner's stock was also high among Braves players. After the last away game of the season against first-place Cincinnati, Turner threw a big party for the team at a local hotel. "He came to me," Bill Lucas says, "and said he was going to give the boys a party. He said they were nice guys and that they ought to go home knowing someone cares."

It would be difficult to find many owners bankrolling a party for a last-place effort. Turner also brings in all his minor league teams every year for a 15-hour baseball festival in the stadium. That costs him $35,000, but as Lucas says, it is great motivation for the young players.

Turner's approach to baseball ownership is paternalistic. After the first season was over he took the team bird-hunting. "He wants the club to be a family affair," Lucas says. "He urges the players to move to Atlanta, live here with their families. Of course that obligates him in a moral way to keep a player longer than he should. That can be a problem."

Everyone acknowledges that Turner revitalized baseball in Atlanta, and the revitalization has cost plenty. A young, energetic fellow with the unlikely name of Bob Hope and a face with mail-order inscrutability is the Braves publicist. He can't help but love working with an owner like Turner. Turner is the publicist's dream, after all. Hope's inventiveness in the promotion department has created somewhat of a carnival atmosphere around the Braves, including weddings at home plate, wrestling after the game, laser light-show sky concerts, and wet T-shirt contests. But even he was stunned by Turner's opening moves.

Hope says Turner was overzealous his first year. "He jumped into the free agent thing, and he made some unwise player deals. It would take a while to learn this business at a normal pace. When you rush in with his kind of charge it's a lot more painful, but you learn a lot faster. He made some grave errors, and he won't make them again. Now he can judge, and reach rational conclusions.

"His image in town is strong," Hope says. "It's a sort of Don Quixote image—the noble effort to build the ball club. He's given it his best shot, and people respect that. Turner is the underdog in baseball for sure. His theory is that you don't get rolling until the big guys get on you. Keep the attack upward, have a fierce dogfight with the people above you, and you rise to their level. Turner figures that none of us put out until we are challenged. This battle with Kuhn hasn't been all bad. I don't think Ted is too upset about being a martyr on a national scale."

Hope says there are all kinds of opinions about Turner around the office. He is considered abrasive, impish, obnoxious, entertaining, refreshing. Others think he behaves like a little kid out of line. But Hope points out that owners generally tend to be too serious about the "product." "It's easy to lose track of the fact that a baseball game doesn't have much of an effect on world hunger," Hope says.

By seven o'clock, as we were sitting down to dinner at the Stadium Club, a light rain was falling, the gauzy streaks of soft drops distinctly visible as they drifted out of the night sky into the man-made daylight of the stadium, collecting below in glistening puddles on the huge plastic tarpaulin advertising Morton's Salt ("when it rains it pours") that covered the infield.

Through the plate glass windows of the restaurant one looked across at the opposite rim of the stadium crater, at the flags flying, at the rows of folding seats in colors by section, bright red, vibrant orange, vivid blue, grape purple, their brilliance heightened by the wetness, then down to the grass of the field below, a glowing emerald under the incandescence of two and a half million watts that were turning several cubic acres of night into day.

A stadium can be a frightening place, containing the festive, often unruly and emotional population of a small city behaving as one as it sits in deathly silence, or explodes into a bone-chilling roar. Especially over football or soccer. But this was baseball, a more sociable event, with broken bones and flowing blood a clear violation of Mr. Doubleday's etiquette, and as the crowd trickled in to fill only one-fifth of the 50,000 seats, the big glowing place felt mellow as can be.

Somewhere, a radio was playing. . . .

". . . So I need ideas, I have to figure out what I'm going to do after I win the America's Cup, if I do win the America's Cup— it's pretty close—because politics, I don't know, it's so sordid, so full of compromise. You have to compromise in politics, don't you? Could I just go straight down the middle and tell the truth? Probably not. I'd have to lie, or I would disappoint both sides."

Turner ordered a steak, and wondered how attendance would be.

"The Braves may not be winning, but they are providing a public service. The Emory Medical Center said that 584 citizens would have died from anxiety if the Braves had been a contender this year. So we're saving lives, how about that? We can't win the pennant, so the deal is to relax.

"Have you seen my scoreboard? Out there in center field. It's amazing. It not only handles messages, we can plug in instant replays from the closed circuit system. It cost a million and a half. Ahh, it's good to be home. There's my man George. Hey George, how's business?"

The rain stopped. The tarpaulin was removed. The show would go on.

Turner shuns the privilege of a private box in the upper deck of the stadium for a field-level seat behind the Braves dugout along the first base line. As he told *Boston Globe* writer Alan Richman later in the summer, "I never could understand why owners like to sit up behind bullet-proof glass sipping martinis. I sit in the front row." He slipped into the seat five minutes before game time, settling himself in like a dog in tall grass. He hollered at a player or two (they waved back, gave the boss a smile), looked around for folks who might want to say hello, found some, rolled up his sleeves, grubbed around in the big Red Man chewing tobacco pouch and stuffed a wad the size of a plum into his cheek, slapped the pouch on the dugout roof, sat his big cup of beer beside it and placed a smaller, empty cup beside that (he would periodically spit tobacco juice into the empty cup), put his feet on the dugout roof, asked Bill Lucas who was pitching, and leaped up with a yell as the Braves took the field.

While watching several baseball games with Turner, my consummate fear was that during a moment of excitement on the field I would mistake Turner's spittoon cup for my cold drink.

The Braves' reliable old knuckleballer, Phil Niekro, was on the mound. Vic Corell, a Braves catcher, recalled that one of Niekro's pitches once hit him twice, hit the umpire twice, and went to the screen. Niekro finished warming up. The catcher Biff Pocoroba made the throw down to second. Play was about to commence. The opposition was the Pittsburgh Pirates, definite contenders in their black and yellow suits with the old-fashioned square-topped hats. Their first batter was Taveras, the shortstop. He hit Niekro's first pitch for a triple. Niekro then struck out Garner. The first pitch to right fielder Parker was wild. A run scored. Parker smacked the second pitch on a line into right. Single. Walter, an usher who makes it his business to see that the boss is happy during a game, brought Turner a portable radio. Turner made a small fuss over Walter, tuned the radio in to the game just as announcer Ernie Johnson was saying ". . . and Ted Turner is in town this week to enjoy the Pittsburgh series. He's got one more month of sailing up there, and we all wish him the best. . . ." Did Johnson have the glasses on Turner, watching for the radio to be delivered?

Niekro picked Parker off first. Niekro, who finished the 1977 season setting new Braves records and leading the league in walks allowed (164), strikeouts (262), games started (42), most runs allowed (166), most earned runs allowed (148), most innings pitched (330), and most hits allowed (315), has one of the slickest and quickest moves to first of any pitcher in baseball. A ground ball ended the inning.

Turner hadn't stopped talking baseball with Lucas and Al Thornwell, a member of the Braves board of directors: trades, positions, strategy, all laced with a great deal of beer, jokes, and spitting.

Jeff Burroughs hit a home run to tie the score. Niekro picked off another Pittsburgh base runner. Perhaps he puts them on base just to embarrass them. At the end of four innings the score was tied at two apiece. Turner was approached by a fan from Jesup, Georgia, (population 9091) who said he appreciated what Ted had done. "We haven't done nothin' yet," Turner told him, "but we're gonna hang in." The Jesup fan was one of a dozen who stopped by in the course of the game.

Braves third baseman Jerry Royster hit a triple. Two runs scored. "Beautiful," the outfield scoreboard read, with explosive graphics. At the end of the fifth inning, the boys in the grounds crew emerged at a full gallop from the right field line, lugging their gear. Their average age was 21, the average hair length was shoulder. Their caps were askew. At double-time they dragged the infield and straightened the bases in two minutes flat. Cavorting among them was a bright green, fuzzy egg-shaped thing with the face of a mutant Muppet, wearing a Braves cap on its pointed head. It was the Bleacher Creature. Fans can buy Bleacher Creature dolls at the souvenir stands. Lucky fans can get the real thing to appear at their kid's birthday party. In the centerfield bleachers, Chief Nocahoma (knock a homer—get it?) pranced around a teepee with two mouth-watering Indian (or perhaps Italian, possibly Irish) squaws in outfits of brief buckskin. The sweet thing in pin-striped hot pants tip-toed around the bases, bouncing, sweeping, smiling, and waving.

On the scoreboard was a reminder of the weddings that would take place at home plate the following night. Once a year, mass weddings are conducted at home plate. Bob Hope says they tried it once, and it was such a hit they made it an annual event. Jeff Burroughs led off the sixth inning with a double. In the seventh inning, Kison, the Pittsburgh pitcher, was pulled. The reliever was Jackson. Gary Matthews hit his first pitch into the seats. The Braves had shown crisp double plays, pick-off throws, home runs, extra-base hits. *They* looked like the contenders. "Hi to all the folks from the Cobb County

Sheriff's Department," read the scoreboard. I leaned over to speak with Lucas. He pointed to the scoreboard. I looked. "Welcome Roger Vaughn." Aw, shucks. I finally get my name in lights and it's misspelled.

The Braves won it, 5–3. No one moved toward the exits until the final out. As the organ played a section from *Rhapsody in Blue,* a small crowd formed around Turner. He signed autographs, posed with three kids while a father aimed an Instamatic, then headed for his ten-million-dollar parking space.

As the last gatekeeper waved goodnight, Turner was saying, "I make people in my organization feel respect for themselves, I make them feel important, don't I? You know why? Because I've been a waiter and a bus boy myself.

"And now I'm on the satellite. That first antenna I had in Marblehead last fall was borrowed. The one in Newport is mine. I bought that one. People wonder if I'm going to spend that kind of money just to watch a few Braves games. Hell no. After the Cup is over that antenna will go to New York and show people Channel 17 off the satellite. I'm like Christopher Columbus. Mine is the first independent station on the satellite. Within 120 days of the beginning of the commercial satellite industry, I figured out the plan. It's a plan calculated to make me the richest man in Georgia. I've got to pass the chairman of Coca Cola first. I figure I'll be worth a hundred million in a few years, but I don't live extravagantly. I drive a Chevy, I live in a $130,000 house. That's not so bad, is it?"

Turner paused. Like a preacher at a lectern, scowling, waiting for the amen chorus. His voice had become louder and raspier than usual as we cruised quietly at 60 through the interlocking concrete maze of Atlanta freeways, the mercury vapor lights casting an eerie glow into the car, highlighting the edges of Turner's features, plunging the rest of him into flickering shadow.

His voice approached a whine, a plea for confirmation of his rightness. Its inflection was a cutting edge held to his listener's throat. He was citing honor and sportsmanship again, Lowell North and the business of sails: "It's fear, it's got to be, doesn't it? Why else won't he sell me sails? He has to have the edge before he comes in. What kind of a deal is that?" (The pause, the scowl, the searching for eye contact in the purple gloom, the eyes pleading, needing that amen chorus; insistent, foundering without it.) "Well, isn't that a raw deal? Huh? Don't you think so?"

Amen.

Ted Turner gained control of Channel 17 in Atlanta by merging Turner Communications Corporation with Rice Broadcasting in January, 1970. It cost him three million dollars. He changed the call letters to WTCG, Turner Communications Group. An independent station (not network-affiliated), it was losing about $50,000 a month at the time. (Of the 146 UHF stations—the vast majority of them independent—reporting to the FCC for 1970, only 47 reported a profit. Of the 47, only 28 stations reported profits in excess of $100,000.)

Turner bought the station against the best advice of anyone who could get his ear. Six months later he bought Channel 36, an independent in Charlotte, North Carolina. It was losing $30,000 a month.

Again, Turner was in up to his lower lip. Will Sanders shakes his head when he thinks about it. "It could have sunk our ass, that TV business," he says. "We were really in it. Our purchase contract included all the debts. There was no way to cut it loose if it didn't work. We all said he was crazy, but Ted is an incredible salesman and debater. For every reason you come up with, he'll come up with five that say you're wrong. That, and the fact that he's in control, overwhelms you.

"Ted was sure independent television was a growth industry.

He thought an independent station had a lot more potential than the billboard business, which had already matured."

Turner bought the stations and weathered the storms. His tenacity combined with his resources gave him immense staying power. He ground down the competition using the cash flow from the billboard company. By 1973, Channel 17 was one of the first independent UHF stations in the country to show a substantial profit.

When Turner bought Channel 17, there was another independent in the Atlanta market, one of five stations in the country owned by United States Communications. It was clear to everyone that the Atlanta market could not support two independents. "Ted knew this," one of the early Channel 17 employees says, "but I doubt he realized how serious the situation was." Only one of the stations was going to survive, and it didn't look like it would be Channel 17, which was running a solid fifth out of five Atlanta stations.

Channel 17's instability was reflected in the fact that in the first 22 months of Turner's ownership, the personnel of the station turned over twice. By the spring of 1971, every spare dollar Turner could find had been poured into the station, and as Will Sanders recalls, the whole show was about to sink. Then overnight, without warning, the station owned by U.S. Communications folded. It was a huge stroke of luck for Turner, a life line for a drowning man.

Bill McGee was general manager of the U.S. station in Atlanta. "We just ran out of money," McGee says. He painted a picture of a large company that had jumped into the development of independent television without fully realizing the resources that an independent would need. "Kaiser," McGee says, "which was the only company that owned more stations than U.S., lost 50 million dollars trying to develop stations. U.S. wasn't willing to spend the money. I remember I had a live basketball telecast arranged, and the phone company was calling to say we couldn't go on the air unless our bill was paid. I went to Philadelphia, the home office, to plead for the money. It was obvious they weren't going to honor their commitment to me. I resigned. They closed Atlanta and the San Francisco station the same day, Pittsburgh a week later.

"I remember having lunch with Ted before I resigned," McGee says. "Our station had the bargaining power to buy films. Turner was making no headway at all. He was in a sorry situation. If we hadn't shut down, he would have been in serious trouble."

In one day Channel 17 went from fifth of five, to fourth of four. As the only independent in Atlanta, the way ahead was clear for development, but the problems were still immense. UHF reception was terrible, for one thing. "We had signal problems," McGee says about his station. "The 'able-to-receive' figures were frightening." It was the same for Turner.

"I can remember going into an advertiser's office and asking him to buy Channel 17," Turner says. "The answer would be, 'We don't buy UHF.' And I'd tell them, 'Why not? It's coming, like FM radio. We're not asking you to pay for the future. We're just asking you to buy our audience at the standard cost per thousand. Our audience isn't very big, but our viewers are way above the average viewers' mentality.'

"And they'd say, 'How do you know that? How come?' And I'd tell them, 'Because you've *got* to be smart to figure out how to tune in a UHF antenna in the first place. Dumb guys can't do it. Can *you* get Channel 17? No? Well, neither can I. We aren't *smart* enough to get it. But my viewers are.'

"Then I'd ask them if their commercials were in color. And they'd say, 'Of course.' And I'd tell them their commercials would stand out better on my station. Why? Because most of the programs were in black and white, and when their commercials came on they would have more shock value, they would catch the viewers' attention. They fell over. They hadn't thought of that.

"And finally I told them my audience was richer. I told them most sets with UHF capability were color, which cost more. Don't you think that was a pretty good sales pitch?"

With the independent competition gone, Turner put more money into strengthening his signal. Then he got his second break. The Atlanta ABC affiliate was forced by the network to pick up the 6:00 P.M. news, which they had not been running. It is a television fact of life that roughly 25 percent of the audience will actively avoid the news. So Turner scheduled *Star Trek* at 6:00 P.M. and not only increased his rating at that hour, but got a few more people acquainted with Channel 17's presence. In Turner's mind, a philosophy was beginning to take shape. As he told *Television/Radio Age* in 1974, "All three stations in Atlanta had big group-ownership money behind them, and they programmed pretty much alike. I felt people of Atlanta were entitled to something different than a whole lot of police and crime shows with rape and murders going on all over the place. I believe that people are tired of violence and psychological problems and all the negative things they see on TV every night."

Turner concentrated his energies on buying films and composing a line-up of old shows that sounded like the sitcom hall of fame: *I Love Lucy, Gilligan's Island, Leave It to Beaver, Petticoat Junction, Father Knows Best, Gomer Pyle,* and *Andy Griffith.* "We're essentially an escapist station," Turner announced to those who hadn't noticed. "As far as our news is concerned, we run the FCC minimum of 40 minutes a day."

Having moved into the void left by ABC's commitment to news, Turner attacked the NBC affiliate (WSB-TV), Atlanta's number-one station. WSB had chosen not to air five network shows, which meant they could be picked up by an independent in the area. Turner grabbed all five, and soon billboards around Atlanta (Turner's, of course) were announcing, "The NBC Network Moves to Channel 17," and listing the five shows.

"We didn't think we could take over as the number-one station in the market," Turner said at the time. "But we felt we could shake 'em up a bit, get 'em to think about us, let 'em know we were in the race." The other stations were shook, and started thinking. The move was splashed all over the papers, and if success could be measured in phone calls from NBC lawyers, it was a hit.

While WSB-TV was still fuming over their public embarrassment, Turner grabbed their rights to telecast Atlanta Braves games. At the time the Braves were paying WSB to run 20 games a year. Turner made the Braves an offer they couldn't refuse, paying *them* $2.5 million for TV rights for five years.

"The Braves games were the top-rated program in the Atlanta market," Jerry Hogan says. Hogan is general sales manager of Channel 17. He is a dapper, precise fellow with styled red hair and the office manner of a Park Avenue physician discussing a social disease of moderate seriousness. He left Chicago broadcasting in 1971 to take a chance with Turner.

"Signing the Braves did a lot for our image," Hogan says. "It changed it from that of a kiddy station. It forced people to tune us in. We became a factor. Atlanta went from a three-station market plus WTCG to a four-station market."

Turner used the same straight-ahead approach to bring wrestling to Channel 17. The ABC affiliate had been off-hand with wrestling, switching air times around, treating the promoters without much regard. Turner made them a better deal (it turned out Turner had once dated a girl who was married to one of the promoters, so he had something of an in). "There's no prestige to wrestling," Hogan says, "but you can't beat it as a rating success. It has more viewers than football or the Braves *or* the Hawks."

As *Television/Radio Age* put it, "The story of how Turner, a man with absolutely no broadcast experience, turned a jumble of grade D film, tired equipment, and a building vaguely resembling a broken-down supply depot from the Civil War into one of the most successful independent stations in the country in four years' time, reads more like a movie script than a prescription for success in the hard-boiled, real world of the broadcast industry."

The operating profit (or, in parentheses, loss) at WTCG over the years tells the story: 1970, ($550,707); 1971, ($531,584); 1972, $181,406; 1973, $1,043,316; 1974, $732,340; 1975, $1,707,987; 1976, $3,687,447; 1977, $3,714,648.

"Ted has controlled programming from the beginning," Hogan says. "He used to select each movie himself *and* schedule it. I don't know how he gets his input, but he gets it."

One might think that such a flamboyant fellow as Turner would take advantage of his ownership to schedule himself regularly on the air. He did so on only one program. "I used to sit in a big wing-back chair and introduce the Sunday morning *Academy Award Theater*," Turner says. "I enjoyed it, and it was great during those winters I was off sailing in Australia. The kids could turn on the set and see their daddy at Christmas. But I didn't really have the time to do it."

With programming developing nicely, Turner began concentrating on signal distribution. From the beginning, Turner had his eyes on television-starved areas outside metropolitan Atlanta, areas where reception was a problem. The only way to reach this large market was to extend the station's range by bringing the signal into existing cable-TV systems.

Cable television is an offshoot of hotel television, where all the hotel rooms are wired to a master antenna. Cable's official designation is CATV, or community antenna television. As the name implies, CATV was aimed at smaller, outlying communities where television reception was limited and inferior. Of the 3400 cable systems in operation nation-wide in 1978, two-thirds of them had fewer than 2000 subscribers. Until very recently, efforts to bring cable into metropolitan areas had not been particularly successful. Cable installation costs were high in cities, and the presence of quality independent stations were usually satisfying viewers' demands.

Typically, a cable company brings in a strong television signal to a "head end," which usually includes a large, tower-mounted antenna. From the head end, the signal is distributed through the community along a network of coaxial cables that can be tapped and fed directly into subscribers' homes. Cost to the cable subscriber runs from seven to ten dollars a month.

Until three years ago, all cable companies imported their signals by microwave. By law, a different company, called a common carrier, ran the microwave setup. Microwave is a cumbersome way to go. The carrier must transmit a signal through a series of amplifying stations. Because a television signal travels a line of sight, elevated land (at least two acres) must first be purchased for each of these stations. A tower must be built and electronics installed at an additional cost of about $60,000. Power lines must be run in. And for the signal to carry properly, the amplifying stations usually can be no more than 25 miles apart. Once a station is completed, maintenance begins. The result is often an unreliable signal, sensitive to weather extremes and weakened progressively as the distance traveled increases. Because of the huge void Turner was trying to fill in the Southeast, estimates were that a microwave system would have cost a carrier eight million dollars to install.

On top of equipment cost, the FCC presented the television stations with a whole book of complex cable regulations that severely curtailed the export of signals.

At Turner Communications, modest progress was being made. From the time he purchased the stations in 1970, Turner had added 462,000 cable customers by the fall of 1976. Then two events transpired that opened up the heavens for Turner. First, in 1975, the FCC lifted some of the 1972 restrictions. The FCC determined that these restrictions had brought cable growth in many areas to a standstill and that lifting them would have a minimal effect on local broadcasters.

Second, in December, 1975, RCA launched its first Americom satellite, SATCOM I, into a geo-synchronous orbit (stationary relative to a point on the earth) 22,300 miles above the equator. The communications satellite is pure magic. A television signal is beamed to the orbiting antenna, where it is reflected back to earth. The signal makes the round trip of nearly 45,000 miles in a fifth of a second, and can be received by an earth-station antenna anywhere in the U.S. Compared to microwave, satellite transmission is cheap, and because the signal travels almost vertically through the atmosphere, reception is always clear.

In the fall of 1975, Turner watched the unveiling of Home Box Office (a subscriber film package for home viewing) being broadcast by satellite. Subscribers paid an additional ten dollars a month for 82 hours a week of movies and special events. HBO was the first service to cable systems via satellite, and one look was enough to convince Turner he wanted up.

As soon as the FCC changed the rule to allow any independent to be brought in by cable systems, Turner took notice. While other independents were fighting the cable, he worked with it. He joined the cable association. He testified in the cable hearings in Washington. "They called me the Quisling of the broadcast industry," Turner says, "because I was the only television station owner who testified for them."

While Turner began scheming, a quiet, studious man named Donald Andersson was making a systematic study of the television industry. Andersson was an official of the cable association in Washington, a well-organized lobby that was examining how the cable industry could benefit from recent changes in FCC regulations. The more Andersson studied the reams of figures, computer print-outs, and maps before him, the more his attention kept being drawn to Atlanta, Georgia. "I kept wondering," Andersson said, "who this fellow Turner was, and if he had any idea what he had down there. I kept wishing I could meet him."

As Andersson explains it, referring to an eight-foot map of the U.S. on his wall that is peppered with small dots of various colors, Tampa–St. Petersburg, Miami, and Atlanta are the only three television markets in the Southeast that are in the top 25 nationally (although St. Louis, Cincinnati, Kansas City, and Washington are lurking along the northern border). The only independents in the above markets that carry significant professional sports programming are Kansas City and Atlanta. Of the independents in the Southeast, only Channel 17 carried sports. "Sports are very big with the cable people," Andersson says. "Plus Turner has a station that's on the air 24 hours a day, and he runs all those movies, which are great for the cable."

Turner had been picking people over full time, and sure enough he came to one with the ball—a young lady, as usual— who connected him with Andersson.

"He came into the office one day," Andersson says, "and said 'Hi, I'm Ted Turner, I hear we think alike.' Within 30 minutes he was positive I would run a cable sales operation for him. 'Would it help us if I bought the Braves?' he asked me. I said it sure would. He said he was going to Australia for an ocean race, and that he would call me when he got back. And he did," Andersson says, recalling his surprise.

Selling Channel 17 to cable systems was part of the job. The other part—the horse before the cart—was getting the signal on the satellite. Turner went to see RCA and discovered that would not be simple. The advent of the satellite was supposed to generate initial interest from the large commercial networks. No one in the industry had suspected that far-flung pay cable schemes like Home Box Office and little independents with wildcat notions and dreams of glory would be lining up for a piece of the sky.

Turner was told RCA would lease him space on their bird, but first an earth-station transmitter-receiver would have to be built—an installation costing three quarters of a million dollars. He began bouncing around the aerospace communications industry, where the technology was expanding so rapidly even the FCC was having trouble keeping up with it. Turner looked at other satellites. But he knew how popular Home Box Office, on RCA's satellite, was becoming with cable systems, and he knew how difficult selling Channel 17 to cable systems would be if it was on a different satellite. (If a cable system wants to pull signals off two different satellites, it needs either a second earth station or a system for continually redirecting a single antenna.)

So Turner went home with a problem that was giving him fits. In such a situation, Turner will unfailingly turn to direct action, simply because he can't stand holding patterns. Patience is not Turner's strong suit. Whether the issue is boats, business, or women, he goes for instant gratification.

If the truth were known, Turner probably just picked up the telephone one Sunday night and ordered an earth station. Monday morning at the office he told one of his executives to drop everything and go find a piece of land to put it on. But the truth will never be known, because the legal intricacies of this little million-dollar, outer-spatial gambit were mighty complicated, and perhaps even a touch questionable.

Turner the business tycoon is no different from Turner the kid who knocked off the Tennessee State Debate Championships at age 17 by redefining the basic question and coming in from left field with a position no one was prepared to debate. People don't change after all. His tactics aren't exactly illegal, but they range deep enough into the gray area to make some people hysterical—especially those who didn't think of his scheme themselves. But a case can certainly be made for Turner's modus operandi following the classical American outlaw-pioneer tradition.

In any event, it wasn't long before an earth-station transmitter-receiver dish standing 30 feet high and measuring 10 meters across was in place on an acre of land ten miles from Turner's WTCG studios in Atlanta. Tucked away in a remote wooded hollow with its nose pointed toward the heavens, its white electronics trailer standing nearby, and its high chain-link fence topped with three strands of angled barbed wire, it had the appearance of a highly classified military installation.

Turner formed a company called Southern Satellite Systems (SSS) that would operate the earth station and distribute his television signal to cable companies. He was well on his way to putting the package together when his Washington lawyers reminded him that a station owner cannot own the common carrier of the signal. So Turner sold the company.

On December 27, 1976, Channel 17, WTCG-TV Atlanta, "The Super Station that Serves the Nation," as Turner dubbed it, went on the satellite. TCG's satellite debut was six months behind schedule. It took that long for the FCC investigation to conclude that Ted Turner was in no way connected with SSS.

Turner's frenzy to get his station on the satellite and the various gambles it prompted would seem more reasonable if his audience had been ready and waiting. The move can be better appreciated as the calculated risk that it was if one understands how far ahead of demand Turner placed supply.

The people at Home Box Office, who are understandably jealous of their ice-breaking efforts with satellite transmission for national television, report there were only two earth stations "out there" when they committed seven million dollars to a long-term contract in April, 1975, to use RCA's satellite. HBO is now rolling along handsomely, reaching more than a million and a half subscriber homes through 576 cable systems in 47 states. But as HBO's public relations director Robbin Ahrold admits, "Up to a year ago, it was a question of survival.

"When Turner started," Ahrold says, "it wasn't clear that the earth stations were going to be there, and federal regulations seriously inhibited independents. Home Box Office paved the way. But you have to hand it to Turner. He surrounded himself with people who knew the cable industry, and he made friends. He had the timing, ambition, foresight, and will to put his money where his mouth was."

Turner wouldn't disagree with that assessment. As he remarked in a speech to the Cable '78 convention in New Orleans, "You have to have a little balls. Hell, I've got 'em or I wouldn't be here."

Both HBO and WTCG found themselves in the right place at the right time. The cable business, which was not prospering in 1975, has been virtually saved by the use of satellite transmission. Teleprompter Corporation, the largest owner of cable systems in the country, made a commitment in 1975 to link a majority of their systems to the satellite. Within six months the other major cable conglomerates made a similar commitment to satellite technology.

The quick and unexpected drop in the price of "receive-only" earth stations helped spur the general momentum toward satellite use. In 1975 a receiver cost around $100,000. In 1978 it was available from between $25,000 and $40,000, thanks in part to FCC approval of smaller dish size. In 1976 there were fewer than 20 cable systems with earth receivers. In January, 1978, there were 181 earth receivers in operation, 90 construction permits granted, and 120 construction applications filed with the FCC. With applications pouring in at the rate of 25 a month, predictions were that 1000 earth stations would be operating by the end of 1979.

Very quickly the quality and variety of programming available to cable operators improved significantly. As John P. Taylor concluded in a January, 1978, article he wrote for *Television/Radio Age,* "The cable operator can put in an earth station, install as many receivers as needed, and take his choice of programs. In one year, he has gone from a lack of program sources to almost more than he knows what to do with." The day when cable can offer *everyone* something they want but can't get with "rabbit ears" or other antennas may be rapidly approaching.

The fragile antennas and circuitry of the communication satellites that orbit magically above us in perfect synchronization with the earth, like lollipops on sticks without the sticks, unquestionably represent the beginning of a technological revolution with serious cultural overtones: soon we will be using television differently, and expecting different things from it. When rates begin to drop for the rental of channels on the various birds, network dominance of individual stations—which is currently maintained by affiliates' dependence on the network transmission lines—will terminate.

Although officials of the three major networks are maintaining their brash, thirtieth-floor stance, the cumulative alternatives of new programs and video systems have got to have an eventual negative effect on the ratings of, say, *Love Boat.* Those who speculate on the industry's future also wonder if WTCG's line-up of sports and movies can stand the heavy onslaught of programming competition that is gathering like a great wave.

Today Don Andersson sits in his office overlooking the playing field of Fulton County Stadium and watches the busy patterns of little green dots accumulating on his large map of the United States. Each dot represents a cable system that is bringing in Channel 17. A recent headline in *TV Guide* read: "Why Are They Watching an Atlanta Station in Nebraska?"

Andersson is WTCG's man in charge of cable relations, and green, significantly enough, is the color of money. "Ted impressed me with his vision," Andersson says. "I knew that *he* knew what he was talking about. To do what he has done you've got to have vision, guts, and money. If he was missing any one of those he wouldn't have made it.

"Look what's happened in a year. In terms of cable homes,

we've done in one year on the satellite what it took seven years to do with microwave. By the end of 1978, when we hit two million cable homes, that will more than double our viewers in the Atlanta market."

The TV station Turner bought seven years ago is worth $30 million today. "The station's worth is appreciating at the rate of nearly one million dollars a month," Will Sanders says. "Theoretically, for every 100,000 viewers we have in the Atlanta market, we figure one million dollars in billings. The cable homes we're adding in the outlying areas are worth about half that, and we're adding about 50,000 homes a month. The rule of thumb is that a station's worth is three times its billings. Of course, this is all based on the assumption that we can interest advertisers in the audience we're building."

WTCG is already making initial billings that reflect its growing coverage. Certain national advertisers are paying higher rates to sponsor Braves games. Turner has opened full-time offices in Chicago and New York to market his station's cable audience.

Turner's "per-inquiry" sales program is already well established and growing. Sold-only-on-TV items like jewelry (mood rings), records (gospel and greatest hits), household items, or your authentic family crest are advertised on Channel 17, accompanied by an 800 telephone number. As many as 3000 calls a day are received, with 60 percent coming from the cable audience. In 1977 the per-inquiry program generated gross revenues of a million dollars.

"Ted sometimes talks about Channel 17 in national terms," Don Andersson says, "but I think our real potential is to be the first regional independent station—from Texas across Oklahoma, Arkansas, Tennessee, Kentucky, North Carolina, and everything south of that line. We're operating just like a network. We send our cable systems endless promotional material, newspaper slicks, advertising ideas, and so forth. We figure that Channel 17 is worth a 30 percent increase in business for a cable operator."

The function of the ball teams Turner has purchased becomes more clear. By owning the Braves, he avoids contract disputes and renegotiations over broadcast schedules. That reassures his cable customers. And if he hadn't bought a piece of the Atlanta Hawks, they might well have left Atlanta and cost Channel 17 one of its most marketable commodities.

Andersson enjoys working for Ted Turner. "He leaves me alone," Andersson says. "He runs the shop, controls the empire, but he tells me I'm the expert. He doesn't look over my shoulder. Often I don't hear from him for months. I just read about him in the papers. I couldn't be more fortunate. I saw the dream and now I'm making it a reality. But I suppose if those little green dots stopped appearing, Ted and I would part company.

"Ted plunged us into this thing and cast us adrift. No one really has any idea of where we're going."

Street Fighting

BY ALL ACCOUNTS, the Ted Turner who steered *Courageous* to victory during the summer of 1977 was hardly recognizable as the harried skipper he had been in 1974. A generous portion of the credit for Turner's defrenzification must go to Gary Jobson, the young man from Toms River, New Jersey, who was tactician aboard *Courageous*.

The tactician is of critical importance on a 12-meter, because to be successful, helmsman and tactician must function as one. Basically, the helmsman steers and maneuvers the boat while the tactician literally calls the turns by evaluating his boat's position on the course relative to the competition and the weather. The steering of a 12-meter is so demanding that if the helmsman were to continually take his eyes and attention off the boat long enough to make such evaluations, it would quickly cost sufficiently in boat speed and direction to lose the race. The tactician, then, becomes not only an extension of the helmsman's eyes, but of his judgment as well, which is damn tricky business.

Lowell North, skipper of *Enterprise,* named himself the tactician, preferring to put an even-tempered fellow known for his powers of concentration at the helm (Malin Burnham). In so doing, North took a page from British aviation. In two-man British fighters in World War II, the commander of the aircraft was the navigator-bombardier. The pilot was the chauffeur. Selecting a tactician was apparently so difficult for Ted Hood, a man known for his compulsion to do everything himself, that it took him until May, only six weeks before the June trials, to pick his man, Scott Perry.

Because the proper utilization of the tactician demands such ultimate confidence from a helmsman, who is usually the skipper, the combination most often falls far short of its goals. The problem is further complicated by the fact that the tactician must be a top-ranking skipper in his own right. He must have the experience and confidence to call the turns, and it is against human nature for such a person not to harbor notions that he could be running and steering the ship better. Such notions are honed by the inevitable and disproportionate amount of credit and publicity heaped upon the skipper.

So into the small cockpit of the 12-meter are placed two very competitive men with egos even larger than the outrageous lump of silver each of their accumulated sailing trophies would produce at a foundry, and fragile as egg shells besides. Each of them is then supposed to give up a very delicate and precious piece of his soul to the other for the duration of this strange marriage at sea. The tactician bows and offers up his self-image as number one. The skipper returns the bow, accepts the gift, and vows to trust the tactician as much as he trusts himself. Mission impossible begins.

Off they are supposed to glide like skate dancers, moving flawlessly together, smiling convincingly; like a brilliant dou-

bles team in tennis, covering instinctively for one another; like
soloist and accompanist, the latter mostly following, but ready
to provide the lead at any time, blessed with an uncanny sense
of where his prima donna is going, filling hesitations with such
skill and subtlety that even the critics might not catch them. In
short, the tactician must be extraordinarily able, supremely
confident, and practically incapable of being ruffled.

In addition to the textbook job description, the peculiarities
of each skipper place more abstract demands on the tactician.
Aside from having his own head screwed on straight, anyone
taking on the job should have a degree in psychology as a pre-
requisite. Turner is very volatile on board his boats. He may be
calmer than he used to be, but he is still inclined to scream and
rave, and to single out crew members for sustained, often em-
barrassingly degrading tirades of abuse. And though over the
years he has overcome his tendency to go left just for spite when
someone suggests he go right, the need for such blind assertive-
ness is ingrained. Even though Turner understands the necessity and logic of the tactician's job, even though he personally
hand-picked Jobson, being in the position of telling Turner
what to do would not be enviable. During the ceremonial bows,
Jobson hung up his guns in good faith. Turner undoubtedly
had a Derringer hidden in his boot.

Jobson wasn't Turner's first choice for the job. He asked Graham Hall, *Valiant*'s tactician in 1974 and former college All-
American from Kings Point. Hall was director of sailing at the
U.S. Naval Academy and was unable to obtain leave to accept
Turner's offer. Hall suggested Jobson, whom he had recruited
and coached at New York Maritime Academy. "A first-rate
skipper like Gary in the role of crew has the toughest job in
sailing," Hall says. "But Gary had crewed in Tempests with a
guy who has many of Turner's characteristics, and on Flying
Dutchmen. He was uniquely prepared for the tactician's job.
But even as strongly as I recommended him, I had no idea Gary

would handle the situation as well as he did."

In college, Jobson was an All-American sailor his last three years. He was named College Sailor of the Year in 1972. In the fall of 1972 he was invited to the first North American Interclass Solo Championship, an event held at Barrington, R.I., which tries with commendable success to bring together the ten best sailors in the country for three days of racing in three different types of boats. Jobson led the whole way, only to lose it in the last race and finish second by one point to Robbie Doyle, who would be *Courageous*'s sailmaker and on-board trimmer. (Turner also raced in the Solo's that year, finishing well behind Doyle and Jobson, and locking their names into his memory.)

In 1973 Jobson never finished worse than second, won the Nationals again, and was awarded College Sailor of the Year a second time.

"Some important advice Graham Hall gave me," Jobson says, "was to start sailing for fun. Once I started sailing for fun I was unbeatable. I was never nervous, I was smooth, I kept plugging away. What a feeling! From the spring of 1972 to the fall of 1973 no one I came across was better than me. Doyle beat me that once, but I beat all the other hot guys."

Jobson's father is the managing editor of the Asbury Park Press, the largest paper in central New Jersey. His mother teaches at Toms River Regional High School while working on a Ph.D. The small wood frame house Tom Jobson bought in 1957 went through eight additions as the family grew. It is a comfortable, welcoming place that was a neighborhood hangout for the Jobson kids and their pals.

Gary learned to sail in an old Atlantic City catboat. "It had a metal brace around the bow to hold it together," Tom Jobson says. The elder Jobson is a stocky man in his fifties with a ruddy complexion and a shock of straight gray hair that covers his ears. He is a most congenial man, a far cry from the classic metro city editor type. "That boat had so much sail we would dredge the bay with the rudder on a broad reach. We had a big pump with a piece of drainpipe for an extension. Everybody got good at pumping because we pumped all the time. I could teach Gary some seamanship, but that's about all. He was always sailing against kids whose parents were sailors. Gary couldn't come home and talk to me about racing. I felt bad about that."

Gary says flunking the second grade provided him with a motivation to excel that remains to this day. "That was a really rough time," Jobson says. "All at once I was older and bigger than everybody in my class. It's the worst thing to get left behind. I really got picked on—that's the age when you get hit over the head with lunch boxes. Those days left a deep scar. The next couple years I really felt challenged to prove myself. That's when sailing became important. I didn't do too well at first, but I was serious."

He joined the local sailing program when he was seven. By the time he was 13, he was winning trophies. When he was 16 he was named the outstanding junior on the bay. "I was stunned," Gary says. "It was a totally major feat. The list of winners is illustrious. Olympic gold medalists and world champions."

Jobson graduated from college with a degree, a 75-dollar Pontiac, a stereo system, and his foul-weather gear. He turned down what could have been a lucrative offer to become a sailmaker because he wanted to coach. Then the job at Kings Point opened up, and he got it.

How does one coach sailing? "I coach attitude," Jobson said one sunny day in Marblehead during the early spring of 1977. The crews of *Independence* and *Courageous* were killing time at the dock, waiting for a small gale to abate so they could go sailing. It was warm and pleasant in the lee of Graves Yacht Yard, and at lunch time we all opened brown bags and relaxed. To an outsider, 12-meter crews can seem an uptight, distant bunch, especially before the final crew-selection process. This is often partly a result of the crew's private suspicion that what people say about 12-meter sailors being the cream of the crop is absolutely true. But Jobson couldn't have been friendlier.

He is relaxed, open, easy-going, which might sound a touch mundane unless it is pointed out that sailors of the first rank usually affect a more arrogant, aggressive approach. Perhaps this is because sailors who make the first rank—like swimmers and tennis players—start very young. It is often a case of too much too soon. Little heads can get twisted easily, producing semi-adults of dubious distinction. Sailing is an individual sport, but unlike tennis and swimming, a sailor can continue to compete in the first rank well into senility (depending on his financial resources) by choosing boats which fit his physical capabilities. And that is a long time to suffer the pressures of being a fast gun. So the affectations tend to be acquired early in this sport and carefully nurtured and developed for the long run.

But not with Jobson. When Graham Hall told him to start sailing for fun, he took it to heart.

Jobson generally looks like he is having a good time. His most common facial expression is shaded with pleasant anticipation, good humor, and often amazement. When he speaks of past successes he gives you the facts, not a chorus of self-aggrandizement, and the narration is usually followed by a raising of the eyebrows and a shrug, as if to say, "Wow, that's me. I did that." His reaction to the America's Cup was the same: "I kept saying, 'No big deal, no big deal.' Then I realized, 'This *is* a big deal—this is really it!' " Jobson was both awed and smitten by the realization. He fell in love with it. It was so beautiful; it was his, and he clutched it with the tenderness which he felt was its due. Of all the participants, Jobson may have suffered the biggest letdown. "I went into a restaurant down home with my family the other night," Gary said in October, after it was

71

all over, "and for the first time all summer, nobody knew who I was. . . ."

He is 6′ 2″, 180 pounds, and carries himself with the relaxed posture of a man who has just had a sauna and massage at the health club. His casual clothes—corduroy jeans, baggy sweaters, flannel shirts—and hands resting easily in his pockets, complete a Columbo-like steadiness.

Some of the posture has to be left-over Jersey high school cool. Squint a little at Jobson standing around the dock in his green *Courageous* "team" jacket with the vertical white stripes running up and over the shoulders from under the arms, and it is easy to place him in a sixties teen scene at the local Toms River juke joint. Until he got his *Courageous* clothing issue (blue-crested blazer, green or white alligator shirts, white sneakers, off-white pants), he favored beige suits with dark shirts.

An attractive young lady I know, who is in the daily throes of making judgments about men, and who is fast approaching the rank of expert in that field, pronounces Jobson as "gorgeous." She says it is mostly his eyes, which are the color of butter rum candies. He really *looks* at you, she reports. It figures that a fellow with Jobson's approach to coaching would be interested in people. He really does look at them, he sees them, hears them, and thinks about them. Puzzling out and being amazed by the intricate ebb and flow of personalities around him is the grist of his daily life.

Even for a man of Jobson's good nature, Ted Turner was an overdose. Jobson had to figure out not only what to do on the race course, but how to tell Turner what to do so he would *do* it most of the time. The second task was the most formidable. While Jobson had been practicing what to do since he was seven years old, he had less than a year to lay the groundwork for programming his skipper.

The first times he raced with Turner everything went very well. Jobson enjoyed it, the two worked together, and the results were the breathtaking SORC series with *Running Tide* and a coveted Congressional Cup win. But two series do not a whole summer make.

It was Turner who suggested the walks. All during the preliminary racing at Marblehead, and in Newport from the time the boats arrived, Turner and Jobson would leave the house together every morning and walk to the boat. After sailing, they would again take their solitary walk. That Turner would suggest such a pattern, and practice it with such determination, reveals a startling knowledge of self. Because if it is real communication of real information one is after—of the sort that should be exchanged between skipper and tactician—it is essential that Turner be alone. Turner in a crowd is useless. A crowd, in this instance, is defined as more than one other person. Turner can no more resist exploring the dynamic potential of a crowd than a child can resist pulling the cat's whiskers.

So they walked and they talked, all fall in Marblehead, and day after day, week after week in Newport. It would be more accurate to say that Turner talked and Jobson listened. But that was okay. Given the groundwork Jobson was undertaking, the information Turner was providing would be invaluable later when two 12-meters with the momentum of very large semi-trailers would be approaching each other at nine knots on opposite tacks.

The two talked about specifics of the boat, of course: how to improve crew performance, evaluation of methods and systems, sails, tactics, starting techniques, better ways to work together, and so on. Then Turner would take off on whatever was in his mind, and that covered a lot of ground. He talked about his family, his childhood, his father's death, whether or not he should trade this player or buy that one, the fortunes of the Hawks, how to make the satellite business work, his political ambitions—he unloaded it all on Jobson.

Often, after dinner, Turner and Jobson would be in Turner's room watching the ball game and drawing tactical situations on paper between innings. On days off the two would go sailing in Lasers and try out various starting situations. Turner got into the habit of barging into Jobson's room first thing in the morning, waking him up, and sitting on the bed waiting until he was dressed and ready to go to breakfast—until Gary's wife Janice began locking the door at night. So intense was their relationship that Jane Turner remarked at the end of the summer that they were in love with each other. Which wasn't quite the case.

Jobson and Turner's relationship was essentially a combative one. Like a cooperative patient, Turner was talking incessantly to Jobson, telling him more about himself than perhaps anyone had ever known, talking about even the dark times and revealing the hidden recesses, giving it all to Jobson to use in his struggle to keep Turner cool. But Turner's very nature forced him then to battle back, having once again stacked the deck against himself, with renewed fervor to keep Jobson from succeeding—or at least to give him doubts about how well he was doing.

Jobson's eyes were open. "I knew I was going to have a struggle with Ted. I knew he was a tough one." There were little things. Jobson would not play backgammon with Turner, for instance. Turner is an accomplished player, and Jobson figured he would lose more often than he would win. But he would beat Turner at Ping-Pong whenever Ted wanted. "It was important," Jobson says, "for me to keep whatever edge I could."

But as the summer wore on, certain things couldn't be avoided. There were the croquet games. Turner cheats at croquet, according to those who bop around the wickets with him. He did so that summer in a friendly, joshing sort of way that occasionally amounted to something more. Having lost a dozen straight to Ted, Jobson was lining up his winning, last shot through the wickets to the stake when Ted walked off, announcing he didn't want to play anymore.

And there were reading aloud sessions. As the press coverage mounted, Turner would ask Jobson to read clips and articles to him. "One of the tough things," Jobson says, "was that Ted never listened if I felt the need to talk about myself for a minute. He only listened when I talked about him. It got pretty far out. One Sunday in July, we stopped at three newsstands on the way to the boat to find *Time* and *Newsweek.* He read about himself in *Newsweek,* then asked me to read the coverage in *Time* to him. We were ten minutes late getting to the dock. He would have a fit if the morning papers didn't arrive at the house on time."

Jobson perceived along the way that more sophisticated moves would be necessary on his part to both hold his edge and nurture Turner's momentum. After the Demi-Tasse dinghy race following the July trials, I needled Jobson a little for having lost to Turner in small boats, remarking how unlikely that was, especially since he had a good lead going into the last race. Jobson had a glass lifted high at the time, and was concentrating on breaking the adhesion of an ice cube to the bottom. He choked and coughed and brought his glass down fast. His smile was a touch crooked. "Yeah, well, there was a really bad wind shift on the last leg and I lost seven boats." Jobson paused, his eyes locked on mine. "Now tell me," he said quietly. "Don't you think Turner needed to win that little regatta?"

As Jobson began receiving his own recognition and press coverage, he had to dig in even harder. Turner was delighted, for instance, when he was able to embarrass Jobson in front of the crew. It began with a bull session aboard the boat one day while she was being towed out. The subject was hackneyed: who was doing what to whom. A particular girl was mentioned, Jobson was asked by Turner if he had scored, and Jobson said yes. A few days later, again while being towed out, Turner announced he had checked with the girl in question, and that Jobson had lied. He had lied! Naturally, with Turner, such a disclosure would call for a fairly long and colorful speech examining the sailing ability, education, diet, geographic heritage, hobbies, music appreciation, and true moral fiber of someone who could hope to peddle such an outrageous, self-serving falsehood.

Jobson grimaces as he tells the tale. "I was really stupid to give him the ammunition. It just seemed like the easiest thing to say at the time."

When Tom Jobson showed up in Newport, Turner found him a handy secondary target. "The first time I met him," Tom says, "he looked at my hair and said, 'Oh, you're a hippie, huh?' After that, he developed a patter that went along the lines of, 'Ho! There's Papa Jobson. I wonder how Gary got so smart having a newspaperman as a father.' I couldn't dislike a guy I didn't really know at all, but I will say I stayed as far away from Turner as possible without falling off the dock."

But Turner had to be careful. There was an edge, a limit, and naturally it was defined by Turner's own needs. As Jobson says, "Turner can't stand anyone mad at him. If I acted angry he would quickly change tunes, fire off a couple compliments, and ask to shake hands and get it back together.

"My deal on the boat, my strength, was to never allow myself to be surprised," Jobson says. "I was always ready with good advice based on plenty of preparation. Ashore, our crew was self-motivated. Turner had selected well. That may be his greatest talent, in fact. He is best at selecting people and telling them what to do. But the crew members had to get their jobs done in spite of Turner. When he left them alone they were fine. But once in a while he would come around and start telling them how to do it. Some of the guys would get mad and take off. So I would grab him and suggest a walk, or an ice cream cone, or remind him the Braves were on TV—anything to get him off the boat.

"My job was keeping Ted from going off the deep end. It got

to be a real pain in the ass playing his game, sucking in my gut in croquet, but it paid off. Toward the end I really didn't know why I was in it. Was I in it for myself? I don't know. I do know that Turner became the real challenge, not the Cup."

In between psychological rounds, *Courageous* afloat was a loose boat. It's easy to be loose when you're winning, but the *Courageous* personnel probably could have stayed fairly relaxed through anything. As Turner told them, in an extemporaneous psyche-up speech from the helm just before the first official race with *Independence*, they were "street fighters."

"We need to win," Turner told them, "because we're just a bunch of bums. Are there any blue bloods here? Raise your hands. None. I didn't think so. Anybody from fancy prep schools? Awright. We could have won it with the latest in computers, but that's not our style. We like to slug it out. These other guys are going to have to slug it out with a bunch of street fighters from the Bronx and Queens."

The analysis wasn't very accurate, but it would suffice. Counting Turner six of the crew were *Mariner* repeats:

● Richie Boyd, winch tailer (age 25, 5′ 9″, 170), Islip, New York, had sailed regularly with Turner for seven years all over the world, including the 1977 Congressional Cup. Boyd was a recent Princeton graduate.

● Carl (Bunky) Helfrich, winch tailer (age 40, 5′ 8″, 165), Hilton Head, South Carolina, had known Turner since they were both nine years old. He, too, had sailed with him all over the world for many years, and was on the 1977 Congressional Cup crew. Helfrich was an architect.

● Robbie Doyle, sailmaker and sail trimmer (age 28, 5′ 10″, 180), Marblehead, won the Sears Cup in 1964 and 1965. He was on the U.S. Olympic Finn Class team in 1968 (he narrowly missed being selected), 1969 and 1970. He won the North

American Solo Championships in 1972 and 1973 and the Canada's Cup in 1972. Doyle was vice president of Hood Sails.

● Marty O'Meara, winch tailer (alternate) (age 50, 5' 10", 170), Hartford, Connecticut. Marty was a former Lightning sailor and president of the class association. O'Meara had campaigned with Turner for years, including the 1977 Congressional Cup. O'Meara's businesses in Connecticut included a gas station and partnership in a dog track.

● Conn Finlay, mast man (age 47, 6' 7", 235), Belmont, California. This was Finlay's third 12-meter campaign. He had two Olympic gold medals, a bronze in double sculls with cox, and a bronze medal in the 1976 Olympics as crew in the Tempest class. His ocean racing background was extensive, including the 1977 Congressional Cup. Finlay's business involved buying, rebuilding, and selling rowing shells.

The others missed the *Mariner* excursion, for which they were undoubtedly grateful:

● John Edgecomb, bow man (age 25, 6', 190), Palos Verdes, California, had been on Congressional Cup winners four times, including 1977, and had been the captain of *Charisma*. His racing experience was extensive.

● Gould (Stretch) Ryder III, mast man (age 29, 6' 1", 195), Port Washington, New York, was a Long Island Penguin champion and won the Bacardi Cup in Stars. A professional helicopter pilot, Ryder had a strong ocean racing background.

● Dick Sadler, grinder (age 23, 5' 10", 160), City Island, New York. An All American sailor from New York Maritime College and a Laser champion, he was also the New York metropolitan diving and gymnastic champion.

● Bill Jorch, navigator (age 32, 6', 165), Northport, New York. Jorch navigated *Valiant* in 1974, with Turner as skipper for the last races. Jorch was East Coast Lightning Champion. He was a computer design engineer for Grumman.

● Paul Fuchs, grinder (age 24, 5' 10", 170), Detroit, Michigan, had won three Canadian Nationals as a lightweight single sculler and had taken a third and a fourth in the U.S. Nationals. Fuchs was a naval architect.

Jobson and Turner rounded out the crew.

Then there was the tender driver, a curly-headed, prematurely gray ocean racer and carpenter with the unlikely name of Mickey Spillane. He was a street fighter himself and a fan of Turner. The tender chartered for *Courageous* was a 45-foot Hatteras originally called *Tragen*. One night in July after Turner had thrown a screaming, beer-can-slinging fit on the boat after another in the sequence of losses to *Enterprise*, two of his crew quietly sandpapered the T and the N off the transom of the Hatteras. The new name, *Rage,* was such a hit that owner John Bushell re-documented the boat at the end of the summer rather than change it back.

With the 50,000-pound *Courageous* strapped alongside, the quiet, cool-handed Spillane would spin the whole lash-up and back it into the impossibly small space at Bannister's Wharf like it was a ten-foot outboard. He often got a big round of applause from onlookers, which always caused the color to rush to his cheeks.

The *Courageous* women were impressive, too, in their multiple and demanding roles of personal counselors, soothers of bruised egos, massagers of muscles, tireless sign makers and cheerleaders, loggers of endless boring hours aboard observation boats, menders of rents in the fabric of personality, patient sufferers of aggressive groupies, and enthusiastic lovers of tired mates. They piled onto the tender with Mickey whenever they could persuade or avoid Loomis, to be as close to the action as possible, and to sing "Go *Courageous, Courageous* rules the waves" over the loudspeaker system on *Rage* whenever it seemed appropriate. They never did come up with the second line.

Turner had his moments of uptightness on the boat, to be

sure, but he was loose enough to agree to a casual suggestion made one morning during practice that it might be nice to have lunch on Block Island, 20 miles southwest of Newport. They were halfway there when the suggestion was made—they could see the hills beckoning—and even loafing along, a 12-meter makes seven or eight knots. Mickey, their constant companion, had taken *Rage* back to Newport for some reason. So Bill Jorch called him on the radio and reported their course and position.

Jorch had given Mickey a set of bearings once they got into Block Island's Salt Pond. A few minutes later Spillane called back, confused. That position line, he told Jorch, goes right over Block Island. What's the story? Jorch didn't bother to answer him. Spillane never did find *Courageous* until later that afternoon when the boat was approaching Newport.

"Turner was like a tour director," Jorch said. "He warned all of us that the boat was leaving at three o'clock sharp, with or without the crew. Then we walked over to Ballard's and chowed down with burgers, clams, french fries, ice cream, just like a bunch of tourists.

"We sent a post card to Lee Loomis and Ted Hood, saying 'wish you were here.' And we bought Loomis a souvenir T-shirt. We would have preferred a satin pillow.

"The crowd at Ballard's was great. Marty picked up a girl using the same line he had been using all summer: 'Hi, I'm Marty O'Meara. How do you like me so far?'"

When it was time to leave, they couldn't find a boat to take them out, so Turner walked down to the Coast Guard station and explained who he was and how he had been in the Coast Guard himself. He came back standing on the bow of one of their 40-footers. The Coast Guard loved it. They stood by until the sails were raised and *Courageous* was cast off, then provided an escort from the harbor.

Turner made time to take in various events he considered important, like the Triple-A All-Star game featuring players from his Richmond team. It was held in August in nearby Pawtucket, Rhode Island, where the minor-league All-Stars would take on a slightly watered-down version of the Boston Red Sox. Here he killed two birds, making the big game a family night as well. Ted, Jane, and four of their five children—Beau, Rhett, Laura Lee, Jinny—my wife, Possum, and I jammed into the Turner station wagon for the 45-minute ride to Pawtucket. No one had taken time for dinner, which undoubtedly increased the restlessness in the back seat. The decibel level in the car was just slightly under the permanent damage range. A lot of attention-getting ploys were being craftily worked by the children as they competed fiercely to talk to their father, who hadn't been in their lives much during the spring and summer. When one of the children would complain to Ted about the treatment being received at the hands of another, Ted would refer them to Jane. "Speak to your mother. She's in charge back there. Janie! Do something!"

Jane, who looked child-weary, had drawn herself into the left rear door, as far as possible from the action, and was concentrating with determination on the fast-moving landscape.

Ted was responding to the children only sporadically, because two evenings before, at the party thrown by the Kings Point Syndicate for the other 12-meter organizations and friends (each syndicate takes its turn hosting such an affair during the summer), co-host Turner had forced a confrontation with Lowell North that had nearly come to blows. The incident was still very much on Turner's mind, and he was raising his voice above the din in the station wagon to rail about the subject one more time.

"North has got to be motivated by fear. . . . It's no better for me than it is for them. . . . They must be afraid they can't beat us without an edge. If we were playing baseball, and North manufactured the balls, we'd have to use rocks."

A wave of conflict exploded from the back seat, causing Turner to scold the children. They quieted. He asked them if they understood his meaning. There was a chorus of contrite "yes sirs."

At the ball park, which was filled to capacity, Turner and his entourage received red carpet treatment. Hank Aaron was already there. The rest of us were ushered into the large VIP field box, where we joined the young mayor of Pawtucket and his wife, Dick O'Connell, the general manager of the Boston Red Sox, and the owners of the other AAA teams. Crackers and cheese had been laid out, and waitresses scurried after drinks. Laura Lee went off to get hot dogs, and Beau, much to Ted's delight, said he would rather sit in the bleachers.

Turner bet Dick O'Connell that the All-Stars would beat the Red Sox. The wager was one dollar. Turner said he didn't think it would offend Bowie Kuhn.

A local television station interviewed Turner, who said he thought the America's Cup was safe.

Turner exchanged banter with the minor league owners. He said the Braves were in bad shape. "It's a good thing losing ball games doesn't kill anybody. Our defense is leaky, we don't have any healthy pitchers, and our salaries are big. I would be happy to trade the whole Braves team for one of your Triple-A franchises," he told O'Connell.

"I sent Kuhn an autographed copy of the picture of me on *Sports Illustrated,*" Turner told the group. "Then I wrote and asked if he received it. I told him if he hadn't, I would send him another one.

"Am I bad for baseball? If you're in this game and losing two million dollars then you ought to be able to get drunk once in a while and have some fun.

"I'm through with this free agent stuff. I was a rookie owner and I made some mistakes. I'll tell you, I've gone to the well for the last time. Hey, people aren't supposed to beat on a rookie!" The minor league owners were chuckling.

At the other end of the box, one of Turner's boys had burst into tears. Janie brought him down to sit next to his father. Ted was concerned. It seemed the boy felt he had finished last in the sibling battle for attention.

"Well, son," Ted told him, "I've only been paying attention to those who talk the loudest, and I guess I didn't hear you. You've got to speak up, son. Make yourself heard. I'm sorry, son, it's been a rough summer for me. You know how it is when you're playing ball, right?

"Come on, let's get some runs! Murder those bums!"

Turner leaned out of the box and caught the eye of Tommie Aaron, Hank's brother, who manages the Richmond team in the Braves minor league organization. Turner patted himself on the cheek. Tommie nodded, disappeared, and then ran over to the box and slapped a pack of Red Man chewing tobacco on the railing. Turner stuffed a clump in his cheek and offered some to his son. The boy declined.

No one on the crew really suspected Turner would go after Lowell North during the *Courageous-Independence* syndicate party. They all knew that the issue of sails had become an obsession with Ted, and all of them knew him well enough to know that he wasn't about to drop it. In fact, most of them had gotten fairly sick of hearing him rave about it. And while he had been threatening to do whatever he could to persuade people not to buy North sails, it was assumed he would either stay away from North at the party, or let it go with an exchange of greetings.

There had been one incident back in June. Turner had taken Jobson and gone to visit *Enterprise.* Such fraternal visits were commonplace. But Turner had turned the visit into what Jobson recalls as a very embarrassing ordeal. The two had looked the boat over and conversed with friends (almost all the crew members on all the boats had known each other over the years, and most had sailed together at one time or another). Then Turner started in on the sail business, and carried on to such an extent that after a few minutes, everyone had found a place to sit and something inanimate to stare at.

When Turner finished, the silence was long and stony. One of the *Enterprise* crew said it felt like it lasted five minutes. Then Turner got up and left, with Jobson trudging behind.

At the syndicate party, people were a little edgy. The overkill had been so extreme on Turner's part that having him and North under the same yellow and white caterer's tent was . . . well . . . chancy. But then a week or so before, Turner had apologized to North on the dock for the extent to which he had carried the whole thing, so perhaps there was nothing to worry about.

I was talking with Lowell North and Lucy Jewitt, the wife of *Enterprise* syndicate principal Fritz Jewitt when Turner approached. It was early in the evening. Turner was stone sober. The two exchanged greetings.

"You know, Lowell," Turner said, "I always thought you were a good guy. And I've been a good customer over the years, right?"

North: "That's right, a very good customer."

Turner: "Well, I'm not going to be a good customer anymore. I want you to know I'm going to do everything I can to work against you for the rest of my life."

Lowell bristled noticeably. He leaned toward Turner, his jaw thrust out. "Listen, Ted, what is all this? What about the deal that was reached at the Congressional Cup? I thought everything was settled at that point."

Turner: "There was no deal."

North: "I thought you came up to me and apologized last

week. Apparently that didn't have any meaning at all."

Turner: "I did. I apologized for name-calling. It had nothing to do with the principle of the thing."

North: "Then it was a meaningless apology, wasn't it?"

The two stood face to face, no more than a foot apart. It was showdown time. *Enterprise* and *Courageous* crewmen had begun to form a loose circle around Turner and North. Turner's hands were clenching into fists and then unclenching.

The random, cocktail-party flow of people broke the spell. A young lady, oblivious to what was happening, simply waded in to exercise her desire to meet Lowell North, and it was all over. Lowell greeted the stranger with his usual charm. Turner came up beside me at the bar. "Well, how'd I do?" he asked. "Should I say more? I wasn't going to attend the party—I came down from my room just to punch him in the nose. Do you think I should?"

After the party, on the way to dinner with the Norths, Kay North couldn't get past the first part of the story. Kay is a trim California woman. Her blond hair is cut close, Mia Farrow style. She doesn't stand a fraction over 5′ 4″ in her socks. She is soft-spoken and very feminine, sexy. But her aggressive tennis game reflects her intensity. Her sense of humor is subtle, and well developed. Her sense of self is strong, having been recently rejuvenated by completion of an EST course, which had a more visible effect on her than on Lowell, who also took it. Kay North's small talk might be unnerving to the bashful. Her focus usually goes right to the center. Her response to criticism for a remark she once made was a shrug: "It took me 35 years to learn how to be honest," she said. "I'm not going to blow it now."

Her reaction to Turner was refreshing. "It was marvelous Ted spent so much time paying Lowell extravagant compliments—screaming nationwide for North Sails when he had Hood in his syndicate. You can't buy publicity like that."

During the incident at the syndicate party, Kay North had been across the tent. "Lowell bristled," she kept repeating with quiet amazement. "Lowell bristled?! How wonderful. I never saw him do that. Hmmm." She looked up at her husband, studying his face. "Will you bristle for me, Lowell?"

Lowell North is just over six feet, and weighs 180 pounds. He considers himself at the minimum of what is physically required for crewing on a 12-meter. He is an erect man who carries his head high, as if he were stretching a bit to see a distant object. He has curly brown hair, freckles, steady blue eyes set close, and radiates a pervasive sense of calm. His nickname is "the Pope." The name was coined one night in a West Coast sailor's bull session. It was agreed that Paul Elvström, the great Danish sailor, was God. "What does that make Lowell?" someone asked. Hence the nickname.

North is a laconic fellow who has found sailing by far the most eloquent way to express himself. He is habitually preoccupied—like the archetypal college professor—with the tangle of lines, gear, sail shapes, hull shapes, wind and sea conditions, minute adjustments, inventions, innovations, and endless variables that make up the sport of sailboat racing and the business of sailmaking.

Whether North is number one or number two in the sailmaking business is a moot question. He and Ted Hood have been staging a close-fought battle over the years that has escalated into rather specific, put-up-your-dukes advertising campaigns run by the two lofts. GM and Ford. Coke and Pepsi. Hood and North. Depending on the yardstick used, one or the other holds a lead too slim to be very significant.

The two share what may be occupational similarities. Hood is also laconic, and even more reticent about talking—ever. They are both first-generation successes in the business. Hood's debut in 1950 came after a shot at the home construction business and coincided with the advent of synthetic fibers. North began in 1959 after hoping to manufacture skis. Hood was 50 during these Cup races; North 47. Hood has four children; North has three. Both their fathers are inventors, North's in geophysics with the American Oil Company, Hood's in chemistry with Monsanto. Hood has been making sails for Cup defenders since 1958, North since 1964. And both of them live in rather grand houses overlooking the home harbors and yacht clubs of their choice.

While Hood's racing successes have been in larger boats, from international one-designs to ocean racers, North has won most of his silverware in smaller boats in fleet racing around closed courses. He has been part-owner of the Star class since he crewed on the winning boat at the Worlds when he was 15 years old. He won the Worlds himself an unprecedented four times, a fact that astounds racing sailors. He has also placed second five times, and third twice. It is a phenomenal record, considering the competition in that class. From 1972 to 1977, North also piled up an impressive record in larger boats. For 1976 he won the Martini and Rossi (now the Pinch Scotch) Yachtsman of the Year honors for the second time (Turner has won it three times).

Racing sailors can be generally divided into two categories: those who prefer as standardized a class as possible, racing in one-design fleets, wherein sails are purchased in lots and assigned by a lottery and where the entire emphasis is on helmsmanship and tactics; and those who would rather tinker with ounces, millimeters, and systems to help develop latent speed. John Marshall, the scholarly fellow who ran North's most productive loft in Stratford, Connecticut, until he was promoted to sales manager of the whole North operation, and who was downwind helmsman aboard *Enterprise,* feels Lowell definitely belongs to the latter group.

"Lowell is much more interested in developing a superior aerodynamic and hydrodynamic vehicle than in sailing a race.

When it is going well for Lowell, the sailing part is anticlimactic. He has it won before the gun goes off."

On the 12-meter, skipper North showed just how anticlimactic he thought the sailing part was. North hardly got his hands on the helm of *Enterprise*. He selected Malin Burnham, an old Star boat competitor and close friend, to sail weather legs, and Marshall drove downwind. This freed Lowell to work full time on tactics and boat speed, his specialties. He did start the boat, although even that was not definite in his mind. He said beforehand he would start unless he found someone who could do it better.

It was an unusual, perhaps unprecedented approach to a 12-meter. North not only disregarded the hand-to-hand combat of the helm, he revealed an ego of amazing passivity for a man of his accomplishment. What 12-meter skipper has ever been able to resist the helm? The helm is the power, the glory—part of today's corporate vernacular.

The *Enterprise* set-up reflects the overall North philosophy. His sail business is decentralized. Each loft (there are 14) is managed independently by a person hand-picked by North. The loft manager is encouraged to set up business where it best suits him and to operate as he pleases. North's list of managers—"tigers," he calls the best of them—reads like a who's who of world-class racing skippers: former teachers, businessmen, and so on to whom North has popped the question, "How would you like to be a sailmaker?" After six to eight months in San Diego learning the business, off they go. The salaries are average, the profit-sharing generous. Marshall, a former math teacher at the University of Bridgeport, drives a silver Porsche 911 and flies his own airplane.

North agrees that sailmaking is a personality business. The customer wants to talk with the star. So he has put a star at every loft.

North's powers of evaluation are keen, and his crisp objectivity includes himself. Doug Peterson, who designed *Pied Piper* and *Williwaw,* boats in which Lowell won the 1975 One-Ton Worlds and the 1976 SORC, respectively, says North is the first one to admit a mistake, as he did after the 1977 Congressional Cup. North thought the mainsail on the Cal 40 he drew was bad. He asked permission to recut it, which was granted. It still wasn't right. "I thought I was smart enough to fix it," North said. "I didn't fix it enough. I should have asked for another sail to begin with." What kind of a sail was it? "An old North mainsail."

Many people with North's bent for the quantitative approach to their vocation have trouble keeping the rest of their life free of it. Such people begin the day by fretting over the amount of milk on their morning cereal, and alienate less precise thinkers without even trying. That is not Lowell North's problem. North puts people off by forgetting their names, even those of good customers, or by not noticing them at all, which is sometimes mistaken for a snub.

"Never drive with him," San Diego boat builder Carl Eichenlaub warns. "It's amazing he gets home at night. I've been on the highway with him and watched the speed go 60, 70, 90 without him realizing it. He's always in a fog. I've seen him walk over from his office and stand here having forgotten what he came for. On the way out he'll run into the gate, or a boat. When he and Kay are going out at night, she'll have to remind him when they arrive who they're seeing."

Kay North describes her husband as a man without a highly developed ego or sense of vanity. "He would still be wearing pants with a buckle in the back if he could find them," Kay says, "simply because he got used to them in college." He does favor white bucks and saddle shoes. Kay predicted Lowell would not put his stamp on the overall defense effort, as past skippers have done. "He actively delegates some things and passively delegates the rest, like what the crew will wear," she says. "He saw a small part for himself: take the boat and make it go fast. Leave the rest for others. He won't take hold of the big picture and have it reflect his personality. He doesn't want that or need it."

Kay's favorite word for Lowell is "level." "Maybe too level," she says. "Sometimes it's not just control; it's that he isn't feeling. It's hard communicating with him. We exchange books. But I don't often venture a precious thought because he'll be off on a different channel, or wherever it is he is . . . wherever that may be. I've never been too sure.

"When he does focus on you it's very flattering. We met skiing. I tested him. I asked him if it was a choice between skiing or sailing, which would he choose? He said sailing, if the competition was good. Lucky I tested, I thought. But he persisted. He wanted me to go to Naples with him for the Olympics. My parents refused. What if I marry her first, he asked then. My mother pointed out that he would have to keep me when we got back. We never talked about religion, politics, kids. I jumped in. We got married between regattas and went to Naples."

At least partly, with Lowell, the way he operates is a matter of good old Southern California style. Nowhere are the toys of childhood so seductive as they are in Southern California, or so accessible. Nowhere are the seasons so long. There is surfing, skateboarding, boating, skiing in the nearby mountains, hang gliding, sky diving. . . . Early in his career North vowed he would do something that was fun. When skis didn't work out, he turned to boats. And to be in one of the pleasure industries of California is to work with other kids who didn't want to leave the toys behind.

In San Diego's man-made Shelter Island complex, where palm trees wave in the steady afternoon breeze, you can have a racing sailboat of any size designed, built, outfitted with gear, and launched practically by standing on one spot and shouting requests in different directions. There, over the delicatessen, is designer Doug Peterson's office, and there's Dougie, shuffling across the parking lot in old moccasins, chino pants, and a faded purple T-shirt, his red beard waving in the breeze, laughing hysterically about something. Down three or four buildings is Carl Eichenlaub, his epoxy-stiffened pants sagging halfway to his knees, turning out an aluminum 50-footer on his postage-stamp lot. Two more doors down is Gerry Driscoll's more austere office. Driscoll skippered *Intrepid* (the *people*'s boat!) to within a crying shame of being selected in 1974. And across the street is Lowell North's loft.

They all work hard, and they all disagree about things, but no one seems to forget he is supposed to be having fun. An obligatory dinner at the home of the man who owned the Cal 40 Lowell was sailing to certain defeat in the 1977 Congressional Cup turned into a full-scale party, with unwilling dance partners being dragged on their backs across the shag rug by wonderfully aggressive ladies. The food was delicious, Mexican, and messy, and not a tie, jacket, or pair of red pants was in sight. After dinner, with their parents' grudging consent, the children of the hosts brought down their pet rats and passed them around.

The endlessly sunny weather has something to do with the good-natured, open-door policy, but it is a far cry from the East Coast approach to "yachting," which is all too often characterized by clenched teeth. But then people on the East Coast don't have a California hot tub to plop into after work or sailing, the latest development in social amenities in which a communal soak in 105-degree water relaxes sore joints and takes the cramps out of jaw muscles.

At the North home, a spacious, angular place built of spruce and redwood and lots of glass, the telephone was ringing. Lowell was sitting at the kitchen table, reducing the day's sail-testing data to plots on a graph. Kay was fixing dinner and asking Julie, the 14-year-old, how the salad dressing she made the previous evening worked out.

"Perfect!" Julie said. "Except there was too much vinegar."

On the porch, Holly, 17, was cooking steaks on the grill with a boyfriend.

And the telephone was ringing, ringing, ringing. No one seemed to hear it except me.

"Does the telephone bother you?" Kay asked. I admitted that it did. I expressed amazement that two teenagers weren't breaking legs to answer it.

"It usually does bother people," Kay said, "including friends who try to call us. Anyone is free to answer it. Apparently no one here wants to talk with anyone else right now."

Dinner was candlelit, quiet. Talk was of college applications, part-time jobs, summer plans. The boyfriend inquired about the 12-meter project. Lowell told about the reporter on board that day who kept asking him why he was doing it. "I guess she figured if she kept asking, she would finally get to the real reason," Lowell said.

"Well, it's all simple enough, Daddy," Julie said, "You just want to create the perfect boat and do the whole thing just right."

Lowell laughed. "That's right," he said, and smiled at his daughter in a reserved sort of way.

After dinner Lowell, Kay, and I went out back and climbed into the hot tub, which Kay had thoughtfully turned on late that afternoon. Up to our necks in the hot water, we looked through tree branches at the moon suspended in the clear San Diego sky, and had a serious discussion about the logistics of shipping a hot tub to Newport, Rhode Island.

Even after Turner beat it into the ground and then continued to jump up and down on its grave, the sail issue must have bothered Lowell North. Because while North has been known to shave various pieces of gear slightly under legal limitations in his dogged fascination with maximum strength-to-weight ratios (and what racing addict hasn't?), he is an honest man. He had, in fact, told Turner he would sell him 12-meter sails. Then he had to accept the syndicate's decision not to do so, which was a turnabout, and in this case it wasn't exactly fair play. And there were some definite communication problems between North, the syndicate, and Turner. But "play," it should be emphasized, is not what the America's Cup is all about.

Despite its sporting overtones, the America's Cup has the same relationship to men at play as the National Football League. As Lee Loomis so accurately pointed out, the America's Cup is a business, and it always has been. Keeping the Cup is an international business of pride, patriotism, and national accomplishment among titans of industry on both sides of the ocean who pour giant sums of money, all the expertise and technology they can muster, and their hearts into the ethereal fortunes of a racing sailboat. That is the bottom line. Before that, U.S. titans combat one another for the privilege of representation, and that struggle has always been the greater of the two. Because when it comes to racing 12-meters, the U.S. is the power. Why we have always won and why we will probably continue to win is a cultural phenomenon. It is the same reason we lose at Nordic ski events, or why a 100-pound, undernourished Nepalese walking barefoot and carrying a 60-pound load can outtrek us in the Himalayas. It is ingrained, practiced, a way of life. The U.S. had a fleet of 12-meters on Long Island Sound in the 1930s. France built her first one in 1969, Australia in 1962, Sweden her first modern one in 1976. The British have had 12-meters since 1923. Why they don't fare better in America's Cup competition is another, more mysterious problem.

Given the unruly nature of a 12-meter, all that is significant. So is the fact that by 1977 sailmakers Ted Hood and Lowell North between them had 35 years of experience making sails for twelves. And before they were edged out of the business, Ratsey and Lapthorn had been building 12-meter sails for an additional 30 years.

People are endlessly fascinated that the syndicate contributors, managers, skippers, and crews participate in such a strange ordeal. And when they stop to think about it, which isn't often, most syndicate contributors, managers, skippers, and crews are equally puzzled. I have yet to hear more than a very few cogent responses to the question from any one of the above. And the cogent responses are personal, not general. As for the rest, some hedge, others shrug, still others mouth pat phrases ("for the good of the Cup") or patriotic clichés that add up to nothing at all.

Wives, friends, members of the press, and people in the sailing business who suffer the long, boring, rolling days aboard the tenders often discuss the question. It usually begins by someone wondering what in hell *he* is doing where *he* is, blowing another potentially productive day lolling on the water, watching grass grow. Peter Barrett, a stout, jocular fellow who now manages the North Sails loft in Pewaukee, Wisconsin, joined such a discussion one rough day in early June aboard *Chaperone, Enterprise*'s tender, and easily walked off with the Charles C. Cogent award.

"People like to attempt anything that is so grandiose as to be asinine," Barrett said, quickly silencing a group of less precise thinkers. Barrett has a law degree, a Master's in engineering, and had completed his coursework for a Ph.D. when North lured him into sailmaking. He has a silver medal in the Finn class in the 1964 Olympics, and a gold medal he won crewing for Lowell in Star boats in Mexico, 1968. He is executive vice president of North Sails.

"If you were to enter a room full of crazy, doing people and suggest any reasonably outrageous idea," Barrett said, "it would stir something in them. They would want to do it."

Chaperone shuddered as she breasted a sea. A torrent of spray smacked against the cabin windows. Underfoot, the deck slanted.

"There is something irresistible about squandering large amounts of money, even for people who may be otherwise conservative," Barrett said. "It's Tower of Babel kind of stuff. Some men like to be known for doing something that may be dumb, but magnificent in concept: singlehanded ocean crossings, balloon flights, mountain ascents, hot-dog skiing. And the opportunities today are fewer than they used to be. Most things involve technology and money that only governments can come up with, like space exploration.

"The America's Cup will have no trouble continuing to attract people, because it is so grandiose," Barrett said. "And of course you have to think of it as war in the traditional sense, which is another irresistible attraction. These skippers are latter-day sailing-ship captains doing battle. The decisions they have to make about safety and tactics are not so different from those made by man o' war skippers in Queen Elizabeth's day."

There was that word again: war. It recalled Lee Loomis talking about the disposition of carriers at the Battle of Midway. It was an image invoked later that summer by as passive a man as Paul Cobel, an engineer, boat builder, and surveyor who has been project engineer on several 12-meters. Cobel is a quiet gentleman whose idea of a good time is cruising the coast on the 37-foot wooden Herreshoff ketch he has rebuilt. But this summer he was doing occasional work on *Enterprise,* and as that unsuccessful effort was grinding to its conclusion, Cobel suggested one reason why. "This group was different from others I have worked for," Cobel said. "In past years I have likened the project to total war. It has to be unlike any other sport. I had never experienced such a degree of urgency or the hours worked outside of wartime. If something broke on the boat, we drove thousands of miles for parts, and worked night and day until it was ready for action again. The *Enterprise* group wasn't quite so cranked up. They were looser. When did they want the boom finished? Oh, Tuesday or Wednesday, it didn't matter too much."

And of course Turner's very life is a war. One evening in Atlanta, after he had won the America's Cup, we had been talking about how sports had taken off in this country, and how television was cashing in on it. We were speculating about what the future might hold. Would Roller Ball replace Roller Derby? Would men fighting to the death with mace and chain replace Saturday night wrestling? Turner wished he had video tapes of the lions and the Christians in the Coliseum to run against NCAA football games on Saturday afternoons.

"I really think man can get through life without violence to the death," he said. "That's why I like sailing. You can have all the thrill of killing somebody without actually killing them."

If it is war we are talking about, then we must consider the slogan "all's fair," as it is in love. And to be more specific, we should consider the business of the elusive North Sails, which were treated as if they were the secret weapon of the 1977 America's Cup.

In 1975, when the *Enterprise* effort was beginning, Fritz Jewitt, a principal in the syndicate, said there should be no conflict of interest with either sails or designer. Olin Stephens should be exclusive to *Enterprise,* and so should North sails. Exclusivity of purchased goods and services is not new per se, but it was a departure as far as the Cup was concerned.

The rationale for exclusivity was the underwriting of an expensive experimental sail-testing program for *Enterprise* that would be conducted by the North loft. Then when Lowell signed on as skipper, the commitment was cemented by the cost of a new instrument package requested by North that would include the data collectors for the sail testing. "We hated to do it," syndicate manager Ed du Moulin said. "It was somewhat like reinventing the wheel. But it was Lowell's first request, and we couldn't really turn it down."

Edward du Moulin is a tall, handsome man in his sixties. A resident of Manhasset Bay, New York, du Moulin enjoyed a productive 44-year business association with Bache Halsey Stuart, Inc., in New York's financial district. Now retired, he continues to serve the firm as a director. He has been a similar mainstay of Long Island's old Knickerbocker Yacht Club.

Du Moulin's manners are courtly, his presence dignified. His charm is exceeded only by that of his wife, Eleanor. Du Moulin is approachable, friendly, and was as open as he could be about syndicate organization, decisions, and business. He is a balanced, even-tempered man. Over the course of what turned out to be a long and painful summer for him, as it usually is for those connected with losing efforts, du Moulin never publicly showed more than a few ruffled feathers.

If du Moulin could be faulted in the eyes of his California charges, it would probably be for his general (Eastern) conservatism. He was at first puzzled by the large pile of two-inch redwood planking that arrived on the overland trailer with *Enterprise* from the coast, then stunned to find out it was, sure enough, a real live California hot tub. Its arrival was followed, the next day, by Gary Gordon of Gordon and Grant Redwood Tubs, Santa Barbara, California, who spent two days putting it together. When the subtleties of hot tub ambience were explained to du Moulin, it was one of those feather-ruffling times. Casual group nudity at the syndicate mansion? Oh my God. "I could just imagine what Turner would have done with that one," du Moulin said one evening after the crisis had passed, shaking his head ruefully as visions of front-page pictures syndicated throughout the country danced before his eyes. And he was probably right. The hot tub saw very limited action.

When du Moulin spoke about the Great Sail Crisis, it was with the same pained intonations he used when talking about the hot tub. We had our discussion the day before the August trials were to begin, sitting in the bright sunshine on the upper deck of *Chaperone*. We sat facing aft, watching the womanly curves of *Enterprise,* hauled out on her slings, being sprayed with a newly developed white substance with a complex chemical name that was supposed to be the latest thing in go-fast hull coatings. Behind us, Olin Stephens was at work on a page of figures he had spread out over *Chaperone*'s instrument panel.

"We simply could not have afforded the sail-testing program without exclusivity," du Moulin said. "*Enterprise* became a test platform for all kinds of exotic cloths and weaves. It wasn't just the dollar cost. It was done at the expense of crew training and tactics. It has been a struggle ever since we got out here to give those other factors their due.

"So the *Enterprise* committee, Archie Cox, Fritz, and myself—without Lowell—sat down and made a decision about it. It had to be our decision to protect Lowell and John Marshall from taking part in it. Then we went on with the test program. Navigation also took a back seat to the sail testing, and we became more determined than ever not to share what we were paying so dearly for. We were giving up too much. But we figured we would have the best sails in the world in September.

"Then Ted started in—why aren't you going to sell a poor old country boy some sails—and we told him we had made our decision. Without exclusivity, there would have been no *Enterprise*. That was it."

A series of meetings took place between the *Enterprise* committee and the selection committee. "They thought it was the wrong way to go," du Moulin said. "But I explained about the test program, explained the benefits, and told them we thought it was in the best interest of the Cup. They said anything in the test program should be ours, but that we should make available to them sails built with 1974 technology."

Du Moulin discussed it with the crew, and none of them wanted to do it. They suspected that with Turner, it wouldn't end there. "First of all, we would have to put a North sailmaker on board," du Moulin said. "And even then Turner wouldn't be satisfied. He would keep pushing."

There were more meetings with the selection committee. The decision was finally made to release 1974 sails if another boat requested them.

"Turner contacted Marshall," du Moulin says. "He refused 1974 sails and demanded the best and newest we could make. He had quite an outburst on the phone. Then the public harassment began, and the name-calling.

"I am tolerant of Turner's shenanigans," du Moulin said. "He can be amusing. He has an amazing personality. But in this case he went far beyond the realm of good taste."

As Commodore Bob McCullough admitted, the whole thing did create "a problem." The problem arose from the fact that the two major producers of 12-meter sails were each skippering a boat. Other sailmakers can make 12-meter sails. But practically speaking, because of the expense and retooling necessary for handling the huge, powerful sails, not many have. If the third boat hadn't been allied with one of the sailmakers, and if a vice president of that loft, Robbie Doyle, who happened to be one hell of a sailmaker, hadn't been signed to sail on *Courageous,* it could have been a lot bigger problem. As it was, even with Doyle's clout at the loft, *Courageous*'s sails were a long time coming. One evening the craftsmen at the loft were told to stop all work on a job they were doing for *Courageous* and start on a new *Independence* sail. It took a little persuasion, a touch of insurrection, and an all-night effort to get the *Courageous* sail finished.

As an official of the United States Yacht Racing Union said, "Those guys spoiled it for the rest of us concerning commercialism in the series. It started with their personal war as sailmakers and carried on into the Cup. In the past, other sailors have been impressed with the sense of fairness they have seen among the principals."

That is an admirably sporting sentiment, but there is an unmistakable feeling that the fierce, open intensity of the 1977 Cup has signaled a departure from the past. Even though it didn't produce a victory, a precedent has been set for buying an edge. And with money getting tougher to raise, the idea of buying an edge is certainly something tough-minded businessmen can relate to. When that sort of thing begins, commercialism is sure to win out, as it does in auto racing and the National Football League. Perhaps in a few more years, the "private" game Lee Loomis spoke about will be selling more than foulweather gear, winches, and watches.

As Ed du Moulin and I concluded our conversation that August day on *Chaperone,* we looked out over the harbor at a small fleet of little boats sailing past. The mainsail of each was royal blue, and each was imprinted full size with the gold lettering and ornate design logo of a popular brand of Scotch whisky. Someone called Olin Stephens's attention to the fleet, suggesting that is what the America's Cup boats would look like the next time around. Olin Stephens, that reserved gentleman who has been designing America's Cup yachts since 1937, shuddered and said he certainly hoped not.

But why not? Why should the America's Cup be excepted from the T-shirt selling of America? The T-shirts, in fact, abounded in the shops of Newport merchants this summer. You paid your money and took your choice. The T-shirt award for the summer went to whoever made the one with the two Australian twelves on it, running right at you side by side under spinnaker. The design was laid out so that a breast fitted perfectly behind each spinnaker. The fullness of the sails depended on the lady wearing the shirt.

Isn't it just a matter of time before some smart advertising man sees those big mainsails for the 1270-square-foot floating billboards they are? Maybe it will be Ted Turner. He is in the business. A trip to the calculator would quickly give him the rates for the space based on prime-time television exposure and newspaper circulation. And you can bet the syndicate would love the money.

Ted Turner hadn't planned to attend the *Enterprise* party. He figured his obsession might get the better of him, and he would end up in trouble. But Loomis's sense of propriety wouldn't permit Turner's absence. He told Turner he *would* attend. It was a great party. Lucy Jewitt flew her favorite band in from California, and everyone danced into the night. Except Turner. He is not a dancing man anyway. As soon as the music starts, Turner begins leaning toward the exits.

Turner stayed for 20 minutes, enough for one tour of the tent. From receiving line to parking lot, he was dogged by the imposing figure of Conn Finlay (6' 7", 235 lbs.), the mast man on *Courageous.* Finlay had been assigned to Turner for the evening. The rumor that he had a set of police handcuffs in his pocket wasn't true. Finlay wouldn't have needed them.

A few evenings later out at Castle Hill, a seaside mansion which has been turned into a grand restaurant, Finlay was off-duty when Turner, who was having dinner with a friend, spotted a man at an adjacent table wearing a lapel button that read, "Beat the Mouth." The button, large as a silver dollar, was one of hundreds which had been made and distributed by people associated with the *Enterprise* syndicate. On it was a caricature of Turner's mustache and mouth (open, of course) and the slogan.

The man with the button was with an *Enterprise* official and former member of the NYYC Race Committee who had known Turner in 1974. With their wives, the two had gone to Castle Hill for dinner. Turner was seated when they arrived. He exchanged pleasantries with the *Enterprise* man while the other man was parking the car. The minute the other man came in and was seated at the table, Turner saw the button and jumped to his feet.

According to the *Enterprise* official, Turner reached across the table and ripped the button off the man's lapel with such force he thought the material had ripped. Looming over the table and continuing to berate the stranger, Turner flung the button to the floor.

"If you want to beat the Mouth, I'll give you a chance to do it right now if you want to follow me into the parking lot," Turner told the man.

The *Enterprise* official tried to calm Turner. He was successful only at returning him to his seat, where Turner continued a barrage of abusive remarks. The flow of the sedate restaurant had naturally been brought to a standstill by the incident. Turner called angrily for his check. It was brought instantly. He threw his money on the table, got up, and left, stopping to pick the button off the floor and place it next to its owner as he departed.

"It was obvious," the *Enterprise* official said later, "that Ted didn't like the sight of the pin. He has apologized to me twice now for the incident, saying he was sorry, but pointing out that the pin just wasn't fair."

It didn't take "Beat the Mouth" lapel buttons to get Turner cranked up for August. He had lost just enough races in July to keep the betting men interested, and to make his whole crew work even harder. *Enterprise* was still the new boat, and new boats have a way of getting it all together in the August trials, which are the only ones that really count anyway. And *Enterprise* had taken four straight races from *Courageous* in July. Those in the *Enterprise* camp who suspected Turner's sail issue overkill had something to do with insecurity were right, of course. "I knew we were good," Turner said after it was over, "but I didn't know we could win until we faced *Enterprise.* I've got a lot of respect for North's ability to diddle with a boat and make it go fast."

Various adjustments had been made. Jobson assumed much of the blame for the July defeats. "A lot of it was my fault," he said. "I started listening to too many people. The tactics got watered down. I collected myself for August."

And after a colossal number of hours on his knees in the sail loft, Robbie Doyle felt the sails were looking right at last. If Doyle hadn't been seen much during the summer, it was because every afternoon after sailing he had hauled a sail back to the loft for adjustment, which meant spreading out 110-pound jibs, or 125-pound mainsails (dry), or 3000 square feet of diaphanous spinnaker cloth, ripping open seams, and carefully marking them for resewing from notes made that day.

Sailmaking is a trial-and-error business. It is painstaking work: an inch here, an inch there (even on such huge sails), working with compound curves and variable stretch factors. Try this. Is it faster? Good. What else can we do? Try that. Slower. Okay then, put it back where it was. Now try this. Ad infinitum.

Doyle also had to practice a bit of psychology, or perhaps simple determination. For weeks he talked to Turner about changing the jumper struts, a pair of small, forward angling struts high on the mast that regulate the bend of the top section, and hence the upper shape of the sails. When Turner stubbornly refused to make the changes Doyle wanted, Doyle recut the sail instead to produce the effect he was looking for.

After it was over, Turner's praise of Doyle was complete. "If it hadn't been for Robbie Doyle," Turner said bluntly, "we wouldn't have won." Others on the boat agreed 100 percent.

If there was doubt in anyone's mind as the August trials began, it didn't last long. *Courageous* won five straight before her only August loss (to *Independence*). It became a matter of time before Turner was selected. Ted Hood and Loomis were still making crew changes. *Independence* was showing occasional bursts of speed, but losing consistently over the distance. And *Enterprise* was not coming together at all. Her sails, while remarkable for their unique qualities, did not look like "the best in the world," as Ed du Moulin had hoped. One jib was made of dark green Mylar, another was baby blue; one mainsail wore a scalloped seam two feet in from the leech where white Dacron and beige Kevlar cloth had been sewn together. Nicknamed "jaws" by the crew, it was later dubbed "gums."

Steering the boat with a hiking stick attached to the wheel probably wasn't such a good idea either. It allowed helmsman Malin Burnham to sit outboard to weather, giving him a good view of jib and seas. But it served to telegraph tacks (Burnham had to come into the boat and secure the stick before he spun the wheel), and as one former 12-meter skipper said, "You simply have to grab the wheel of these boats in both hands and make it go where you want it to go."

And the last-minute experimental hull coating had reacted adversely to something in the waters of Newport Harbor (oil, perhaps) and congealed in globs. A panic party that included wives, sons, daughters, and passersby spent many hours scraping the stuff off.

An even bigger mystery was some of North's tactics. Even average weekend sailors know that in a two-boat race, the boat ahead should "cover" the boat behind; staying between her rival and the mark, tacking when she tacks, etc. North often failed to practice this golden rule, and was never terribly forthcoming as to why, except to admit with typical honesty that he had made a mistake. And word was that Lowell was still roaming the boat taking pictures of the sails, even during races.

But North continued to be the gentleman. When he lost, he offered no excuses. When he won, he refused to crow. Turner, on the other hand, was still swinging from the knees. Once when asked about a protest North had lodged against Turner (which North ultimately lost), Turner told the press it was to be expected: "Lowell North's and John Marshall's financial futures are at stake. They'll do anything to win."

Four days into the August trials, Turner beat North in a big one. The breeze was so light that an official America's Cup race would not have been sailed. But the selection committee let the boats go to watch the effects of the very light air. As happens in such conditions, the boats ghosted along, one drifting past another in wisps of private breeze, until at the last turning mark of the shortened course, North rounded ahead by 30 seconds, perhaps three boat lengths in the slow going. North stayed on his tack until Turner rounded. Turner went left, and North covered this time. Then in the fluky breeze, the wind shifted in a manner that put North almost directly astern of Turner.

Instead of hanging on (the left side was closest to the finish line), North chose to tack and go off in search of some breeze. Turner made short tacks in the shifts all the way to the finish line. North's flier produced nothing. Turner's margin of victory was more than eight minutes.

That evening, Turner was the featured speaker at an annual 100-dollar-a-plate Football Association dinner at Brown University, his alma mater. He rode to the affair with the McCulloughs (Bob McCullough also went to Brown), which pleased Turner for its political possibilities.

The dinner was held at the Dunes Club, a posh summer watering spot in nearby Narragansett. Dinner was hardly worth even a small fraction of the hundred, and there were endless speakers to endure before the main event. The dinner was really a celebration of Brown's first Ivy football crown in decades (Brown shared it with Yale), and winning was perhaps so long in coming it seemed to have brought out the worst in some people. The master of ceremonies had a voice like an Excedrin headache. "Whadda ya say about Brown-Dartmouth, 35–21, first time in 20 years!" he yelled at us over a peaked-out P.A. system. He told a story about a business contract he had won on the strength of Brown's reversed football fortunes: "I told 'em I'm a Brown man! We know how to make winners out of losers! Think about it! Maybe we can help your products! I got the business!"

A long-suffering administrator sitting next to me turned and said quietly, "There *were* advantages to losing."

When Turner finally walked to the podium he looked weary. It had been a long day sailing in the frustrating light air under a hot sun. But he quickly warmed to yet another task. The speech was a typical Turner ramble, with sentiment approaching the maudlin intermixed with worn snappy one-liners, played for maximum effect.

At the end of his speech, Turner said, "All right, I've got five more minutes, and maybe somebody would like to know something about anything."

Q: How did you win by eight minutes today?

A: Well, it was mostly luck. Really. It was light fluky air and we went the right way. We told the press today that we won because of 30 years of checking weather maps. Where there's smoke there's fire, so we try and make as much smoke as we can.

Q: Could you evaluate the foreign competition?

A: There's no press here, right? I get in a lot of trouble when there's press around. Mostly at cocktail parties is when I get in trouble. If you had as much to say as I do, you'd get in trouble, too. I think the foreign competition is good, but whoever represents the U.S.—well, I think the Cup is pretty safe.

Q: What about computers?

A: Computers have as much to do with winning yacht races as winning football games. They can give you the statistics—we use one that mixes a lot of variables and tells us actual speed made good and a few other things—but when you get out between those white lines, you have to play ball. When computers start winning yacht races, I'll take something else up, because I hate the damn things.

"Give me one more," Turner said, "and I'll disappear so we can see the film. I want to see it because I ain't seen it before. Another question, or I could close on a story of sorts if I could think of one. I'll tell you what, if you haven't seen *MacArthur,* it's an old man's movie, it's pretty good, even if you didn't like MacArthur. I went to see it last night to get pumped up, and it did pump me up. Sport and good sportsmanship and doing your best are the most important things any man can learn in his life. The friendships you make in good competition and everything, well, you can't beat it anywhere, and if Russia had this kind of a deal we'd be in trouble, but they don't and they ain't got a chance."

Lowell North was fired a few days after his eight-minute loss to Turner. That such things happen in August on losing boats doesn't reduce the shock value of the event. The firing of a 12-meter skipper is unique. There is a note of finality about it, first of all. Turner is an outstanding exception to the rule that once fired, a 12-meter skipper's career is over. In other sports, tackles, goalies, coaches, forwards, shortstops, even quarterbacks who don't work out with one team can usually find productive employment with another. The 12-meter skipper sits atop the narrowest of pyramids. Losing skippers have enough trouble returning. Those who are fired don't have a prayer. If Turner hadn't been steering a radical boat in 1974 that was widely acknowledged as slow, he would never have made it back either.

Twelve-meter skippers are generally highly paid executives, company presidents, or owners of productive businesses who have more or less outdistanced the threat of being fired. They are not immune to being moved around, to be sure, but for men who have reached their station in life, kid-glove devices with names like "early retirement" are employed. In Newport during a Cup summer, August is the cruelest month. Egos of successful men with financial security and the world at their feet are severely tested. It's not just a job they are fired from. They are fired from the literal helm, ultimate symbol of machismo and the spirit of staunch individualism since the days of Columbus and John Paul Jones. No wonder fired 12-meter skippers have made such willing candidates for the psychiatrist's couch.

Possum and I were supposed to have dinner with the Norths the evening Lowell was fired. Knowing nothing of the day's events, we arrived at the house to meet them and were told the news. We found Lowell and Kay and several crew members in the lounge of Newport's Chart House restaurant in the midst of a wet and teary wake. Lowell was composed, but he looked gaunt. He had known for four days he was through, and had been asked to keep it to himself, which he did. He had suspected it before that. "Each morning when the laundry arrived," Lowell said, "I kept asking Kay to look and see if they were still returning my red *Enterprise* shirts."

Kay was awash as the terrible pressure of the last four days was released.

"We've had a good time," she said. "We figured from the beginning that if we were stupid enough to do this thing, we may as well have some fun."

"People told me I should have gotten a no-cut contract like Turner's," Lowell said. "I said no, it would be better for the boat if I didn't have that. Now I wish I had." He laughed. "It wasn't a bad decision to fire me. We were losing."

The selection committee chose to eliminate Ted Hood and *Independence* a few days after Malin Burnham began skippering

Enterprise (Halsey Herreshoff, who had been *Courageous*'s navigator for the 1974 win, went on board as tactician). It was a Hobson's choice, but they wanted to give the new afterguard a chance to see what they could do. *Enterprise* and *Courageous* were then paired every day. *Enterprise* came close a couple of times, but *Courageous* kept winning. Her record for August was 9–1, and time was running out.

The last day of August, selection fever was in the air. The largest crowd to date gathered on adjacent docks and nearby rooftops to watch *Courageous* get underway at Bannister's Wharf. Or more specifically, to watch Ted Turner, whose folk hero magic was beginning to seduce Newport.

At least a dozen photographers had begged or stolen their way past Loomis, and were barely giving Turner walking room on the narrow floating docks alongside *Courageous.* Turner didn't really have any specific dockside duties prior to casting off, but he was acting busy, shouting an order or two, studying things aloft, leaning on this or sitting on that, strolling, swaggering, strutting, and posturing—all in the interest of good pictures. And the snapping of shutters and the whir of motor-drives were all but drowning out the cries of seagulls on the neighboring fish docks. In his white shorts, white sweater with "Courageous" embroidered across the heart, his blue Greek fisherman's cap and dark glasses, he was this morning the living picture of the nickname, "Captain Courageous," that had been hung on him by the press and that was soon to be emblazoned in four-color on a T-shirt made possible by his own financial backing.

Having temporarily run out of moves for the photographers (who were grateful for the chance to reload), Turner strolled over to speak with John Bushell, owner of *Rage,* who was a guest aboard his own boat for the day.

"So John," Turner said, "have you decided to sell me this old boat yet? It's a wreck anyway. Have you seen all the places the twelve bumped into it? The engines are shot, the canvas is ripped—have you seen below decks? It's a mess. I'll buy it if the price is reasonable and use it for a tender the next time. Meanwhile you can have full rights to it. Go fishing any time you want, and in exchange I'll teach you how to sail."

Towing out, Turner spotted *Australia* just ahead and radioed to Mickey, asking him to catch up with them. Spillane pushed the throttles to the wall, and at ten knots we slowly caught *Australia*. Mickey lined up the two twelves side by side, and close. Turner could be seen standing on the afterdeck of *Courageous*, leading his troops in *Waltzing Matilda*.

At the starting line, Turner cruised by the selection committee yacht and gave them an exaggerated doff of his cap. With that amenity checked off, Turner took the start from *Enterprise*, covered her to the right for a few minutes, picked up a shift, tacked left, and beat her to the weather mark by 1:13. *Courageous*'s spinnaker set was perfect. *Enterprise* rounded and set an hourglass, so-called for the shape a spinnaker takes when it has a twist half way up. At the third mark, *Enterprise* again had sail-handling troubles as the jib came a third of the way down after it was hoisted. It was an easy win for *Courageous*, whose record improved to 10–1.

In a violent late-afternoon thunderstorm, the selection committee paid a call on *Enterprise*, telling her crew thank you and so long. The sun poked through and the rains stopped when the selection committee arrived to tell Ted Turner and his crew they had been selected to defend the America's Cup. Champagne was broken out as the committee boarded *Courageous*. The crowd on the dock was at maximum. The adjacent rooftops were dangerously loaded. A thousand cameras snapped and clicked as the green-shirted *Courageous* crewmen happily wrestled each other into the water.

A large delegation of red shirts from *Enterprise* graciously came to pay respects to the winners. I congratulated Loomis, who confounded me with an inane remark. "Make sure you stay out of any pictures being taken," he said. "You weren't part of the effort, and you don't deserve to be in the pictures."

Dick Enersen, from the Offshore Productions film crew, who had been doing his best to shoot a documentary on the Cup all summer, found himself hustled off the dock once again by Loomis. Loomis hadn't been able to get past the fact that Offshore, a West Coast group, had started out to make a film on the *Enterprise* effort. Enersen was also one of the few people around who matched Loomis in size. That, and Enersen's full beard and quietly aggressive nature helped make him instantly unwelcome on the dock. Enersen was irate. "Christ, Lee," he said to Loomis, "can't you even be gracious in victory?"

When the initial celebration was finished, overloaded tenders left from the *Enterprise* and *Courageous* docks for Goat Island, across the harbor, where the selection committee had set up a dockside bar. Turner almost didn't make the boat. He came running down the dock as *Rage* was pulling out. He climbed aboard *Rage* with new excitement brimming. "Hey, Roger— want to go on the Vineyard Race? Be at the marina in Stamford at ten o'clock on Friday." He began grabbing others. "Gary, you all set to go? I've got the Hood brothers lined up."

One just doesn't get into an overnight race at the last minute. Turner had his secretary call the race committee the day before to see if they would accept *Tenacious* as a late entry. He figured he was going to be selected, so why not make the Vineyard Race? It was a perfect example of a favorite Turner saying: "If any one thing is responsible for my success, it is that the minute I land on one plateau I immediately start trying to jump to the next one." As his successes piled up, he began making a subtle change in this philosophy: he was beginning to jump before he landed.

The dockside cocktail party was a great success. Handshakes were exchanged all around. The *Enterprise* people cloaked their obvious disappointment under genteel wraps. North said Turner deserved to win.

Then the emotional day was over, and *Chaperone* sounded her horn, calling all the *Enterprise* folks back on board for the short trip across the harbor. Lines were cast off and glasses were raised and everybody waved at everybody else. But Turner, of course, couldn't resist the old parting shot. He corralled a couple of willing crew members, and as *Chaperone* backed off the dock, they serenaded the *Enterprise* group with a chorus of *California, Here I Come,* "right back where I started from."

Interlude

PETER CLEMPNER, CAPTAIN of *Tenacious,* left for Stamford, Connecticut, with the boat the day after Turner was selected. It was a 20-hour trip under power, and after arriving, he worked around the clock to convert *Tenacious* from summer-camp quarters and observation craft to ocean racer. There were still some loose ends, but the Vineyard Race isn't a particularly demanding outing. From the starting line off Stamford, the course runs east up Long Island Sound past Block Island to the Buzzards Bay light tower at the entrance to Vineyard Sound at the top of Martha's Vineyard, and back. It is 135 miles each way, all within sight of land.

At noon on Friday, Turner arrived at Yacht Haven, where *Tenacious* was berthed with other race boats, and looked over the crew he had collected. For heavies he had Rick and Fred Hood, navigator Peter Lawson, and Bob Campbell, all from *Independence,* and Jobson. There was Dick Enersen, who had sailed on Cup winner *Constellation* in 1964, and Jay Broze, both from the film crew. John Mecray was a marine artist from Newport who Turner would commission to do the official painting of *Courageous* after it was all over, having worked out a deal for selling a limited edition of prints, on which Turner would take a cut. There was also a stout fellow named Blaise who had been a crewman on Baron Bich's big schooner *Shenandoah,* John Winder, who worked on the *Independence* project, Clempner, John Bushell, and me. Marshall Winder, John's wife, who had answered the phones all summer on Bannister's Wharf, would do the cooking.

As we motored out to the starting line, Turner stood on the deckhouse and gathered us around him. First he went over some basics—don't leave handles in the winches, and so on—"not for you experts, but for all the artists and writers we've got here."

"We aren't really in shape, but we'll do all right," he said. "The sails are the biggest problem. We have to get all new sails for the circuit, Hood sails, but we'll make do. I don't even know where the sails lead anymore. The track numbers for the cars used to be posted on the bulletin board below, but they're gone. We'll just have to fool with the leads.

"Now most of our sails are North sails, and Peter, every North label *will* be ripped off, taped over, or otherwise done away with. I don't want to see one damn North label on this boat. Get the ripper out.

"Okay, crew assignments. We need a bow man: Fred Hood. Bobby Campbell, you handle the mast. Blaze, is that your name? I don't know what you can do, but you sure are short and fat."

"Mass confusion," Turner responded to a competitor motoring alongside who hailed him. "I don't know how we'll do. We're all used to sailing 24 miles. After that we'll probably fall apart."

The crew members discussed their jobs with each other,

working out the details of spinnaker sets and sail changes and studying the location of lines and gear. Turner, Lawson, and Jobson were planning the start. Clempner was busy obscuring the big North label on the mainsail with silver duct tape. The jibs never did get de-labeled. There were too many of them.

The start was downwind in light air. We were tight on the line with a clump of boats between us and the race committee. We hoisted the chute just before the gun, and it filled nicely. Thirty seconds after the gun we had good speed and were moving on the fleet. There was a lot of hollering from back aft. Turner was screaming at Fred Hood, who was on the bow, watching the line. Fred was trying hard to be positive about not being over early. Turner pressed him. Fred obviously wasn't sure. He hadn't been able to see the line because of other boats. But there had been no hail from the race committee.

Turner wasn't satisfied. "Get the chute down," he yelled, and spun the boat before anyone could get to the halyard. The chute backed against the shrouds as we turned toward the line. In the light air, it came down without fouling.

"Get a jib up," Turner yelled, and Campbell dove below to manhandle one of the floppy, 100-pound monsters toward the hatch so men on deck could get a hand on it. As we approached the line to re-start, the race committee waved us on. We hadn't been over early. "Never mind that jib," Turner yelled as we were ready to hoist it. "Get the chute back up." Jobson was shaking his head.

The start was at five o'clock. At eleven that night, Turner was still at the helm as we slipped quietly down Long Island Sound under spinnaker at five knots in the light breeze. It was a gorgeous, warm night, bright from a profusion of stars. I was lying on my back on the foredeck, my head propped on a jib, holding the spinnaker sheet and calling trim to the man aft on the winch.

Beneath me, this half-million-dollar state-of-the-art racing machine of awesome beauty was rock steady as her fine entry parted tons of water, moving the mass aside, pressing it outward along the smooth gentle curves of her hull, then letting it squeeze in behind the buttocks of her underbody where it began to accelerate with a little burble of anticipation as it gathered speed along the upward, narrowing taper of her run, slid quickly past the slick blade of the rudder, and exited spent behind the tapered transom in a small confusion of intermingling eddies, alive and glowing with phosphorescence this night. As *Tenacious* surged through the swells of the sound she felt solidly airborne, like a jetliner at altitude. Only the sound of her small bow wave, gurgling beneath my head like a mountain spring, linked her with the planet. How fortunate, I thought, that Turner hadn't taken up auto racing.

Watching the spinnaker, I was looking into the heavens past sails, lines, mast, and shrouds forming a pattern of photographic clichés against a sky alive with the sulphurous trails of speeding meteorites. And I realized that I had not felt such complete and cosmic peace since the last time I was sailing on the ocean for an extended period. I smiled to myself in the darkness of the foredeck at the sublime comfort afforded by such knowledge.

"How's the trim, Vaughan?" The voice was Turner's.

"Couldn't be better."

"Watch it carefully. We're passing *Tatoosh,* the hottest boat in the sound. She started way ahead of us. So we aren't doing bad. Not bad at all.

"Oh, you should be goin'," (Turner was singing the refrain of a local advertising jingle), "to Kennedy and Cohen. . . . That was a Hebrew trick, you know. There was no Kennedy. They figured if they threw in a Scot, people would think they were getting a deal on major appliances. They cost more than in a regular store. Haw haw haw.

"Do you know what the blown-out jib said? I haven't a clew."

Jobson strolled to the foredeck for relief. "Remember, I've

been with him all summer," Gary said. "When you hear that for the fiftieth time . . . whew!"

At eight o'clock Saturday morning there wasn't enough wind to extinguish a match. The last few hours below had been punctuated by the staccato bursts of winch gears as sail after sail was hoisted, dropped, repacked, hoisted, dropped, repacked, and so on, as the wind backed and veered, waxed and waned. The boat was strewn with lines that had been used to tease various light sails into action. Three or four headsails had accumulated on the foredeck. The weary, frustrated four-to-eight-o'clock watch went happily below for breakfast, as we continued the charade of shadow-boxing the wind. The hoist-athon went on all day as Block Island drifted past at a trekker's pace. At eight that evening, over a slick, oily sea, we approached the light tower. Standing 110 feet high on spider legs, it blinded us with its brilliant flashing eye every two and a half seconds like a demon out of *Star Wars*.

As we closed the tower, the wind suddenly came ahead, what there was of it. We quickly doused the chute and raised a light jib. Turner, who had been cutting it fine all summer, announced a tack. Jobson told him we couldn't make it. Turner said he thought we could. Crew members spoke up, suggesting that we hold on. In wind so light there was barely steerageway, Turner tacked the boat.

It was a distracting scene. The light was strobing across us, the sails were flapping noisily as the swell snapped their weight from side to side, and the engine was running to charge the batteries. And naturally as the tower came within hailing distance, Turner started a conversation with the Coast Guard personnel.

"Are we first around?" he asked them. They said we were. We cheered. Their small dark forms peered down at us as they asked who we were.

"*Tenacious,*" Turner said, "two days out of Stamford with 18 idiots on board. You guys got any women up there? No? Not yet, huh? Hey, I used to be in the Coast Guard. If I'd stayed in, I'd be retired by now."

The new tack was taking us dangerously close to the tower. Turner had no steerageway. Two boatlengths from the tower the situation looked grim. We could hear the surge of the swell sucking at the round metal legs of the tower. On the foredeck we tried to backwind the jib to swing the bow, and we might have made it, but aloft, the mast tip was swinging to within a few feet of the tower's superstructure. Turner prudently threw the engine in gear, and for five seconds we motored away from the tower. Then he threw it out of gear. Our joy of being first to the tower was chilled by the use of the engine. One doesn't use engines in sailboat races. Oh well, maybe the race committee would just give us a time penalty.

Less than a minute after clearing the tower, the northerly came in strong. After the long spinnaker run to the tower, it would be a spinnaker run home. Soon *Tenacious* was on a sustained run of ten knots, tracking smoothly.

Turner's lighthearted mood hadn't been affected by the near miss at the tower. At dinner he told "Jimmy Brown" stories, which always please a crowd.

"So I was trying to get laid, it was after the 1966 transatlantic race, and Jimmy was drunk as hell. I told him to bag it. But he wouldn't. So I fired him, it was the first of many times I fired him, and I took this girl into the park where there was a gun emplacement. I remember I banged up my knees on the cement."

We raced past Block Island that night and cruised through Race Point at the end of Long Island Sound making 13 knots over the ground with full current in our favor. We finished Sunday around noon with only one boat, a 70-footer, in front of us. We averaged nearly nine knots for the 135-mile run. As we crossed the finish line, we handed the race committee a written account of the incident at the tower.

By the time we reached the slip at Yacht Haven, the boat was clean. After showers, we returned to the boat to find a couple of cases of frightfully cold beer waiting to be consumed. Soon all the crew was sitting around on the boat, along with two ladies in marine advertising who had known Turner and others in the crew for years. They had arrived in their black BMW shortly after we docked.

Turner showered and dressed quickly. He was playing it close, as usual. Before the race he had made plans to attend the Sunday afternoon Mets-Braves game in New York. He and Gary were waiting for Frédérique, an old friend of Ted's, to pick them up. But she was late, of course, and one damn fine audience was assembled there on the boat, and it was a beautiful day, and Turner happened to have a copy of the current issue of *Broadcasting* magazine with him, which included an article he wanted to share.

"These winches make great seats," he said, coming on deck into the cockpit. "Come on back and grab a winch. I want you to hear what they have to say here about the TV business."

He opened the magazine and read: " 'MPAA,' that's the Motion Picture Association of America. 'Out to Stop WTCG-type Spread via Cable, Satellite. Movie producers seek FCC rule that would examine phenomenon of "Super Station" and determine whether it violates commission's policy to foster localism in TV.' How about that? Super Station. Strong, huh?"

The super station referred to in the article was, of course, WTCG Channel 17 in Atlanta. The gist of the argument was that Turner was buying films for local programming, then splashing them around the whole country by satellite. The article called WTCG a "relatively small UHF station."

"Relatively small . . . ." Turner dropped his chin onto his chest and uttered a long string of high-pitched, nasal chortles, something he does when particularly delighted. "What I am trying to say here, gentlemen," he said, looking around the group as if he were addressing a board meeting, "is that I may have hit the jackpot." He laughed with his audience.

In the article, the MPAA was petitioning the FCC to determine whether the development of cable-system stations using satellite delivery systems was in the public interest. Appropriate corrective measures were urged.

"Appropriate corrective measures!" Turner shouted to the mast tip. "There *are* no corrective measures. They haven't even written *laws* about this stuff."

Word came from the dock that *Thunderhead,* a class A competitor, had just finished. "What time is it?" Turner asked. Someone told him. "Hell, we beat the piss out of them. What I am telling you is . . . this [he brandished the magazine] is a lot better than sailing.

"And who, let me ask you, has the devious and cunning mind that figured out how to upset the world?" Turner paused and then went into a little sing-song: "Me me me me me me me me me." He put his head in his hands and chuckled to himself.

"They want corrective measures. Ha ha. I'm telling you, there could be inconceivably large profits from all this which could make me into one of the world's richest men, and to tell you the truth, it couldn't happen to a nicer guy.

"Listen, this is what the MPAA claims: 'Satellite delivery systems can be expected to result in the importation of national super stations with super-expensive programming made possible by a national advertising base against which many local stations will not be able to compete.'

"I can't be responsible for the economic impact of a great idea, can I? They can't stop me. The FCC is like the selection committee. They've been to ball games with me. I'm in like Flynn. The Atlanta Station that Serves the Nation. How do you like that? I've already got our slogan figured out. Pretty soon we'll be billing 14 million dollars a year. A TV station is worth ten times earnings, which is 140 million dollars, which ain't peanuts."

Thunderhead cleared the breakwater. She was 20 minutes behind on corrected time. "Her only mistake," Turner said, "was entering the race with us." He flashed a big grin. "We've got 'em all on the run. When does *Love Machine* have to finish?"

Turner began talking randomly about his sports teams ("The Hawks are so bad *I* was going to play. I would have been the only 6′ 2″ slow white ever to play the game."), which led him to thinking about Bowie Kuhn. "I went to see Kuhn. He said be like everybody else or be gone. I'll fight him to the end. I don't know if I'll win, though. Kuhn did what Loomis couldn't do— he got me out of there.

"Do you know what George Hinman said to me after I was selected? He said don't change, I'm glad you're like you are. After this summer the cloud hangs over Brit Chance, designer of *Mariner*." Turner lifted his beer bottle. "Let's drink to a large measure of ill will for Brit Chance. All he did was make a mistake. He just didn't admit it.

"I'll never forget how it all started. It was back in 1964 when we chartered *Scylla* from Charlie Ulmer for the Montego Bay race. All we had was a radio direction finder that wouldn't pull in one station. After two days we were completely lost. We sailed into the first harbor we came to and asked the natives where we were, and we were off again.

"We only had one good watch on board, a Bulova Accutron we were using to navigate with, and we couldn't figure out why we were lost again. It turned out the watch captain, who owned the Accutron, had moved it ahead 20 minutes to get off duty early.

"Seven days later we were out of food and water and looking at the loom of some lights somewhere. They had already announced on the radio that *Ticonderoga* (a 70-footer) had finished. So we dropped out and motored into what turned out to be Georgetown in the Bahamas, which wasn't a legal port of entry. We motored into a slip at two knots and couldn't stop. But *Scylla,* bless her sweet heart, she took it.

"That's the best way to learn. You think Florida is on your right going south? Not if you're in the waterway.

"Jimmy Brown was my captain. We were down there for the circuit the second year, and Jimmy came running back to the boat. Mr. Ted, Mr. Ted, he was yelling, I heard how to win races. You do it at night. The other guys don't sail very hard at night. Jimmy had gone to visit this captain on one of the hot boats, and had got him drunk. He learned a bunch of things. Like not to sail with the water tanks full. Then we read all the books, 'how to ocean race,' and we won the other five races and the circuit.

"Then I bought *American Eagle* for 70,000 dollars. We hit Hens and Chickens rocks off Larchmont one night in the sound at nine knots. I was thrown into the wheel so hard I bent it. Dislocated my shoulder. We figured the worst that could happen is we would sink, and we had life rafts. But we won that one, too.

"You just have to keep going. I remember in the One-Ton Worlds a few years ago we had a good chance to win the last race if we could tack for the finish line, but *America Jane* was on top of us. Burke Sawyer was sailing her. I was yelling at Burke, come on, we've gotta tack or we'll lose everybody on the left. Let us tack, I told him, and we'll let you finish first. So Sawyer tacked and we beat him across the line. Was he pissed. I told him finishing second was better than losing all those other boats.

"The only sad thing is there are no more races until the fall series in October. Well, there *is* the Cup. I had dinner in a Chinese restaurant the other night, and you know what my fortune was? 'A very famous possession will soon be yours!' "

Frédérique arrived in something long and tie-dyed. Frédérique is a flamboyant, outspoken woman of French extraction. She is independently wealthy, and uses her money to travel around the world with the ocean-racing and auto-racing schedules as her Michelin Guides. As she once explained, "I happen to have been born with good looks, lots of money, and a good enough mind to enjoy them both."

She is somewhere between 28 (her preference) and 40, with one of those firm, olive-skinned, size-ten, killer French-girl bodies, and an assertive personality to match. She never misses a chance to chide American men for being marriage-oriented, or their wives for being protective and jealous. She has a throaty, heavily accented voice that carries like a bullet over water.

An exhibitionist of the first magnitude, Frédérique has been known to undress in public at the slightest provocation. Her clothes are either the most diaphanous of garments, or soft, wash-worn fabrics that fill her creases like the plastic film on a mozzarella cheese. More than once she has distracted the crew of an overtaking boat during the spinnaker leg of a race by standing at the backstay and slowly getting naked. A good backgammon player, she often wins beyond her talents and good fortune by playing topless against male opponents. "My tits are all right," she admits with some modesty, "But my ass is better." She and Turner have been friends for years.

Frédérique scurried onto the boat and hustled below to comb her hair, talking rapidly as she moved. Turner suddenly looked glum.

Turner and Frédérique are useful to one another. Their relationship, a unique one for Turner in both its longevity and its degree of real exchange, is rooted in their amazement at each other; Turner's discovery of someone who is perhaps more self-centered and more on-stage than himself had to be a startling recognition. When we encounter someone with the potential to let us off a hook of well-worn but dubious distinction, it is a relief—but a disquieting experience, as well. We may despair our less attractive or obsessive traits, but we have learned to love them, too. There is always the nagging question, what would become of us without them?

Frédérique is the only person I have seen Turner with who

can quiet him, almost cow him at times. She elicits his most
conservative posture. Frédérique makes concessions, too. She
is on her best behavior around Turner.

Apart, the two of them swing from the knees. Their antics
keep the ocean grapevine buzzing. When they are together,
each steps back a pace, measuring, assessing. People who run
rats around electric grids call it approach-approach conflict,
and like two champions of the breed, Ted and Frédérique become wary in each other's presence.

Fascination has sustained their relationship. Frédérique's
aggressive independence makes it impossible even for a master
of categorization like Turner to put her in a role. Turner is al-
lergic to her: knowing her flamboyant, competitive nature
could burst impulsively from its hastily constructed confines at
any moment must give him anxiety fits. But hay fever doesn't
curtail the true romantic's passion for flowers. Fascination continues to overcome prudence. For once Turner is as much moth
as candle. And so their encounters are infrequent, short, and
wearying.

Frédérique bounced up from below and started toward the
car with Gary, rushing around to make up for her late arrival.
Shrilly, she called after Ted. Turner was standing on the dock,
leaning on the lifelines of *Tenacious,* talking to one of the girls
from the BMW. He rested his forehead on the lifeline a moment, then he looked after Frédérique. "Feel sorry for me," he
said quietly to the girl, and walked down the dock.

We dropped Frédérique off at a mid-town hotel for her pre-
game preparations, and drove on to the ball park. During the
fourth inning she arrived at the stadium, and even in the Big
Apple her arrival did not go unnoticed. The flight of steps leading down to our box seats were long and steep. Frédérique proceeded down them with Duchampian care in deference to the

dizzying height of her hot-pink platform sandals with leg straps. Over brief white shorts and a red and white striped elastic tube top that exposed her midriff, she wore a short gold lamé jacket and carried a matching shoulder bag. Her reddish brown hair fell to her shoulders.

Frédérique sat down, lined up the bottles on the railing, and began doing her nails.

When Ted left to speak to people he knew, I asked her how he had changed over the years.

"On boats," she said, "if someone said to go right, he would go left just to prove he was in charge. Now he will take advice if he knows the person admires him and doesn't know more than him. He is so big now, no one discusses it, they give advice in a more humble way. The people he sailed with used to be more aggressive about it.

"He still won't allow people to tell him what to do. He is insecure. Americans are brought up to be first. He has to keep proving it. He wishes his father could see him.

"I remember in Australia one year, I was there during the Sydney–Hobart Race, and Ted was not doing so well. Before, when he raced *American Eagle,* he won everything and set records and he was the star attraction. This time he had a smaller boat, a One-Tonner, and he was doing fair, that's all. And when he realized that I was getting more attention than he was—boy, did he get mad!

"But I admire him. I admire his success, and the fact that he can laugh about himself. He is an overall good person. The money hasn't turned him into an asshole at all. He works hard. He doesn't ask anyone to do something that he won't do."

The sports page of the *Providence Journal* the following day contained a story about how *Tenacious* had won the Vineyard Race by an overwhelming margin and had then been thrown out for using the engine to avoid collision with the tower. The headline: "Turner's Honesty Costs Race."

When you're hot, you're hot.

When we picked up Frédérique for the second game of the Braves-Mets series, she was apparently ready to head for the ball park in a red polka-dot shorty see-through pantaloon outfit, with nothing under it but the evenly tanned, size-ten killer French-girl body. When he saw her, Turner choked on a puff of cigar smoke. At a rare, momentary loss for words, he sternly waved her off to change, flashing, in her wake, the sheepish grin of a man who has just dropped a hundred-dollar bill on the subway. Frédérique protested just enough to savor the moment thoroughly.

In the car she finished changing into a long, off-the-shoulder tie-dyed garment. A large flower design spread its petals over her lower belly. On the way to the stadium the two argued about who was more selfish. Ted maintained that he was giving a lot of people pleasure with his sports teams, that on the other hand, Frédérique did nothing that wasn't for her own pleasure. Frédérique would have none of it. She said he was deluding himself if he thought his teams were for anything other than to make him rich, and get himself publicity.

"You're either a lot smarter than me or a lot dumber," Turner told her after a while, and because his best defense is a loud voice, he waded through a transition about how maybe he wasn't so smart after all, having never graduated from college, having been kicked out for harboring a girl in his room, "which was certainly a bad deal since these days dorm rooms practically come with girls in them." He recalled the administrator who kicked him out.

"I was going to go piss on his grave when I heard he died," Turner said, "but there hasn't been time. For a while I considered sending it to Providence in a bottle and having someone pour it on for me, but I never got to that."

Talking about the hapless administrator gave Turner a passing fancy about death. "I'm going to call in the priest when I'm on my death bed, just to cover my bets. It doesn't cost much, and it's only a million-to-one shot that it'll pay off, but you never know." He asked Frédérique if she would call in the priest. She said she wouldn't bother.

Back at Conley Hall, Turner was standing naked in the middle of his room lighting his pipe. He was getting ready to fly to Washington for a state dinner with President Jimmy Carter, fellow Georgian, to celebrate the signing of the Panama Canal treaties by the U.S. and Panama. Loomis was getting a kick out of the fact that aside from Turner, the only other special "outsider" invited to this informal dinner for 200 was Muhammad Ali.

Jane was flying up from Atlanta to attend the dinner with Ted. Although he had supported Ford in the election, Turner contributed equally to both campaigns and had met with Carter on previous occasions. Shortly after Carter was elected, the Braves played softball and ate barbecue with Carter and his family and staff at Plains, Georgia. Turner was enthusiastic about dining at the White House, but what had really been on his mind all day was the attendance at the previous evening's Braves game in Atlanta: 845.

"Eight hundred forty-five," he said, shaking his head as he walked toward the bathroom and the shower. "Pretty bad, huh? I should be home."

If he had second thoughts about doing the Cup, with business at home being neglected and the team faltering, he didn't show it.

"I know exactly what I'm doing. I planned it all out. My priorities are in order. I've never had any problem with priorities. Mine are sailing, business, and family, in that order." He flashed an impeccable smile at the bare-faced truth of it. "Don't you imagine a lot of guys who wouldn't admit it feel that way? Sailing, business, and family. That's why I succeed so well at stuff other people don't give a shit about."

Turner toweled off and jumped to thoughts about the White House. "You know, it's frightening how easy it would be for me to become president. You have to be known—that's the toughest requirement. Now Son of Sam is known, but that's certainly a bad deal. Or take Ronald Reagan, he was a movie star, which isn't such a good way to be known. All movie stars do is mouth stuff other people write. And if you're known as a politician, odds are you can't be trusted.

"But take me. I'm known in a good way. As a sailor, a businessman, a guy who owns sports teams. People like me, they relate to me. What I do makes sense to the average guy. I mean, if the average guy had a ball team, he'd want to manage it, wouldn't he? And I'm nice to the average guy. I understand him. The average guy has to be nice or he'll get shit on. Only the rich can afford to be shits.

"Look at the selection committee. They like me because I'm an amateur. I put money in it just like most of them have. I've paid my way. I'm there to defend the Cup, not promote my business. I serve on various committees, and give of my time just like they have. Last time we got nothing done. This time we're going to tune up the world."

At Newport's small airport, Turner paced around kicking tires, shaking wings, and marveling at the frailty of the light machine that would take him to Providence to catch a jet for Washington. "After it was over," Turner said, strolling around in the sunshine, "Loomis wanted a testimonial. He said, 'I've been fair to you, haven't I? Hasn't it been all right?' And I told him, 'Lee, I hate to tell you, but it hasn't been perfect.' He's a stubborn bastard. And smart, too. I'll do it again, but not with Loomis. He'll want Hood anyway."

How many times, I wondered, would he keep doing the Cup.

"I don't know. I'll know when to step down. No, I won't. I guess I'd rather be knocked down, like in those movies about old quarterbacks."

Back in Georgia for the weekend, Turner decided we should stop for breakfast on the way into Atlanta. Ted's wife Jane, four of their five children, and Jimmy Brown had been in Newport all summer, as they were now, and under the bachelor regime of house-sitter Terry McGuirk, a young fellow who is director of cable relations for WTCG, the refrigerator at Turner's home didn't have much to offer. In fact the house lacked all vestiges of homeliness. It seemed like a shell of a place, a strange mixture of luxury motel and highway furniture showroom. General disarray was complemented by kitchen cabinets that contained amazingly little of anything, from dishes to staples. Even in repose it hardly seemed like a place normally geared to nurture a family of eight.

The house is nicely situated in a hilly area of lush undergrowth and tall trees in the suburb of Marietta, 40 minutes to the northwest of downtown Atlanta. Turner accepted it in partial payment of a debt. But when Turner said he lived simply, he meant it. There is no Betamax replay unit attached to the TV console in the den, nor does the garage door open at the touch of a dashboard button. If there is a stereo system—aside from the one McGuirk brought with him—it wasn't in evidence. But then Ted Turner doesn't keep his toys at home.

The plan of the day was a quick, late stop at the office (it was Saturday), then on to the stadium, where one of the Braves farm teams was in for an afternoon game prior to the second Pittsburgh game that evening. Driving toward Atlanta at eleven in the morning, Turner suggested a pizza might make a good breakfast. Fortunately, Georgia's pizzerias don't open until later in the day. We settled for Chinese. The only other patrons in Eng's Dragon Lounge were a mother and two children. One of the kids, a boy of 11 wearing a numbered jersey, approached our table. He extended an autograph book toward Turner, explaining he was one of Ted's fans. It was determined that the boy played short or second when he wasn't pitching.

"And I never even played!" Turner said after the kid left. "People really need a hero. People can't believe I don't have a public relations outfit. I didn't plan to be idolized. I don't have a press agent. I just jumped up and down a little, and people hadn't seen that in so long they got turned on."

At the office Turner sat at his overloaded desk and shuffled through a huge stack of papers. Occasionally he tossed something across the desk.

"There's a deal on TV vs. the cable. It's pretty complicated. Don't try to get into it. It would scramble your brains. I just hit the high spots. I'm what's causing the trouble. But I can't worry about the economic impact."

Turner smacked his hand to his forehead as he read a memo about one of his Braves farm teams. "Hell," he said, "my teams are playing six games a day in six cities. I'm doing a horseshit job because I can't keep up with it all."

The ball park simmered in the midday sun. July in Atlanta, not a cloud in the crisp blue sky. Maybe a thousand people—players' parents and friends and a few baseball die-hards—had come to watch the Greensboro (N.C.) Braves take on the Asheville (N.C.) Tourists. These are A teams, the bottom rung in baseball's farm-system hierarchy, comprised of kids out of college or high school who have just signed. They make $6000 a year, live four to a three-man apartment to save money. Turner brings each team into the stadium once every year to pump them up.

Turner's mood changed as we arrived. The stack of paperwork could wait, the America's Cup was next week's problem. Right now it was a carefree summer afternoon at the ball park. Peanuts and Crackerjacks. Turner wasted no time settling in between Hank Aaron and Bill Lucas behind the first base dugout, working a big chew into his cheek and talking baseball. Earlier Turner had bragged about being included in a *Sports Illustrated* piece that had named him as the only front office tobacco chewer in the sport. Now he shrugged and said with some difficulty through a wad that would trigger the gag reflex of a grizzly, "When in Rome . . . ."

One of the Asheville players hit a single to the outfield. The throw in went through the Greensboro second baseman, past the shortstop, and was fielded by the third baseman. "Well," Turner turned to Aaron, "the third guy got it, 't's okay." Aaron cracked up.

Dick Ruthven was slated to pitch against Pittsburgh. "Ruthven's father never comes to a Braves game to watch his son pitch," Turner said. "He wanted his son to be a doctor, and he's never gotten over it. I told him Dick has enough trouble being a pitcher. Make a wild pitch as a doctor and they bury you."

The radio was warming up again. Turner began pondering the fact that the entire Greensboro team cost less than Jeff Burroughs's and Andy Messersmith's combined salaries. "I should have bought these guys, saved a million and a half, and we'd probably only be a few more games out. Messersmith cost half a million, and how many games did he win altogether, Bill, 15? Fifteen. Right. So how much did that cost me? You can only count the wins. You don't get anything for appearing. Anyone can appear. What is it? Thirty-three thousand per win. I'm not too dumb, huh?"

Turner hailed catcher Vic Correll, who had arrived at the

park early for the game with Pittsburgh. Turner waved him over. Correll hesitated a moment, then came our way. Braves players were still getting used to the idea of fraternizing with the club owner. Correll made the trip to Newport with the rest of the Braves on June 23 and watched the boss go one for two against *Enterprise* ("That day we were up there," Bill Lucas recalled, "he lost the first one. There was no way he would lose two with his team up there watching, even if he had to suck the water from in front of North's boat.") Correll asked how the sailing was going. Turner said he had about a one-game lead into August.

"It's close, real close, but we're doing okay. The sailing isn't so bad, or rather it's good enough, but there's a lot of hassle. One night I went out and insulted some people who were trying to rip me off, and this guy Loomis who runs the syndicate, he's a typical baseball owner type, you know, a real sour guy, he told me he wished I was a dog so he could beat me. A dog! I said to him, 'I'm not a dog, Lee, I'm a person.'"

The story reminds Correll of one of his bad moments. "I was playing winter ball in Venezuela, and going through a period when I wasn't hitting the ball too well, about .215 or so, and the fans were on me. One day I came to bat, and this big buzzard that had been circling came floating down and landed on the backstop. I took one look at him and said that's that. I left town the next day."

As usual Turner the non-listener hadn't heard Correll's story. Turner doesn't intend to be rude. He has simply determined, over the years, that very few people have things to say as interesting as he does. He had flipped channels and was digging a spirited girl in her late teens who had cruised by, tossed her long brown hair, and given Turner a look. She had on a high school sweatshirt and blue jeans and she was having a good time. She was walking fast but she wasn't in a hurry.

"Hi, beautiful," Turner said.

She stuck a hand on her hip in mid-stride, threw him a wink down the middle, and kept going.

A few minutes later she was back, moving toward the target this time. "Hey would ya mind autographing my leg? I've gotta bet with my friend that you will. You too, Hank."

Turner held the curve of her calf in his left hand, gave her a serious, questioning look, got nothing back, and signed with his right. Aaron giggled as he signed. "Who says signing autographs ain't any fun?" Turner said. "If you don't like people, Bill, this is the wrong game. Am I right?"

Whether or not Ted Turner really likes people is open for debate. But he certainly wants people around him, and he wants people to like him (folk hero!), and in some instances he works hard at it. He also wants to fill the ball park, and while he is a long way from that goal, attendance grew the first two years Turner has owned the Braves. That growth is in the face of two last-place finishes, with 1977 marking the first year since 1935 that the Braves lost more than 100 games (101). In 1976, Turner's first year, attendance was up a whopping 60 percent from 534,672 to 818,179. With ten more home games in 1977, attendance was 872,310.

Watching Turner stroll through the stands stopping to chat with people and sign autographs, I wondered if there was a city in the major league circuit besides Atlanta that would support Ted Turner's ownership of its ball club. Maybe Los Angeles. Maybe. But how would arrogant old Boston react to an owner sitting shirtless behind Fenway Park's first base dugout chewing tobacco? The show would bomb in hostile New York, especially with a losing team. Could an owner finesse racing an ostrich in humorless Cincinnati? Cozy Philadelphia? Bill Veeck flew midgets under kites in Cleveland, but *he* didn't hold the string himself.

Turner is without question a big hit in Atlanta. During every game I watched with him in the stadium, people kept passing by, people from the Georgia hills and hinterlands who think saltwater is something to gargle with, to wish him luck in the "American Cup," or "in them sailin' boat races up there." And after each game, 20 to 50 of the folks would line up with banners, bats, hats, even twenty-dollar bills on which to collect Ted Turner's autograph. Fans in most ball parks would be hard-pressed to tell you the club owner's name, let alone recognize him, and the last thing most of them would want would be his autograph.

Like Turner says, people relate to the way he enjoys his ball team. "They look at me and they figure that's how *they*'d do it if they owned the team, takin' their shirts off and hootin' and hollerin', having a chew and a good time."

Turner's is the same kind of out-front Cadillac hustle those black, ermine-clad evangelist preachers use on their flock. With diamonds glittering from their hands and wrists, alligator platforms on their feet, and breathtaking showgirls on each arm, they pass the collection plate among the downtrodden while telling them, "I'll show you the way." And the flock: "right on, brother," as they ante up.

Turner's credo is apple pie, hard work, Horatio Alger, kids, good ol' boy All Southern American. He has taken the most simplistic of life's little slogans, the ones you see written on small, rough-edged wooden plaques in truck stops, and forged them into a workable, day-to-day philosophy. Of course, the convenient thing about those slogans, the reason they have been around so long, is their extreme flexibility. Perhaps Turner's favorite among them, the one that sits on his desk framed in a miniature billboard facing visitors, reads "Either Lead, Follow, or Get Out of the Way."

Instead of ermine and Cadillacs, Turner's garb is ill-fitting mufti—even his secretaries nag him about buying some decent clothes—and Chevy sedans. The old soapy country song written some years ago, "A White Sport Coat and a Pink Carnation" ("I'm all dressed up for the dance") could have been written about Ted Turner.

Like all good hustles, the act has to be together, the role has to fit. You can't be a folk hero without being one of the folk, and in spite of Turner's frequent and therefore suspect protestations that he is one of the folk, he indeed is. Turner is, first of all, something of a professional Southerner. As he told the press the day he bought the Braves, "Atlanta is my home. I love it here. I've been all over the world racing and stopped in Tahiti on the way back from Australia, which I read a lot about as a little boy, and I decided the closest thing to paradise on this earth is Atlanta, Georgia." He means it.

His idea of a good time around town is taking the family or visiting firemen out to the Cyclorama, a round building in Grant Park which contains a 500-by-50-foot, 18,000-pound wraparound painting of the battle of Atlanta. For a small fee one can stand on a platform in the middle of the building and listen to the taped stentorian tones of Victor Jory telling it like it was. It's like listening to Howard Cosell do Martin Luther King's funeral, and Turner always listens with reverence. Turner took visitors out there during the America's Cup summer of 1974. "If we had won the Civil War," he gleefully told them, "we'd be challenging for the Cup, not defending it."

There are moments when it seems as if he is trying to relive as much of *Gone With The Wind* as possible, at least up to the part where the war is lost. To Robert E. Turner III he adds a "Lee" when he thinks he can get away with it. He named two of his sons Rhett and Beauregard (the third is R.E. IV), and his wife Jane barely kept him from naming his youngest daughter Scarlett. They settled for Sarah Jean. The oldest daughter is Laura Lee.

In the light of this pose, Turner's good-ol'-boy side might seem like a put-on. His family was well-off, and he attended a Southern military prep school prior to an Ivy League college.

His racial heritage deviates only a boat trip across the Channel from pure Anglo-Saxon: English, Scottish, and French on his father's side; Irish, Dutch, and German on his mother's. "I get my thrift from the Scots, my work ethic from the Germans, and my colorfulness from the French and British," Turner says. "My judgment and conservatism comes from the Dutch, and the Irish, well, they're off their rockers, unbalanced."

But early, day-to-day influences sustain, and Ted was supervised constantly during his childhood by Jimmy Brown, a back-country Southern black man. The country heritage goes deeper. Turner's father was born and raised in Mississippi, the son of a Depression-struck cotton farmer. As Ted once remarked, "My father was 20 years old before he knew a chicken had anything but necks and backs." The result is an interesting blend of Southern gentleman and funky down-home goofhead cousin, in whose vernacular the words "sir" and "ain't" nestle compatibly.

It is an ideal combination for selling baseball in Atlanta. Those who wish to plumb the cultural idiosyncrasies of a particular metropolitan region should begin by spending time at the local sports arena. Here one sees the people of the region at play, a telling activity. Atlanta's Fulton County Stadium does very well, for instance, with promotion ideas that involve the fans' participation.

One evening during the Pittsburgh series, Bob Hope recruited me to help him find six attractive women who would be required to dive into a small haystack placed on the field before the game, in search of a diamond hidden inside it. This was to highlight "Diamond Night" (several thousand rhinestones were being handed out to ladies at the turnstiles—among them were 250 chip-diamonds). We cruised around the stadium getting a look at tight-fitting jeans and halter tops, pant suits, and various double-knit leisure combos, with "done" or retouched hair being the most common denominator. Make-up was very much in vogue. There weren't many women who weren't put together in a noticeably dressy or cosmetic way.

The ladies of this city where Miss Pittypat's Restaurant still does business were surprisingly approachable and friendly, and while a few prime candidates demurely said no thanks, out of embarrassment rather than pique, we had no trouble at all finding six willing diamond divers.

While we ogled, Bob Hope recalled great moments in Braves promotions, especially the wet T-shirt contest, won by a little honey who offered to display her more profound talents to several nervous Braves officials. With apologies and a shrug of the shoulders to Tennessee Williams, Erskine Caldwell, William Faulkner, and others, it turned out she was a minister's daughter, and it took several weeks to cool off her old man, who naturally claimed she'd been led astray.

Hope's current problem was the multiple weddings scheduled to take place at home plate the following afternoon before the game, an annual event. One of the brides-to-be had called Hope that afternoon in tears, having belatedly confessed to her intended that she was already married. Her husband was in prison, so she didn't think it mattered that much, but it sure enough scared the new boy clean out of the state.

Pearl Sandow wouldn't be caught diving for diamonds, even in her younger days, but she likes Ted Turner. Pearl Sandow has missed very few ball games in Atlanta in the last 37 years. She used to fret over the fortunes of the Atlanta Crackers in the Southern League, then the International League. She goes to Florida to observe a month of spring training every year. Just before Turner bought the team, she was awarded a lifetime pass for her devotion to the sport. Pearl is a smart lady. She knows her baseball, and a few other things. She is a handsome white-haired woman, sitting very happily in the hot sun with a great pile of Bleacher Creatures, hats, and banners (presents for various children, she says) taking up the seat next to her lifetime aisle position, 20 rows up from the field and halfway between home plate and first base, watching the smattering of "A" baseball being played on the field before her.

Turner honored Pearl's pass, for which she is grateful ("he didn't *have* to do that, you know") but she is unhappy that Turner has spent so much on a team that just won't jell, for some reason. She speaks quietly and with good sense about the starting line-up, the pitching rotation, and the effect of manager Dave Bristol, and finds no easy solutions to the problems.

Milo Hamilton stopped by to see the Braves' most loyal fan. Milo Hamilton was the radio announcer for the Atlanta Braves for nine years until he left shortly before the change of ownership to become the voice of the Pirates. Hamilton, whose sharp dress matches the edge of his tongue, says it was lucky he left when he did.

"I wouldn't have been able to work for Turner," Milo says. "No one can tell me how to broadcast."

Does Turner do that?

"That's what they say. He's tried broadcasting, among other things around here. Brought his chew of tobacco and his little cup into the booth. He did some color for two innings during a game in Pittsburgh this season. He filled in a few words about Willie Montanez. He said with all the high-money boys on the team, it was great to have Willie—Max, they call him. He said you give Max enough money to buy a few burritos and he's happy. He did a quick fade-out after that.

"And when he decided to manage, I would have stuck it to him. It was real tough on Dave Bristol. Bristol should have walked right the hell out of there."

Ted Turner took over managing the Braves on May 11, 1977. His tenure in the position lasted one game, the seventeenth game of a 17-game losing streak the Braves accumulated. Turner was available because the occasion fell between spring practice 12-meter racing in Marblehead and tune-up racing for the June America's Cup trials in Newport. And he was able to participate for a short time in Braves affairs as the team's owner because Commissioner Bowie Kuhn had temporarily lifted Turner's suspension in the light of an injunction filed by the Braves in Atlanta U.S. District Court against the commissioner's office. The Braves argued that the commissioner's decision was "contrary to the weight of the evidence and that he abused his discretion and violated the mandates of natural justice in disciplining Turner." In other words, the punishment exceeded the crime. Until the hearing, which would be held on April 25 and 26, and the subsequent ruling, Turner was free to participate. Or almost free. Kuhn cabled the Braves the moment he heard Turner was in the dugout:

"Given Mr. Turner's lack of familiarity with game operations, I do not think it is in the best interest of baseball for Mr. Turner to serve in that capacity."

Turner phoned the commissioner. Kuhn told him he didn't have the necessary experience. Turner asked him how he was going to get it. Kuhn told him, "In the stands, like other owners. Why can't you be like everybody else?"

"Because," Turner said, "I'm in last place."

Turner was disappointed. "I was ready to argue with the umps. The fans would have loved it."

Turner's managing was more than a stunt. When there is a problem somewhere, he likes to check it out himself. He had spent a fortune to buy the team and pay the players, and now the club was having trouble. He wanted to find out why.

"Ted had called me on the phone," team manager Dave Bristol says. "He was hesitant. Then he said he wanted to manage the club for ten days. I told him sure, come on into the dugout and sit with me and we'll talk about the game and I'll show you how it works. But that wasn't enough. I couldn't persuade him. He wanted to manage. He wanted me to be gone from the dugout. I said okay. I didn't think it was the right thing to do, but it's his money, his ball club, and he can do what he wants."

At the time Bristol told the press, "It's a strange thing to happen to a man. I'd rather not answer questions. I'm taken aback right now."

Bristol was sitting in his large office in the Braves locker room before game time, half-dressed in his Braves flannels, spitting tobacco juice into the nearby wastebasket. He is a hard, stocky man near six feet tall, with the calm weathered face of a range cowboy. His voice is soft, the deep North Carolina accent pleasing. His twinkly blue eyes do half the talking over his slow, captivating grin. He is at once fatherly and firm, a classic coach figure.

Underneath the hanging rack for Bristol's street clothes a pair of white, ostrich-skin, high-heeled cowboy boots sat directly beneath the straight legs of faded, starched and pressed blue jeans, which had been buttoned and carefully suspended by a hanger inside the waistband so as not to disturb their shape. The embroidered western-cut shirt hung beside them.

"He's up there in Newport winning and we aren't," Bristol said, "and he wonders why. I went up there with the team. That New York Yacht Club Selection Committee is going to grade him tough. That's no dog and pony show up there. That's tough going.

"When he bought the team he called me and we met at noon. I brought my wife along. He said to bring her but I guess he forgot. He went and called Janie, and she and my wife went off. Ted and I were together until 6:00 P.M. My head was hurting, he talked so much.

"I thought he came into the clubhouse too much from day one, and I told him so. He wanted to be one of the boys, develop a family scene. It doesn't work. I told him he should back off. He paid everybody real good—real good—and I don't know about that. Maybe they should learn to produce first, then get paid, huh?

"Feeling the way he does about the team is great, but you can't make it work overnight. This is a ruthless game. It's hard to buy a pennant. This game is one of survival of the fittest, for the players and for the teams.

"It has been hard for Ted. I figured this year we would have competed with the Reds and Los Angeles. Then we had an unbelievable string of injuries from Messersmith on down. Messersmith fell on his pitching elbow going after a ground ball. Bone chips. We gave up two good young players for reliever Mike Marshall, and then he left. He *was* the bullpen.

"So Ted tends to jump into the problems with both feet. He makes quick judgments. He has to learn to be patiently impatient. But he knows a lot after one short year. And he's got a lot of qualities I like. He never gives up, and I love that."

An example was the Kuhn suspension. Turner was willing to take on the baseball establishment's front office and the powerful mandate of its commissioner. The commissioner operates under the Major League Agreement, which is signed by all clubs in both leagues and which includes each club's waiver of the right of recourse to the courts over disciplinary decisions made by the commissioner. The Braves challenge raised important legal questions, and created an interesting decision.

The hearings, held in Atlanta in April, 1977, interrupted spring sailing in Marblehead, which caused various Kings Point Syndicate members to rattle their cages a bit, especially when the press gleefully reported that Turner had offered to deliver a "knuckle sandwich" to Kuhn's lawyer if he persisted with a particularly tough, repetitive line of questioning.

District Judge Newell Edenfield spent 17 pages of his 25-page decision on legal considerations of the baseball commissioner's authority, material which will be useful to those who take issue with the commissioner in the future. Recalling the remark of one judge, who had written that the commissioner of baseball has "all the attributes of a benevolent but absolute despot and all the disciplinary powers of the proverbial pater familias," Edenfield concluded that the commissioner did issue fair warning, and that "there is no evidence that the Commissioner's decision was the result of bias or ill will, although during the same period one other tampering violation was dealt with much less severely. The Court concludes with some misgivings that under this provision, the Commissioner did have the authority to punish the plaintiffs."

With tongue screwed noticeably into cheek, Edenfield went on: "The Atlanta Baseball Club is called the 'Atlanta Braves'; and considering the severity of this punishment, the casual observer might call this an Indian massacre in reverse. In their encounter with the Commissioner, the Braves took nary a scalp (except, of course, the Matthews contract), but lived to see their own dangling from the lodgepole of the Commissioner, apparently only as a grisly warning to others. At about the same time and for an identical offense, though perhaps not as flagrant, the venerable owner of the St. Louis Cardinals was fined $5000."

But in the matter of the denial of the Braves' first-round draft choice, Edenfield ruled against Kuhn. The judge said that "denial of a draft choice is simply not among the penalties authorized for this offense. . . . Accordingly the court concludes that the Commissioner was without the authority to impose that sanction, and its imposition is therefore void."

By picking up the gauntlet, Turner had reduced his penalty by one-half, not counting his own court costs.

During the first inning of the game with Pittsburgh, Walter again delivered the radio. Turner placed it on the dugout roof, flipped it on, and quickly reached for the volume knob as it roared with unexpected new strength. "New batteries!" Turner yelled, elated. "Where'd we get the money, Walter? I must owe you a couple bucks."

While Pittsburgh was putting together a first-inning rally, Terry McGuirk, the cable executive who had been house-sitting for the Turners, talked about trying out for the Braves. It seemed reasonable. McGuirk is a fine athlete, tall and lean—he'd been a memorable tight end at Middlebury—and he could pass for a ballplayer easier than some of the Braves themselves. He explained it wasn't a serious effort. "Turner came into my office on a Monday and told me to leave for spring training the next day," Terry said. "He just wanted to see how it worked. I was his alter ego. He would have gone if he could have, but he didn't have the time with the sailing going on."

The Braves held the Pirates even at six until the top of the eighth. Then Bristol made an unlucky pitching change. Suddenly Pittsburgh loaded the bases, and Robinson's grand slam settled matters for the evening.

As the stadium emptied, caterers began rolling large pots and steaming containers and cases of beer and Coke into the picnic area along the right field line. Turner was treating his minor leaguers to a post-game barbecue. The players gathered nervously, some of them with their parents and friends, and Turner quickly circulated among them breaking the ice, remarking on a good catch or a timely hit from the game that afternoon. Chief Nocahoma and two of his lovely squaws had come in from the teepee in center field to open the beer, and soon the sound of laughter and good times was bouncing around in the huge empty stadium.

Dave Bristol and his wife were making the occasion a family affair with a vacationing daughter and her friends, who were talking animatedly about college plans for the fall.

"Up there in Newport," Bristol said, leaning close so he didn't have to raise his voice, "when Turner lost that first race,

Skip Caray, who does the Hawks games on TV, said to me, 'I hear Turner's gonna go scout the Pacific Coast for us for ten days, and you're going to sail *Courageous.*" Bristol grinned.

"How come," I asked him, "you didn't walk out when he insisted on managing the team? Lots of managers would have."

"Well, that's true," Bristol said. "Lots would have. But one thing I've found is that pride isn't too hard to swallow if you chew it good first. You have to be bigger than the situation. You've got to be a man first. I love him, I really do. There's no animosity between us." Bristol tugged at his beer.

"I'll tell you why I love him," Bristol said. "It's the same reason he gets away with all the stuff he pulls. It's because he isn't afraid to fail. Now you can't say that about too many people, can you?"

Turner had moved away from the crowd and was standing next to the railing surrounding the playing field. He motioned me over. He raised an arm and swept it in an arc which took in the whole immense place, the high crater walls surrounding us, the tiers of blinding lights on their steel mesh towers, the well-clipped turf, the gonzo scoreboard, now in darkness, the 50,000 empty seats, the grounds keepers shutting down for the night, the squaws walking together toward the exit (buckskin bottoms twitching in unison), the last of the barbecue eaters, the caterers packing their wares, and his smile reflected his astonishment as much as his pure joy. "So how do you like my big playpen?" he asked.

The story goes that shortly after his suspension by Bowie Kuhn, Turner was driving home late one night. He impulsively took the stadium exit, and drove in, using the electronic gate-opening device that should have been forfeited by then. He parked in the tunnel, in his space, and took the elevator to the Braves offices. He ran into a cleaning woman upstairs, who he made vow not to tell anyone she had seen him there. He let himself in, and walked down the long, curving corridor to his private office. He opened the curtains to reveal the playing

field below, and sat at his desk in the semidarkness, contem-
plating the trophies and plaques and framed testimonials from
the Urban League ("Employer of the Year"), the Stanford
Graduate School of Business Alumni Club ("Entrepreneur of
the Year"), the Cobb County Sheriff's Association, the Rock-
dale County Girls Softball League, the National Foundation
for Ileitis and Colitis, Ted Turner Appreciation Night, the
Chattanooga Cable Television Company, the 100% Wrong
Club; the autographed baseballs and bats and pictures; the
books kept next to his desk (Charles Colson's *Born Again, The
Magic of Believing* by Claude Bristol); and he thought about
what had been taken away from him, and he put his head on his
desk, and he wept.

Sunday morning at 10:30 Turner was settled in front of the
television to watch *Mr. Deeds Goes to Town* on Channel 17's
Academy Award Theater, a film he had been looking forward
to seeing for several days. *Mr. Deeds* is a Frank Capra film that
came out of the Depression. Gary Cooper stars as Deeds, a rich
eccentric from the Midwest who attracts considerable attention
in New York with his free-wheeling style and with the way he
hands out money to those who seem to need it. There is a pretty
newspaper lady who cons him, then falls for him, and some bad
guys who try to lock him up and steal his money.

Turner was beside himself with pleasure as the film un-
folded. "Isn't this great? It's so uplifting!" Cooper hitches a
ride on a fire truck in his tuxedo. Cut to the city editor talking to
the reporter: "He's either an idiot, or the grandest thing alive."

"See," Turner said with glee, "he's winning everyone over. I
know who I am. I'm a character from a Frank Capra movie. No
bullshit. You know anything about Capra? What other films
did he do? There were a bunch of them."

In the film's climactic scene, Mr. Deeds' sanity is on trial in a
courtroom. Deeds, who has refused to defend himself, finally

speaks up and articulately retains the right to remain at large. When the judge asks him if he has any final statement, Deeds walks over to the bad guys' lawyer and decks him with one punch.

"Awright!" Turner roared his approval from the couch. In the past few years Turner has resorted to the occasional punch-out himself. He backhanded a well-known yacht designer during the SORC a while back. It wasn't a serious punch, but it was a serious swing. And he hung one on arch-rival Dennis Conner at the Congressional Cup in 1976, after Conner had persistently harassed him with protests. Turner says it was a glancing blow, delivered after Conner refused his invitation to put up his dukes and defend himself. Turner won't acquire a reputation as a brawler based on two uncontested swings and one courtroom threat, but in these placid times the record is worthy of note.

Turner was excited by the TV punch-out. "I'm like Gary Cooper, and Bowie Kuhn's lawyer is like the guy who gets punched."

That afternoon at the stadium we passed up the hot sun behind the first base dugout for the cool of Bill Lucas's private box. After a few innings of a slow game, Turner got restless and went wandering. On the way to the press lounge to get a Coke, I heard the sound of a familiar voice coming from the direction of the radio booth. Turner had dropped in on announcer Ernie Johnson to provide a little color for a few innings. He was punctuating base hits ("awright!") and talking about the evils of artificial turf (Fulton County Stadium uses real turf). Then during a pause in the action on the field he turned to Johnson and said into the microphone, as if they were having a private conversation over a drink, "Ernie, this isn't a very hard job, this announcing, is it?"

Johnson looked at Turner, who was staring right at him, his head tilted back slightly, his expression serious, his cigar poised near his mouth, and knew he was being picked over.

"It's a snap," Johnson said, and went back to the game.

The Braves won it handily, adding four unnecessary runs in their half of the eighth to make the score 8–3. In three games they had played well, taking two out of three from the Pirates. Perhaps energized by the rare experience of seeing his team knock off a contender, The Radio was playing as we left the stadium. The subject was war, never far from Turner's mind, and the new Time-Life series on World War II he was reading, and Adolf Hitler, who intrigues Turner.

"He had more imagination than anyone to come along in a long time. He was deranged about racial superiority to a degree. He was ruthless.

"Did you ever read about his plans for rebuilding Berlin? He was going to build a lake in the middle of the city. The rotunda of the capital building would be five times the size of the one in Washington. The drive leading up to it would be three times as wide as the Champs Élysées.

"During the Depression in Germany, 300,000 people turned out for his rallies. He hypnotized people. He built huge sets with lights and fountains. Each appearance was greater than the last. The rallies were like Martin Luther King and Muhammad Ali on the same bill. His plan was to give the people their pride back. His followers were willing to die because it had been so colorful."

We were in the tunnel now, climbing into Turner's Chevrolet Caprice.

"Hitler was the most powerful figure of all time. He knew how to use movies and radio. I know how to use TV. I understand the media. I just about have the media in this town eating out of my hand. Really. Hey, there's Wayne, Wayne Minshew, he writes sports for the *Constitution*. Hey Wayne!"

Turner pulled the car to the right-hand curb of the tunnel. Wayne Minshew approached. Turner leaned across the passenger seat. "Hey Wayne, don't I have the press in this town eating out of my hand?"

Minshew bent down so he could look into the car at Turner. "Yes," he said, "you just about do."

"You see?" Turner said, and pulled out of the tunnel.

Turner from Savannah

FLORENCE TURNER, MOTHER OF TED TURNER, was enjoying a glass of cream sherry before lunch at the Cincinnati Club. To combat the two-degree January weather, she was wearing a round pillbox hat of black and silver fox that nicely complemented her black outfit and set off her pastel blond hair. "A light hair color softens the lines in your face," she said. "That's why your hair turns white when you get older. God figured that out. I just keep helping Him along."

Mrs. Turner is a handsome woman, tall and erect, with the bold facial features inherited by her son. She is a formal, dignified person. Her breeding was precise, and indelible enough so that strangers, even younger ones, are addressed with "Mr." until permission to use first names has been earnestly solicited. Even in her sixties, her wide-eyed, schoolgirl naïveté is not a pose. When an account of one of her son's remarks during the America's Cup summer was reported in print with "bleep

bleep" inserted for stronger rhetoric, she had to inquire about the meaning of "bleep bleep."

Her grandfather (Ted's great-grandfather), Henry Sicking, was the first chain grocer in Cincinnati. At one time he owned more than twenty stores. He also owned a livery stable. He went off to work each morning in frock tails and top hat. A full-length portrait of him, so styled, is in the family album. He is standing in right-hand profile with one foot subtly but aggressively planted ahead of the other. His left hand thrusts the frock coat aside and is wedged into a high, slit pocket in the front of his pants. His right hand rests on a thin, knobby cane of darkened bamboo. His head is erect, and below his small mustache, a large cigar protrudes straight out. The resemblance to his great-grandson is striking.

Henry Sicking died at the age of 40 after stepping off one trolley into the path of another coming from the opposite direction. He was down to three grocery stores, having sold the rest in order to play the stock market, and was said to be terribly preoccupied with his losses at the time he was struck.

Florence Turner's childhood memories are of Gibson girl dresses, frilly sunbonnets, and a sequence of elegant pony-drawn carts. Again, the photo album speaks eloquently. And although her courtly manners and demure posture were reinforced by the nuns at convent school, her passion for parties, dress balls, and the string of suitors that accompanied the social whirl was in no way diluted by her stern schooling.

She met Ed Turner when he came to rent quarters at the 100-room apartment hotel owned by her family in Cincinnati. It was an elegant place. A string quartet played for dinner. In the mornings, the chauffeurs lined up their limousines in the courtyard and scrubbed them.

Ed Turner was a dynamic young man who came to Cincinnati at the urging of the owner of Queen City Chevrolet, who intended to make him a great car salesman. Ed was from Sumner, Mississippi, the son of well-educated cotton farmers who had been reduced to poverty by the Depression. Ed had to quit Duke because of the financial difficulties, and finished college at Ol' Miss. To help pay his way through college, he had worked in a butcher shop, run a laundry, strung tennis rackets, and worked in a woodshop. After college he took a job in Memphis making traffic counts for the General Outdoor Advertising Company. He often complained that he made more money his last year in college than his first year out.

Ed Turner courted Florence Rooney with the same ferocious intensity he applied to every project. The courtship lasted eight months, morning, noon, and night, Saturdays, Sundays, and holidays. Once Ed had to go to Detroit on business. He drove to Detroit, did his business, turned around, and drove back straight to Florence Rooney's house. He made the trip in 23 hours with no sleep. "He said he was afraid I would have other dates," Florence says. "He was amazing. Anything he wanted he would get. I didn't have the sense to be frightened.

"I was in love with someone else at the time, and it appeared we would be married. The poor fellow came up from the South to propose, and Ed wouldn't leave me alone with him. Finally the fellow proposed in the kitchen while Mother was with me. I told him it looked like I was going to marry Ed. Mother said not without her consent."

A few days later Ed arranged to drive Florence and her mother to Mississippi to meet his parents. The other suitor announced he would be traveling the same route to go back home, so he would tag along, stay at the same hotel, and if Mrs. Rooney didn't give her consent to the Turners, the party could journey on and meet *his* family.

The nature of their courtship—and perhaps the ways of a genteel maiden and a Southern man of the 1930s—was such that it wasn't until long after they were married that Florence Turner discovered her new husband drank excessively, and that he couldn't abide the Catholic Church, in which they had been married. He told her to pick a church, any other church. She settled on the Episcopal.

The Turners had two children: Ted, and a younger daughter, Mary Jane. Like many a traditional father, Ed Turner was very tough on his son, and gentle with his daughter. Ted was a devilish child who enjoyed pranks like muddying his hands and leaving perfect hand prints on the neighbor's freshly laundered sheets drying on the line. As a Turner cook once remarked about the little boy, "He sure looks good to be so bad." Such behavior strengthened Ed Turner's belief that a spared rod produced a spoiled child, and the beatings he administered were fierce and frequent. Fierce enough, in fact, to cause Mrs. Turner concern.

"I would say that 90 percent of the arguments I had with Ed were over him beating Ted too hard," she says. It was a concern that apparently Ed Turner could not resist exploiting. There was the day he sternly called his son into a bedroom and locked the door. Outside, Mrs. Turner heard the sounds of a terrible beating and young Ted's outcries. Beside herself, she pounded on the door. Finally the two came out, laughing. Ed had been striking the bed with a coathanger. Ted had been hollering on cue.

"Oh, I used to fuss a lot when Ed would send Ted out at the age of ten to cut weeds around the signs that were in swampy places full of snakes," Florence says. "But he would jolly me along. He really was witty. With that thick Southern accent of his he could be hilarious at times. He called me 'the avenging angel,' and 'his little nubbin.' I thought that was cute until I found out a nubbin is a deformed ear of corn."

A pattern of shipping Ted off to boarding school started early. When the Navy assigned Ed Turner to the gulf coast, he took his wife and Mary Jane, leaving Ted, age six, in a Cincinnati boarding school. Ted, who is loathe to talk about his childhood, once singled out this incident as particularly unhappy.

After working for several billboard companies in Cincinnati, Ed started his own by purchasing a company in Savannah. When he decided to expand his business, he located a house big enough for three. At age nine, Ted was off to Georgia Military Academy.

Mrs. Turner found a bigger house and Ted came home, where he attended local schools, hunted and fished happily in the Georgia woods, and indulged his passion for animals. Ted also took a correspondence course in taxidermy and, according to his mother, became quite proficient at the craft. But a year later he was sent off to the McCallie School, then a military-oriented prep school in Chattanooga, Tennessee.

"There was nothing I could do," Florence Turner says. "I cried. It did no good. Ed told me he had the purse strings. I had to do what he said. Ted hated McCallie. He was a devil there. I had to buy him new shoes every time he came home. He wore them out walking punishment tours. He would hide his tickets in his cap on the way to the airport, hoping he wouldn't have to go back. It seemed that Ed was always trying to separate Ted from me. Maybe he was jealous of my love for him."

At the age of 12, Ted started working a 40-hour week at his father's billboard company, cutting grass around the signs and creosoting poles. He was paid a pittance, and charged rent at home. "One summer I made 50 dollars a week, and my father charged me 25 dollars a week rent," Ted recalls. "I asked him if that wasn't a little high. He said if I could do better than that for food and lodging seven days a week I could move out.

"Aside from working, I had to read a book every two days. I never considered not doing it because I was instructed with wire coathangers when I didn't get them read. I learned quickly not to question the word of the big chief."

One of Ed Turner's few really close friends, Dr. Irving Victor of Savannah, says Ed's treatment of his son was puzzlingly inconsistent. "He idolized Teddy," Dr. Victor says. "He was his whole life. He would have hung the moon for him. He bought him guns, boats. Yet he was tremendously difficult with him. I think he took out a lot of hostility on him."

Judy Nye Hallisey, Ted's first wife, knew Ed Turner. "He told me once that he wanted Ted to fear him," Judy says. "He said if Ted feared him, then he would respect him. He wanted Ted to be insecure, because he felt that insecurity breeds greatness. If Ted was insecure then he would be forced to compete. When I knew Ted, he admired his father and wanted to emulate him. Emulate is a Turner word. I think they coined it."

According to the school's catalogue, "The McCallie School provides Chattanooga and the South with college preparation for boys in a Christian context." There is an honor system: "Honor may be the most valuable lesson McCallie teaches. Boys clean their own rooms, occasionally serve detention on Saturdays. Hair is long enough to satisfy most boys and offend some alumni; some of the dress is prescribed some of the time. . . . McCallie is the school for the boy who wants to work—and be known by his work." McCallie has changed some since Ted Turner attended the school in the early fifties. Gone is the military gear and bearing affected by many private schools during wartime. But the basic philosophy is the same.

Several of the older masters at the McCallie School know the Ted Turner stories, but none know them as well as Elliot Schmidt, the school's senior faculty member and a teacher of American history, and none tell them better. Schmidt is a short, stocky man wearing thick tweeds. He walks leaning heavily on a stout cane.

Blessed be Schmidt's philosophical nature, for Schmidt not only taught Turner, but was his dorm master for three years, a fact that still causes him an involuntary grimace. He recalls

Turner as a smart, inquisitive boy. He wasn't at school more than a few nights when the dorm proctor saw the light under the door after hours and asked who was responsible for it. Turner's voice was heard replying in proper, military fashion, "Edison, T., sir." The master dutifully wrote the given name on the demerit board.

"He kept a shallow, aluminum pan in his room," Schmidt recalls. "He put dirt in it, and grew grass, *lawn* grass, which he clipped with manicure scissors. I told him it didn't add to the military decor. He asked what was wrong with having it. I let him keep it.

"All the boys had metal bunk beds. Ted experimented with welding a length of brass chain to his bed. He succeeded, but he blew out every circuit in the building. When we got furious, telling him he could have electrocuted himself or burned down the building, his attitude was, 'why me?'

"He tried to take in dogs, birds with broken wings, gerbils, snakes, anything he found. Then I moved to a new dorm, and Ted followed me. It was thought being with older boys would calm him down. But he started leading them. There was a Latin master in this dorm who was a bit of a misfit. He always wore white shirts and bow ties. Ted organized the hall into a group called 'Spastics Anonymous' whose sole purpose was to make this master's life miserable. They found when they reversed their uniform blouses it gave them a penguin effect—naturally the Latin teacher's nickname was 'the Penguin'—and they would waddle up and down the hall tormenting the man."

When it appeared that Schmidt would have Turner in his dorm a third year, he appealed to the headmaster with a long letter that concluded it would be better for both Ted and himself if their relationship was terminated. "The news reached Ted," Schmidt recalls, "and he was somewhat offended."

But Turner's attitude at McCallie was changing. He was beginning to spend more energy on academics and military bearing than on scheming how to place alarm clocks around study hall set to go off at ten-minute intervals, or how to unobtrusively release live parakeets from under his desk top. After his third year, no longer would he be detained each spring for several days after school was out, walking off punishment tours. As Ted recalls, "For several years I was absolutely the worst cadet in the place. I didn't do anything, and what I did do got demerits. Then I turned it around. I'd been the worst cadet, and I determined to be the best. I became a believer. I ended up with 'best cadet' honors. When I left there I cried. It was such a perfect place."

Elliot Schmidt got Turner again despite his plea. But the relationship became more productive. Schmidt was also the debate coach, and when Turner came to him with the ambition to take the affirmative side of a subject upon which he desired to construct a perfect, non-debatable argument, Schmidt was somewhat startled. He told Turner that the subject should be debatable.

"The question dealt with federal aid to higher education according to need," Schmidt recalls. "Most of the students who were debating the affirmative side of the question defined 'need' as the need of students—those passing the entrance exams who did not have enough money to go to college.

"Ted went to English teachers at McCallie and the University of Chattanooga and asked them to verify the fact that, in the wording of the query, 'according to need' could relate to either students *or* the government. He chose to build his case on the government's need; that is, if the federal government felt that the country would 'need' civil engineers, the government could offer scholarships for students who would major in civil engineering."

Turner produced his argument at the Tennessee state secondary school debating championships, and left the girl who was supposed to debate him both speechless and in tears. He won the state championship with a score of 97 out of 100. "It was a little below the belt," Schmidt says, "but he won with a perfectly legal, non-debatable subject. For some years McCallie was in disrepute. Many area coaches felt that we had been unethical in not using the popular definition that their teams were prepared to debate."

Turner's other notable accomplishment at McCallie, aside from being voted the "neatest cadet" his junior year, and "Captain of the Corps" his senior year, was the way he overhauled his College Board verbal exam. Disappointed with the score he achieved junior year, he set up a goal of learning a number of words a day during the summer while he was working at the billboard company. When he took the test again senior year, he had raised his score by 162 points, considerably more than test administrators say one is likely to improve it through effort.

"He was known as 'Terrible Ted' at McCallie long before *Sports Illustrated* called him that," Elliot Schmidt says. "But for all his scrapes here, none were really serious, and if Ted told us he wasn't involved in something—'this time'—we could be sure he wasn't. He was honest as could be, and never malicious. And he had that incredible drive. When he became determined to do something, he would do it.

"His father? I don't recall that he ever set foot here. He was too busy. Jimmy Brown always brought Ted to school. This year, Ted's son Teddy started at McCallie. Jimmy Brown brought him to school just like he had brought his father."

About the time Ted went to McCallie, his sister was taken ill with a rare and terminally debilitating disease called lupus. One effect of lupus is to make the body susceptible to other diseases. Mary Jane contracted encephalitis. Hospitalized at Johns Hopkins, she recovered from almost certain death—but with brain damage. For twelve weeks she was in a coma. At full recovery she was often violent, and was given to sustained, uncontrollable fits. She lived at home in a gradually deteriorating condition requiring intensive and expert care for eight long years before she died.

When Ed Turner purchased the outdoor company in Savannah as a way of expanding his business, his plan was to set it up with a management team and run it from Cincinnati. He rented a house in Savannah, hoping to wrap up the details in three months. But neither the advertisement in the billboard trade publication, *Signs of Our Times,* nor Ed Turner's subsequent investigation revealed the ill will that existed between the former owner and the executive he refused to sell to, a man named Schumann. Schumann wasted no time setting up a rival company. To make money, billboard companies need a virtual monopoly in a given area. Schumann belonged to the Outdoor Advertising Association of America, which was worth a certain amount of business, and he knew the territory, he had the connections. Embittered over being shut out of the deal Turner closed, he wasn't above jumping billboard leases that belonged to Turner, and employing other hard-nosed tactics. Ed Turner realized he had a fight on his hands. He moved his family to Savannah and dug in.

Ed Turner didn't mind moving. He quickly got to like Savannah, and the idea of a good fight didn't bother him at all. James Hogan, who eventually bought the Savannah company from Turner, had firsthand experience of the Schumann-Turner battle. Hogan recalls that one of Ed Turner's hobbies was contesting the Internal Revenue Service. Most people consider themselves fortunate if they never do business with the IRS. "Ed figured if they didn't call him every year," Hogan says, "he was doing something wrong. His theory was to take full advantage of the tax laws. If there was any doubt, he took advantage of it, and figured it was up to the IRS to prove him wrong. He functioned as his own attorney, and I doubt if he ever lost to them."

Hogan, now retired, is a heavy-set, poker-faced man who masks a fisherman's caginess behind a mumbling drawl and the manner of a slow loris. Ed Turner hired him away from his newspaper advertising job "for local color," Hogan says. "He brought me up to Cincinnati when he was trying to hire me, and we did the town. We must have hit every night club. He was drinking Scotch with a buttermilk chaser so it wouldn't bother his ulcers.

"He had a killer instinct. He was smart, shrewd. He put up the first flip billboards in Savannah. He gave people the impression he was out in front of them by a long head. Maybe he was too smart, too sharp. He would take customers out on that boat of his, and instead of a leisurely cruise down the waterway, he would sail into the ocean and make them sick. His fight with Schumann was the longest and the toughest in the industry's history. It probably killed them both. I remember three weeks after Ed sold out to me, Schumann had a brain hemorrhage and died. Ed told me if he had known Schumann was sick, he wouldn't have sold out."

One of Ed Turner's Savannah friends was Carl Helfrich, an architect. The two met at the Savannah Yacht Club, where their sons were racing Penguins. Bunky Helfrich, who has sailed with Ted ever since, was a winch tiller on *Courageous.* Ted had avoided the Penguin his father gave him until Jimmy Brown suggested using it to explore a nearby island for hunting and fishing. After that he began sailing and racing in the yacht club's junior program.

"Ed had a big schooner named *Merry Jane,*" Carl Helfrich says. "He would line up a bunch of Penguins behind it and tow them to the regattas. The kids would sleep on board. Then Ed and I would sit on the bank and second-guess the racing tactics.

"Ed didn't race. He really didn't have any diversions. He was a ladies' man, but he was quiet about it. He liked beauty. I think he just liked having women around. We played golf some, but not in a group. Just the two of us. He loved competition. We played for a nickel a hole, and he fought it out like we were playing for thousands. He really lived to make money. I would kid him, tell him he needed some recreation. He would say that making money was his hobby."

"Ed was a real good friend," Helfrich says. "He helped me a lot. Ed had an idea for the first big shopping plaza I ever heard of. He wanted to open a K-Mart type of store. I drew up the plans for him, and I was paid well for it. But he got nervous, the control got out of his hands, and the deal fell through. Ed was like that."

Jimmy Brown came into the Turners' life when he was just 17, a young Geechee black out of Isle of Hope, Georgia, a small community on the coast near Savannah. He was hired to tend the schooner, and has been invaluable to three generations of Turners. As Judy Nye Hallisey said of Jimmy, "If he could have nursed our children, he would have."

Once when Ted was bargaining for a boat he wanted to charter, the owner suggested he throw in his wife Jane, the five kids, and Jimmy Brown. Ted considered it, and said okay except for Jimmy.

Jimmy Brown today is a rotund man with a keen eye and a big laugh. "That's me," he says, "free, black, and unattached." Despite the crippled left arm he has had since birth, he sailed everywhere with Ed Turner, and went ocean racing as cook on Ted's boats for ten years. Jimmy has retired from racing, scoffing at the smaller boats and the stripped-down racing machines of today's circuits, opting for the comforts of dry land duties.

"Now Mr. T., ohhh, he was a handsome man," Jimmy says. "Tall, always well dressed. He wore Irish linen suits, white shirts, and green ties. And Panama hats. Real ones. Not b.s. Panama hats. He was a Southern gentleman. He made sure I was dressed well, too. He took me up to his tailor in New Orleans and had me fitted for suits that cost 200 dollars apiece.

"He had a black limousine. I drove. He did all his work in the back seat. He called me 'Sport.' He had real class. He was a man. There was no b.s. about him. He was outspoken. He would say to me, 'Sport, I blew that one, didn't I?' And I would say, 'You sure did, Mr. T., you sure did.'

"He had two plantations down in South Carolina, one across the road from the other. I had my own place on the grounds. I used to go over and fix him breakfast. He got me a red Borgward, a real sporty car. And you see this watch? It's one of the first Accutrons. He gave that to me. I'd as soon lose my hand as this watch."

Ed Turner made it possible for Irving Victor to have the house in Savannah where he resides today. He offered his house to Victor when he was moving, taking out a second mortgage so the young doctor could pay off the equity as he was able, with no interest involved. Most people found Ed Turner friendly but closed, a conservative who kept things to himself. But as Victor says, "If he really liked you, he liked real hard."

The Turners forced an Ivy League education upon Ted, a decision none of them were later happy about. College was the first time Ted's life hadn't been monitored by either his father or military school disciplinarians, and it was a big disappointment. The shock of any Northern liberal institution would have been considerable to anyone with Turner's background and emotional sympathies. The accident of his birth as a Midwestern Yankee notwithstanding, Ted began a lifelong love affair with the South when he moved to Savannah at age nine. He showed up at Brown University a strange mixture of states' rights revisionist, rebel, war-lover, Dixiecrat, and humanitarian—an unmistakable Southern Man.

Ted and I were fellow students at Brown in the 1950s. We met at the old Brown Yacht Club, which perched on the banks of the grimy Seekonk River. Diseases like sailing bring all kinds of unlikely people together, and Turner and I existed as an example. At 18 he was more outrageous than he is today. He was too loud, too red in the neck (or so it seemed to an equally provincial Northerner), he talked too much, he was an on-stage drunk, and he won more dinghy races than I did, none of which endeared him to me.

Ted had wanted the Naval Academy at Annapolis. His father said no. He wanted his son trained for the business. There were other complications that would pile up and cost Turner his degree. His first year out, Ted won his first nine regattas on the college dinghy circuit. His ability came to the attention of the Noroton Yacht Club, where he was offered a job for the summer and a chance to race in a hot Lightning fleet. His father said no. He had to work at the billboard company. It was a keen disappointment. That, and the divorce brewing at home, was enough to make Ted throw away the $5000 bonus his father had offered him if he didn't have a drink until he was 21.

Figuring the price of the first drink would be reduced proportionately by subsequent drinks, Turner and some friends got rowdy and landed at a nearby women's college. Ted was suspended from Brown for the ensuing fracas.

His father's solution to that problem was a tour of duty in the Coast Guard. Ted did six months active duty, then went back to Brown and decided to major in classics. His decision was based on the presence of John Rowe Workman, an urbane, entertaining man, a classical scholar, and one of the few Brown professors for whom Turner maintains any regard.

Workman has a marvelous sense of the absurd, a basic clarity about man's meanderings, thinking as he and his fellow classicists do in two-thousand-year increments. Workman's hobby is disaster. He has collected over 400 books on the subject. He will tell you that if the *Titanic* or an equivalent vessel had not met such a spectacular and horrible end, ships at sea would still not have enough lifeboat space for all passengers. Or that without a Coconut Grove or similar conflagration, strict fire codes for public places would still not exist. Workman is not depressed by his thesis that disaster is what usually precedes social progress. Quite the contrary. For Workman, the knowledge is a reassurance of what is inevitable about man, himself included. Pondering his growing library on disaster, he is benevolently amused like a parent watching the frustrating struggles of an infant learning to walk.

It is not surprising that Turner would choose Workman as a mentor, because Turner has always had a similar quality, a comprehensive and underlying sense of the absurd that certain lucky people are born with, and that only fails him on occasion.

It only takes John Workman a moment to sort Ted Turner out of his mental files of several thousand faces. "Oh yes, Mr. Turner," Workman says. "He's a handful, as we say in Pennsylvania. Did he ever graduate? I'm not sure he did. And I'm sure it was for something colorful, and I'm in favor of that, to be sure. I remember he had quite a time with his father.

"The father took a strong view of Ted's desire to major in classics. So he wrote him a letter, the object of which was to warn Ted that he should major in something that was practical, something which would stand him in good stead in the business world, and not get mixed up with those freaks and queers that everyone knows populate the field of humanities. It was a strong letter. Ted gave it to the student newspaper to publish."

My dear son,

I am appalled, even horrified, that you have adopted Classics as a Major. As a matter of fact, I almost puked on the way home today. I suppose that I am old-fashioned enough to believe that the purpose of an education is to enable one to develop a community of interest with his fellow men, to learn to know them, and to learn how to get along with them. In order to do this, of course, he must learn what motivates them, and how to impel them to be pleased with his objectives and desires.

I am a practical man, and for the life of me I cannot possibly understand why you should wish to speak Greek. With whom will you communicate in Greek? I have read, in recent years, the deliberations of Plato and Aristotle, and was interested to learn that the old bastards had minds which worked very similarly to the way our minds work today. I was amazed that they had so much time for deliberating and thinking, and was interested in the kind of civilization that would permit such useless deliberation. Then I got to thinking that it wasn't so amazing after all, they thought like we did, because my Hereford cows today are very similar to those ten or twenty generations ago. I am amazed that you would adopt Plato and Aristotle as a vocation for several months when it might make pleasant and enjoyable reading to you in your leisure time as relaxation at a later date. For the life of me, I cannot understand why you should be vitally interested in informing yourself about the influence of the Classics on English literature. It is not necessary for you to know how to make a gun in order to know how to use it. It would seem to me that it would be enough to learn English literature without going into what influence this or that ancient mythology might have upon it. As for Greek literature, the history of Roman and Greek churches, and the art of those eras, it would seem to me that you would be much better off by learning something of contemporary literature and writings, and things that might have some meaning to you with the people with whom you are to associate.

These subjects might give you a community of interest with an isolated few impractical dreamers, and a select group of college professors. God forbid!

It would seem to me that what you wish to do is to establish a community of interest with as many people as you possibly can. With people who are moving, who are doing things, and who have an interesting, not a decadent, outlook.

I suppose everybody has to be a snob of some sort, and I suppose you will feel that you are distinguishing yourself from the herd by becoming a Classical snob. I can see you drifting into a bar, belting down a few, turning around to the guy on the stool next to you—a contemporary billboard baron from Podunk, Iowa, and saying,

"Well, what do you think about old Leonidas?" Your friend, the bill-board baron, will turn to you and say, "Leonidas who?" You will turn to him and say, "Why Leonidas, the prominent Greek of the Twelfth Century." He will, in turn, say to you, "Well, who in the hell was he?" You will say, "Oh, you don't know about Leonidas?" and dismiss him, and not discuss anything else with him the rest of the evening. He will feel that you are a stupid snob and a flob; and you will feel that he is a clodhopper from Podunk, Iowa. I suppose this will make you both happy, and as a result of it, you will wind up buying his billboard plant.

There is no question but this type of useless information will distinguish you, set you apart from the doers of the world. If I leave you enough money, you can retire to an ivory tower, and contemplate for the rest of your days the influence that the hieroglyphics of prehistoric man had upon the writings of William Faulkner. Incidentally, he was a contemporary of mine in Mississippi. We speak the same language—whores, sluts, strong words, and strong deeds.

It isn't really important what I think. It's important what you wish to do with your life. I just wish I could feel that the influence of those oddball professors and the ivory towers were developing you into the kind of a man we can both be proud of. I am quite sure that we both will be pleased and delighted when I introduce you to some friend of mine and say "this is my son. He speaks Greek."

I had dinner during the Christmas holidays with an efficiency expert, an economic advisor to the nation of India, on the Board of Directors of Regents at Harvard University, who owns some 80,000 acres of valuable timber land down here, among his other assets. His son and his family were visiting him. He introduced me to his son, and then apologetically said, "He is a theoretical mathematician. I don't even know what he is talking about. He lives in a different world." After a little while I got to talking to his son, and the only thing he would talk to me about was his work. I didn't know what he was talking about either, so I left early.

If you are going to stay on at Brown, and be a professor of Classics, the courses you have adopted will suit you for a lifetime association with Gale Noyes. Perhaps he will even teach you to make jelly. In my opinion, it won't do much to help you learn to get along with people in this world. I think you are rapidly becoming a jackass, and the sooner you get out of that filthy atmosphere, the better it will suit me.

Oh, I know everybody says that a college education is a must. Well,

I console myself by saying that everybody said the world was square, except Columbus. You go ahead and go with the world, and I'll go it alone. . . .

I hope I am right. You are in the hands of the Philistines, and dammit, I sent you there. I am sorry.

Devotedly,
Dad

"We lost Ted in a sense," Workman says. "He changed to economics. But we didn't really lose him. The real humanist will always go out of his way to be different."

"Ed was simply furious that Ted gave that letter to the newspaper," Florence Turner says. "Our divorce had gone through, but he came over to rave about it. I guess Ted was mad at his daddy at the time. I think the divorce had a lot to do with him breaking the drinking agreement. Before that, he wouldn't have so much as rum sauce on ice cream."

Divorce had crept up several times in the life of Florence and Ed Turner. Each time Florence countersued, and nothing came of it. Sometimes it was amazingly casual. Once Ed arrived home and told Florence he was leaving her. He suggested she come sit on the bed and chat while he packed. Then it finally happened. Ed Turner took up residence in Reno, Nevada, for the necessary period. The morning the divorce was final, he called Florence. "He said it was official," Florence says. "I told him I knew. He said, but I don't want a divorce. He said he was coming east. He arrived in a few days and handed me the keys to the black Chrysler Imperial I had been wanting. He said we were going to drive to Florida and get married. I told him the curtain had come down. He said it could go up again. I told him the players had changed."

After having burned down his fraternity's homecoming display, Turner moved into a dormitory, where he entertained the troops one evening by broadcasting the extra-curricular love-life of a dormitory-mate's steady girl. The guy held a grudge. When Turner took a girl to his room a few nights later, the guy called the campus cops, and Turner was asked to leave Brown a second and final time.

This time, Ed Turner wasn't that upset. According to Peter Dames, one of Ted's classmates who had made an unscheduled departure from the university at the same time and who was traveling with Ted, Ed Turner killed the fatted calf when the two arrived at the plantation to pick up Ted's Lightning. Dames is a big, husky man with dark, wide-set eyes that one suspects could burn holes in a plank.

"Ted's plan," Dames says, "was to sail the Lightning to Europe. He had it all worked out. We were going to be the first ever to cross the Altantic in a Lightning. We would be the toast of Europe. The women would fall at our feet. We couldn't miss." Dames, who has never been fully convinced that sailing is a sane way to have fun, still registers subliminal terror at the vision of himself and Turner alone in a Lightning in mid-Atlantic. "Luckily," Dames says, "a big limb had fallen on the boat during the winter, so the transatlantic trip was out of the question."

Dames was struck by the plantation. "Ed Turner was a colorful guy," Dames says. "He might meet you out front of the house in a silk robe or maybe a white linen suit with a mint julep in one hand. Sometimes he drank Scotch from the bottle. There was duck hunting, and barbecues, lots of food and drink. He really knew how to do it. He was a great host. He laid the red carpet out for us. I think he was happy Ted had finished with Brown.

"He intimidated Ted. I remember him bragging one night over dinner that he had screwed every debutante but one in

Cincinnati one year, and he would have gotten her if he had had more time. Ted asked him how many women he figured he'd been with, total. The old man said maybe 300. Ted was amazed."

In the car Turner had purchased in Providence for $125, he and Dames left the plantation and traveled south to Florida. They discovered jobs were difficult to find in that chamber-of-commerce dreamland. They rented a couple of rooms over the White Horse Bar in a Cuban neighborhood. They had money for the deposit and one month's rent. "We used a phone book for toilet paper and ate peanut butter on shirt cardboard," Dames says. "We collected bottles and turned them in for the deposit. On special occasions, we had hamburgers and birch beer at the Royal Castle for dinner." When a change of luck didn't materialize, Turner gave himself up to the local Coast Guard office (the Coast Guard had been after him for missing summer cruises) and Dames started looking for jobs in New York.

After his cruise, Turner went home. "I didn't know how good I would be at knuckling under," he said, "but I knew I didn't want to be a bum, living on the road doing odd jobs. My father brought me to my knees. He brought me to my senses."

Ed Turner also hired Dames. "That was some change," Dames says. "I was assigned to the company in Charleston. What a different world. I was a snotty New York kid. Now I was hearing about the war of Northern aggression and hanging out at whorehouses for want of something better to do." Dames has been running Turner Advertising since 1970.

Ted was sent to work in the billboard company in Macon. The first thing he did was sell his Lightning and buy a Y-Flier because Macon had a racing fleet. "I really played local businessman in Macon," Turner recalls. "They loved me. I was a director of the Red Cross, a member of Rotary and some other clubs, I played poker once a week with the boys—did the whole thing. I was into the business. I worked fifteen hours a day, six and a half days a week. We doubled our sales in two years. It was phenomenal."

Ted also married Judy Nye from Chicago, the daughter of Harry Nye, of Murphy and Nye Sails. When I called Judy Nye to ask her if she would meet with me to talk about her years with Turner, she sounded friendly, almost familiar. Toward the end of the conversation she said, "Well, that advice you gave me years ago about Ted Turner was just right, I want you to know that." I told her I didn't think we had ever met.

"Sure," she said. "It was at the Timme Angstrom Regatta in Chicago in 1958. You and Ted came out representing Brown. I was that girl sailing for Northeastern." I remembered. "You remember what you told me?" I didn't. "You told me I was crazy to get serious about Ted Turner."

Judy and Ted met at that regatta, and they got serious. Judy is an ample blonde, about 5′ 5″, with straight hair that hangs well below her waist, and a pronounced overbite that makes her lips naturally pursed. Her attitude fluctuates between a cool wariness and a relaxed, newly achieved confidence that evidently has been hard-won. She is intense, thoughtful. "Looking back," she says, "I'm not sure any love was involved from either Ted or me. It was a business deal. We were both looking to get married for our own reasons."

The fact that Judy was a first-rate sailor was convenient. With Judy crewing, Ted won the Y-Flier nationals after his first year in the class. It was his first big win. And a man starting in business needs a wife as part of the second-line support effort.

"It was the taming of the shrew," Judy says of her care and training in housewifely duties at the hands of Ted Turner. "I was spoiled. I was born with a silver spoon in my mouth. That changed rather quickly.

"First of all, Ted ate three meals a day at home. He refused to eat canned food, and he wanted a full course lunch. I didn't know how to cook, which made things difficult. Many was the time I palmed off Stouffer's chicken tetrazzini as something I had whipped up.

"He also wouldn't eat anything that wasn't advertised on the billboards. I liked Kellogg's cereal, but Post was the client, and Post it was. Ted told me, '*I* bring home the money—*you* do what I say.' I even argued with Ed Turner about it, but he said Ted was right. I asked him if one damn box would make a difference. He said it just might. Ed wouldn't eat any mayonnaise except what his wife made, and nothing but fresh vegetables unless it was an emergency.

"I pressed Ted's undershorts and ironed his shirts on an old card table, and shined his shoes. Those were daily duties. Ted picked out the clothes I wore—nothing but straight, tight skirts, nothing full—and sent me to get my hair and nails done so I would look right.

"It's so horrible to live in the South as a young married woman. There were coffee klatches or afternoon bridge games. The more racy set got into boozing it up with black russians at the country club. I didn't, but I was beginning to think I could get into it."

Judy worked for Ted for a while and drew a measly check each week, which he would take. He decreed it was rightfully his. He gave her $500 a month to make mortgage payments and pay all house expenses including utilities, fuel oil, and maintenance. She was allowed to keep what was left for spending money.

"After a while I felt like my entire ego had been robbed. I was living with heavy criticism day after day. Ted is the kind of person who will identify some feature on your face and shoot an arrow right into it. Then when his father bought the business in Atlanta, I was delegated to run the house in Macon while Ted went and played in Atlanta."

The final straw was sailing. Judy was racing in a frostbite

series in Macon and leading the fleet on points. Ted was only racing occasionally. One Sunday Ted was racing against her. "He got to leeward of me," Judy recalls, "and suddenly luffed me hard, hitting me, and I was out of the race. It was legal, but real dirty. That was the end. I thought, if a guy is going to do that to his own wife . . . We were divorced. I took the child and went to Florida."

Ted didn't want Judy to leave. "I don't think he was emotionally upset," Judy says. "He was losing property. Ted needs to be married. He needs his dog, clean socks, Jimmy Brown, home cooking, a wife, kids. If not me or Jane, it would be Betty, Alice, or Mary."

Judy was in Florida less than three months when Ted called her and suggested she come back and live with him. It was a response that smacked of déjà vu. Ted didn't suggest marriage. Just cohabitation. "I said okay because I was pregnant," Judy says. "But our second try was short-lived."

When Ted went to work for his father full time, he already had ten summers' worth of experience. He knew the operation from the ground up. He knew the condition of every truck, every sign location, every old painter and maintenance man. And because he was his father's son, he worked hard and he had ideas.

Richard McGinnis remembers meeting the two of them at a convention of the Outdoor Association in Atlanta in 1959. McGinnis is in his mid-forties with a head of curly hair and a subdued, down-home, drawling delivery that would make most Dixie politicians envious. He is general sales manager of Turner Outdoor Advertising. "They weren't members," McGinnis says. "Ed didn't agree with some association policies. But they would come and mix with people. I met them, and talked with Ted. I remember I was sitting on the red steps leading down to the Dogwood Lounge of the Henry Grady Hotel, and the two of them came along. We probably exchanged some conversational banter, I don't really recall. But as they moved on, Ted turned to me and said, 'McGinnis, someday you're going to be working for me.'

"I said, 'What'd you say your name was?'

" 'Turner from Savannah.' "

McGinnis was working for General Outdoor at the time. "In September of 1962," McGinnis says, "the two of them walked in the back door of the office. Ed Turner was wearing a tan tweed suit, and he had on those highly shined, square-toed shoes he always wore. Ted hollered, 'Where's McGinnis?' Then he saw me and came over. 'We're here,' he said. 'We bought the place. You're working for me now.' I've been believing him ever since."

The first assignment Ed Turner gave McGinnis when he got to Atlanta was to find a new headquarters building. He wanted something on Peachtree Street with white columns. Then he wanted an apartment, the finest in Atlanta. He didn't care about the cost as long as it had a classy address, quarters for Jimmy, and a space for his Caddy. He wanted to know who his neighbors were, and he didn't want to endure the smell of chickens cooking in the hallways. He wanted to move up from a small pond to Atlanta, and he wanted to be accepted.

Ed Turner and Bob Naegele, a friend of his in the outdoor business in Minneapolis, had conceived a plan to buy General Outdoor through a third party. They would take the pieces they wanted, and spin off the remaining assets to other buyers. At the time, General Outdoor was the biggest in the country, but Naegele says it was an outmoded company with unaggressive management. The plan worked. Turner got Atlanta, which he had always wanted, and Richmond and Roanoke, Virginia. Naegele got Minneapolis and other cities.

Five months after the purchase had been made, Ed Turner called Naegele. "He called me from an institution in Connecticut where he had gone to stop smoking," Naegele says. "He was terribly upset. He had sold Savannah and borrowed against other properties to buy Atlanta. He said he didn't want to lose everything. I'll never forget what he said: 'It's a long way from the master bedroom to the cellar.' I told him not to worry. His cash flow was good, he was making his payments. Hell, Atlanta is the Chicago of the South in our business."

Turner asked Naegele to buy him out. Naegele says he protested. Turner insisted. So Naegele sent two of his executives to the plantation in South Carolina where Turner had gone after leaving Connecticut. When they delivered a down payment of $50,000, Turner was pacing around like an animal. He pressed Naegele to conclude the deal, which involved about a million dollars.

Meanwhile, Ed Turner was setting the rest of his life in order. He put the real estate portion of the Savannah company in his second wife's name. He also wrote her a long and detailed note. On March 5, 1963, only six months after he had purchased Atlanta, Ed Turner arose, shaved, got dressed, ate a hearty breakfast, went back upstairs, and killed himself with a pistol in the bedroom of his plantation. Jimmy Brown found the body.

Ed had called Florence Turner a few days before he took his life. He told her he had lost face in his business deal and that he was planning to kill himself. She was unable to talk him in off the ledge.

Judy Nye Hallisey says Ted carried his father's death well. "I think he felt challenged," Judy says. "Now he was in a position to carry on, to outdo his father."

For weeks, Ted had known his father was considering selling out, and he was furious. He had been thrilled by the purchase of Atlanta. He had been running things while his father was in

Connecticut, and doing well. What had quickly become an intolerable burden for his father was Ted's sustenance. He couldn't stand the thought of a sale, and began to bully his father into hanging on or selling the business to him. Ed Turner had been determined to raise a competitive son. Now he was suffering the full onslaught of his creation.

"Ed thought Ted was too young to run the business," Bob Naegele says. "And if his son wasn't able to pay him off, Ed visualized losing everything. Their arguments were fierce. Ted called his father cowardly. He thought his father was insulting his intelligence."

Ed Turner was not a man to go half way. When he pursued, he did so fiercely. When he liked, he liked really hard. When he joined the Navy, he was ready to give his life. When he made commitments, they were deep. He was a willful, dogmatic man, a man interested in control who seems to have left very little of his life—or his death—to chance.

He was also a man who confessed to a crisis of mission: nothing, he told Peter Dames, had been worthwhile. He was a success by most measures. But underneath brooded a man of mercurial temperament, struggling without gain to find purpose in his life. Suddenly he was staggered by his own surprising limitations in a business venture he thought would rejuvenate him. Then he became locked in combat with the beloved son he had so carefully programmed for greatness. Imagine his further surprise when he realized that this young, ruthless warrior was not allowing blood to stand between him and his goal. Imagine the cascade of emotions, from shock through comprehension to grim appreciation—perhaps even pride—as he felt the numbing force of a tribal hammer lock that was more than ceremonial. No doubt the potential of the child he had nurtured exceeded even the imagination of the creator. Perhaps in him he at last found something meaningful, something worthy of all he had to give.

174

Right after his father's death, Ted made two calls. The first was to Bob Naegele. The $50,000 down payment was all that had gone through. Ted told Naegele he didn't want to conclude the sale. Naegele said he was only doing what his father had asked him to do. Ted cited Naegele's friendship for his father, and threatened a legal battle on the grounds that his father's suicide indicated mental incompetence. Naegele withdrew, and Ted Turner had a business.

Amid a myriad of details—Ted had to sell the two plantations to help pay estate taxes, and complex financing had to be reaffirmed—Ted made another call, to Dr. Irving Victor. Victor's equity debt to Ed Turner on the house purchase had been reduced to $2000, and Victor was in the process of moving offices and reorganizing his practice. As a timely gift for Victor's new enterprise, Ed Turner had told Victor he would wipe the slate clean of the remaining $2000.

"Ted said he didn't doubt my word," Irving Victor recalls, "but he said it was still listed as an obligation on the books, and he expected it to be paid. I told him you're damn right I'll pay it. He is a hard-nosed businessman, all right. It always amazed me that in all the turmoil he had time to take care of that minuscule item."

Many people in Ted Turner's position would have concluded the sale of the business and indulged their pleasure—sailing, in Ted's case. Why didn't he do that? "Well, my father had worked all his life trying to make the big time," Ted explains. "That's what he wanted. He went as far as he could, and when he dropped the baton it was up to me to pick it up. Plus I'm a fighter. I was raised that way. I could never be a dilettante living off the fat of the land. My business is really important to me. I don't know where I'd be without it. Off the deep end, I suppose."

But it wasn't to be all business, as it had been. "I remember confronting my father about his doing nothing but working," Ted said. "One night I said to him, 'You're not leaving the business to me—you're leaving me to the business.' He was a wise bird, and he looked at me and said he had never thought of it that way. Things got better after that, but he still wanted to work all the time."

Ted decidedly did not want to work all the time. In fact, the very first summer that he was in charge, the summer right after his father's death, he won club championships in both the Y-Flier and Flying Dutchman fleets, the first time it had ever been done. The Atlanta Yacht Club, which conducts business on Lake Altoona, has since passed a rule making the feat impossible.

As a sailor Ted was quickly establishing a reputation as one who either won or went down trying. For a while, he spent as much time in the water as on it. The word prudence was not in his vocabulary. When other skippers yielded to squalls and doused their spinnakers, Ted would keep his sails full until he crossed the line, or dumped the boat.

Warner Guedry, a fellow who sailed with and against Turner in Dutchmen, recalls one race in heavy air when they went over. Ted stood on the centerboard to right the boat while Guedry straightened out the wet tangle of lines and sailcloth. Guedry heard a crack and saw Ted slip, then get back on the centerboard. They righted the boat and got going again. Ted was hiking out, pumping the main, gaining on boats that had passed them. Guedry looked back and noticed Ted's leg was drenched with blood. His knee had been sliced to the bone on the splintered edge of the centerboard. Guedry called his attention to it.

"Just a scratch," Ted said. Then he looked down and saw the

white showing through the blood. "I guess we better stop," Ted said. Either that or bleed to death, Guedry told him.

"If Ted couldn't beat you one way, he would beat you another," Guedry says. "Mostly it was by talking to you. He would either unnerve you by yelling something simple, like, 'You can't do that!' or just be sneaky and engage you in casual conversation. Next thing you knew, he would pass you."

Turner left the lakes of Georgia in search of heavier competition in accordance with his theory that exposure to defeat is character-building. He found plenty of it. Then, at the 1964 Olympic trials, Ted and a friend decided to charter a big boat. For Turner, that first experience in larger, offshore boats was like a potential addict's first skin pop. Sailing, particularly ocean sailing—like flying, skin diving, rock climbing, and other sports where the awesome natural phenomena encountered often have the lasting impact of a religious experience— is more obsession than hobby, recreation, or sport. And Turner was obsession-prone.

Some of his taste for sailing was acquired aboard his father's schooners, and he was encouraged by gifts of sailboats and the tutelage of Jimmy Brown and Savannah Yacht Club instructors. But there was deeper stuff. Sailors tend to be lonely people who prefer their lot to the disquieting rigors of life ashore. They are outcasts of a sort. The loneliness of his childhood—the progression of boarding schools, the enigmatic father, the rigid discipline, the dying sister—had also prepared Turner for the sea.

That, and his romantic nature, his love of battle, his preoccupation with self-image (lustiness—cutlass clenched in teeth), his continuous search for historic figures heroic enough to be part of his own roots. Like his father before him, Ted has committed several hundred feet of poetry and prose to his ample memory, and while a live microphone at a banquet or press conference will suffice, what better platform for recitation can there be than the teak grating behind the wheel of a sailing vessel at sea?

High on his list of favorite authors in Joseph Conrad, whose sailors toil against nature in a masculine world of initiation and transformation. Their tests are of physical and moral courage, honor, loyalty, and will power in the most wretched of human circumstances.

Ahh, Captain Hornblower. Where are you, Lord Nelson, Ahab, Bligh, Queeg, Nemo? Not a savory fellow among you. All were obsessed, logically enough, when one considers what it takes to forsake the comfort of dry land for the perilous challenge of the world's oceans. Who could possibly stand such loneliness or endure such hardship, or sleep in the endless discomfort of motion and damp but a man who felt himself an outcast upon the land? Who would have the gall to think he could harness the wind and waves to his purpose but a man in headlong pursuit of his very spirit?

Once, in a moment of depression, Turner said he didn't want to spend time ashore anymore. "I'm a man without a country," he intoned. "I want to switch ships on the way into port and live like the Arctic tern."

Oliver Wendell Holmes is another of Ted's favorites. He loves to recite "The Chambered Nautilus":

Build thee more stately mansions, O my soul,
As the swift seasons roll!
Leave thy low vaulted past!
Let each new temple, nobler than the last,
Shut thee from heaven with a dome more vast,
Till thou at last art free
Leaving thine outgrown shell by life's unresting sea!

"You just keep continually expanding until you get so big you pass on" is Turner's summation. Again it is the plateau theory, and Turner quickly put it into operation on the water. Each of his vessels was indeed nobler than the last. He went from Penguins to Y-Fliers to Flying Dutchmen to 40-footers to 70-footers in the space of time it might take an ordinary mortal to organize and understand properly one medium-sized boat. With paid crews struggling to sail often immense distances between races, and Turner jetting in at the eleventh hour, often leaping onto the boat just as she pulled away from the dock, he managed an unthinkable race schedule beginning in 1964 by simultaneously owning as many as three ocean racers and a variety of small craft.

Consider the following partial record.*

RACE	WHERE	BOAT	RESULT
1964			
Montego Bay	Florida–Jamaica	*Scylla**	retired
1965			
SORC	Florida	*Scylla**	
Nationals		Flying Dutchmen	3rd
Nationals		Y-Fliers	6th
North Americans		Flying Dutchmen	1st
1966			
SORC	Florida	*Vamp X*	1st overall
One-of-a-Kind	St. Petersburg	Flying Dutchmen	3rd
Bermuda	Newport–Bermuda	*Vamp X*	5th in class 9th overall
Transatlantic	Bermuda–Denmark	*Vamp X*	1st in class 4th overall

* Asterisks follow the names of boats that Turner chartered. The race results have not been included for those races in which Turner did not finish well.

RACE	WHERE	BOAT	RESULT
North Americans	San Diego	Flying Dutchmen	5th
5.5 Nationals	Stamford, Conn.		5th

1967

RACE	WHERE	BOAT	RESULT
SORC	Florida	*Vamoose*	7th overall
Montego Bay	Florida–Jamaica	*Vamoose*	1st overall
Edlu Trophy	Long Island	*Vamoose*	2nd overall
Annapolis–Newport	Maryland–R.I.	*Vamoose*	Did not finish
Transpacific	Cal.–Hawaii	*Vamoose*	4th in class 8th overall
U.S. Open	Buffalo	Flying Dutchmen	5th
5.5 Nationals	Milwaukee		3rd
5.5 Worlds	Bahamas		4th
Congressional Cup	California	Cal 40s	3rd

1968

RACE	WHERE	BOAT	RESULT
SORC	Florida	*Bolero*	25th overall
Olympic trials		5.5-meters	
Olympic trials		Flying Dutchmen	

1969

RACE	WHERE	BOAT	RESULT
SORC	Florida	*American Eagle*	broken mast
Congressional Cup	California	Cal 40s	8th
Montego Bay	Florida–Jamaica	*American Eagle*	6th in class 21st overall
Annapolis–Newport	Maryland–R.I.	*American Eagle*	1st in class 1st overall
Transatlantic	Newport–Ireland	*American Eagle*	3rd in class 3rd overall
Skaw Race	Norway	*American Eagle*	
Fastnet	Great Britain	*American Eagle*	3rd in class 4th overall
5.5 Nationals	Annapolis	*Tiger*	1st

RACE	WHERE	BOAT	RESULT

1970: Yachtsman of the Year

RACE	WHERE	BOAT	RESULT
SORC	Florida	*American Eagle*	1st overall
5.5 Worlds	Australia	*Tiger*	2nd
Gold Cup	Australia	*Nemesis*	1st
Bermuda	Newport–Bermuda	*American Eagle*	2nd in class 9th overall
Chicago–Mackinac	Lake Michigan	*American Eagle*	2nd in class 2nd overall
Vineyard	Stamford–M.V.	*American Eagle*	4th in class 4th overall
5.5 Nationals	Annapolis	*Tiger*	1st
Fall series	Annapolis	*American Eagle*	

1971

RACE	WHERE	BOAT	RESULT
SORC	Florida	*American Eagle*	4th overall
Montego Bay	Florida–Jamaica	*American Eagle*	
Annapolis–Newport	Maryland–R.I.	*American Eagle*	2nd
Stratford Shoal	Long Island	*American Eagle*	
Edlu Trophy	Long Island	*American Eagle*	
Block Island	Rhode Island	*American Eagle*	
Admiral's Cup	Great Britain		(alternate)
Fastnet	Great Britain	*American Eagle*	4th overall (course record)
Plymouth–La Rochelle	England–France	*American Eagle*	
5.5 Nationals	Stamford	*Skat VI*	3rd
5.5 Worlds	Seawanhaka	*Tiger*	1st
Gold Cup	Seawanhaka	*Tiger*	1st
Sandy Hook–Hampton	New York	*Running Tide**	
Fall series	Annapolis	*Running Tide**	2nd
Miami–Palm Beach	Florida	*Running Tide**	
Southern Cross Cup	Australia	*American Eagle*	
Sydney–Hobart	Australia	*American Eagle*	30th
Hobart–Auckland	Australia	*American Eagle*	2nd (clinched World Ocean Racing Cup)

RACE	WHERE	BOAT	RESULT

1972

RACE	WHERE	BOAT	RESULT
SORC	Florida	*Running Tide**	2nd in class 4th overall
Congressional Cup	California	Cal 40s	
5.5 Nationals	Annapolis	*Tiger*	1st
5.5 Worlds	Geneva	*Tiger*	2nd
Vineyard	Stamford–M.V.	*Elixir**	1st in class
One-Ton North Americans	Newport	*Elixir**	4th
Rio Circuit	Brazil	*Charisma**	
Sydney–Hobart	Australia	*American Eagle*	1st overall

1973: Yachtsman of the Year

RACE	WHERE	BOAT	RESULT
Clearwater–St. Petersburg		*Lightnin'*	2nd in class
SORC	Florida	*Lightnin'*	1st in class 2nd overall
Montego Bay	Florida–Jamaica	*Lightnin'*	1st overall
Southern One-Ton	Miami	*Lightnin'*	1st
Annapolis–Newport	Maryland–R.I.	*Lightnin'*	1st in class
Skaw Race	Norway	*Lightnin'*	1st overall
Admiral's Cup	Great Britain	*Lightnin'*	1st boat of 3rd-place U.S. team
One-Ton Worlds	Sardinia	*Lightnin'*	6th
Middle Sea Race	Malta	*Lightnin'*	1st in class 2nd overall
Miami–Palm Beach	Florida	*Robin**	2nd overall

1974

RACE	WHERE	BOAT	RESULT
One-Ton North Americans	Florida	*Robin**	1st
SORC	Florida	*Lightnin'*	2nd overall
Congressional Cup	California	Cal 40s	
America's Cup trials	Newport	*Mariner, Valiant*	
Cork Week	Canada	Flying Dutchmen	
Sandy Hook–Hampton	New York	*Recluta**	
Fall series	Annapolis	*Recluta**	

RACE	WHERE	BOAT	RESULT

1975

RACE	WHERE	BOAT	RESULT
SORC	Florida	*Tenacious*	1st in class
Montego Bay	Florida–Jamaica	*Tenacious*	
Edlu Trophy	Long Island	*Vamp*	1st in class 3rd overall
Block Island	Rhode Island	*Tenacious*	2nd overall
Annapolis–Newport	Maryland–R.I.	*Tenacious*	dismasted
Two-Ton Worlds	Michigan	*Notre Dame Du Lac**	3rd
Larchmont Race Week	New York	*Vamp*	2nd in class
Admiral's Cup team	Great Britain	*Tenacious*	U.S. team 3rd
Plymouth–La Rochelle	England–France	*Tenacious*	2nd overall
One-Ton North Americans	Newport	*Vamp*	3rd
One-Ton Worlds	Newport	*Vamp*	6th
Fall series	Annapolis	*Tenacious*	
Skippers' Race	Annapolis	*Tenacious*	1st overall
Miami–Palm Beach	Florida	*Tenacious*	
Southern Cross Cup team	Australia	*Pied Piper*	U.S. team 1st
Sydney–Hobart	Australia	*Pied Piper*	4th overall

1976

RACE	WHERE	BOAT	RESULT
SORC	Florida	*Tenacious*	4th in class
Congressional Cup	California	Cal 40s	4th
One-Ton North Americans	Annapolis	*Pied Piper*	3rd
Block Island	Rhode Island	*Tenacious*	
NYYC Regatta	Long Island	*Tenacious*	
Onion Patch team		*Tenacious*	U.S. 1st
Bermuda	Newport–Bermuda	*Tenacious*	
5.5 Worlds	Norway	*Sundance*	2nd
Pt. Huron–Mackinac	Lake Huron	*Tenacious*	
Chicago–Mackinac	Lake Michigan	*Tenacious*	
One-Ton Worlds	Marseille	*Pied Piper*	2nd
Fall series	Annapolis		

RACE	WHERE	BOAT	RESULT
1977: Yachtsman of the Year			
SORC ·	Florida	*Tenacious*	2nd in division
Congressional Cup	California	Cal 40s	1st
NYYC Regatta	Long Island	*Tenacious*	1st overall
Demi-Tasse Cup	Newport	Dyer Dhows	1st
America's Cup	Newport	*Courageous*	Winner
Vineyard	Stamford–M.V.	*Tenacious*	Disqualified
1978			
SORC	Florida	*Tenacious*	2nd in class
Congressional Cup	California	Cal 40s	5th
Edlu Trophy	Long Island	*Tenacious*	1st overall
Bermuda	Newport–Bermuda	*Tenacious*	2nd in class

Turner figures he has spent $100,000 a year on racing since 1964, probably a conservative estimate. And maybe as much as $20,000 a year on plane fares. Boat builder Bob Derecktor, who has gone some of the distance with Turner, sums it up this way: "Some people put in a lot of time, some people put in a lot of money, and some put in a lot of effort. But nobody puts in as much of all three as Turner. He has the drive. Not many want to win as badly as he does."

Consider a few footnotes to Turner's racing career:

1. The 1967 Montego Bay Race was sailed in a full gale. Turner kept the chute up all night, and everything somehow held together.

2. An icebreaker was hired to hammer a path out of Long Island Sound for *Bolero* before the 1968 SORC. The trip south in freezing weather nearly ended on the rocks off Cape Hatteras. The Coast Guard had to tow the boat off a lee shore.

3. By telephone, from Florida, Turner had *Eagle*'s spare mast (90 feet, 1000 pounds) brought from Massachusetts to

Bob Derecktor's yard in New York before the 1969 SORC. Derecktor prepared the mast in three days and had it trucked to Florida. In the same time, Ted Hood built Turner a new mainsail and genoa.

4. Turner chartered a plane to meet him at the end of the 1969 Skaw Race to take him from Norway to Sweden for the 5.5 World Championship. The Skaw Race was slow. The crew had to talk Turner out of launching a dinghy and rowing (with his 5.5 crew) 12 miles to shore so he could get to the other race on time.

5. Turner won the first race of the 1970 SORC on *Eagle,* flew 16 hours to Australia for one crucial race of the 5.5 Gold Cup (if he didn't win it he was out of the series), and made the flight back in time to sail the next SORC race in Florida. (Also in 1970, Turner purchased the two TV stations that were losing from $30,000 to $50,000 a month. It was a busy year.)

6. To ship *Eagle* to Australia in 1970, Turner and navigator Perry Bass spent $20,000.

7. During one hectic period in 1973, Turner commuted from Atlanta to races in Cowes, Oslo, Sardinia, and Malta.

As the *Atlanta Constitution* observed in a feature article on Jane Turner, "While [Ted's] been sailing around the world as a champion yachtsman, dishing out millions to buy struggling athletic teams, and running a television station and advertising company, he's had Jane, his wife, cleaning his modest but impressive Marietta home and diapering his five children."

In the waterfront home of friends she is visiting in Annapolis, Jane Turner is more relaxed than in Atlanta or Newport. We sit in the comfortable living room of the well-appointed yachtsman's home, sipping cold orange juice from goblets and enjoying the proximity of cruising boats parked in their berths only 20 feet beyond the plate glass window with its engraved border. Books in floor-to-ceiling cases warm the room. An array of silver trophies add a glow. Paintings and photographs of ships and sailing yachts provide the motif. The setting complements a woman of Jane Turner's traditional Southern heritage and formal bearing. In black sweater and pants with gold accessories, Jane Turner blends with the ambience like an artfully selected wine. "My children," Jane says without exaggeration, "have been my whole life."

Ted and Jane had been married six months when Ted's children came to live with them. Less than a year later, when Laura Lee and Teddy were seven and four, Rhett was born. When those three were eight, five, and one, she gave birth to Beauregard (named for the Southern general). When Beau was four months old, Jane discovered she was pregnant again. "I cried a lot when I found out," Jane says. "My friends thought it was vulgar. I love babies but I nearly died. I thought my back was broken. I stayed home for five years. It would have made anyone crazy.

"Ted copped out," Jane says. "He was gone all the time racing. But I never thought of leaving. Ted had been divorced once. It was important for him that our marriage work out. But it did look like he was trying to kill me with all the babies. And Jimmy Brown was always with him. I was alone. The children were always born in January, February, and March, when Ted was sailing. When Jennie was born Ted finally came home because I cried so much."

Ted Turner married Jane Smith of Birmingham, Alabama, on June 2, 1964, a date which happened to be Ted and Judy Nye Hallisey's wedding anniversary. But that didn't seem to matter. If Ted was about to launch himself into the most ambitious ocean racing schedule ever attempted, he had to have someone at home to raise the children and run the house.

Ted and Jane were introduced at a gathering of young Republicans in Atlanta by Peter Dames. Jane, who graduated from the University of Alabama (1958) in home economics, was a stewardess for Delta Airlines at the time. "I liked him a whole lot," Jane says, "and my daddy, who had never liked any of my beaus, thought he was wonderful, and that was good enough for me."

As one might expect from an enduring wife of Ted Turner, Jane is a quiet person whose life as a homebody seems to agree with her. Jane has naturally pursed lips, a useful confirmation for Turner wives. She, too, is a blonde, although Jane's hair is professionally lightened and styled with considerable care. It is swept up and back from her forehead, Atlanta-style, heavily back-combed on top for height, and sprayed into place. And in her eyes there is the same wariness that again one suspects is an occupational hazard.

Jane's reserve can be read in her erect, careful posture. She walks as though she were balancing books on her head, and even overstuffed chairs can't induce her to slouch. Jane's spareness of movement is partly breeding, partly anxiety, and partly to keep her hair in place. There is a feeling of hesitancy about her. In conversation she must be drawn out; she is not quick to laugh. Jane Smith was raised in the tradition of Southern womanhood in its most inhibiting, ante-bellum manifestations, and marriage to Ted Turner has done nothing to divert her from those magnolia-scented paths.

As Jane talks about her life with Ted she uses words such as "responsibility," "sacrifice," and "necessary adjustment," or she speaks of her preference for anonymity and her complete and willing deference to Ted's business career and needs. Only rarely does the word "frustration" creep in. Society-page writers chronicle her life of car pools, cooking, household chores, and bedtime stories, then quickly point to her handsome, man-about-town husband, who is seen at countless social functions in the company of attractive female companions. "He always comes back to me," Jane has been quoted as saying about her errant husband. "I trust him. I'm confident he is faithful to me."

Listening to Jane Turner I am astounded by the degree of bygone tradition she possesses. At a time in history when women as a group have emerged so noticeably as a liberated entity, Jane Turner's self-image sounds positively anachronistic. I am reminded of a passage in *Gone With The Wind*, a Turner family favorite I prudently re-read some months before. I ask Jane how long it had been since she read it. Years, she replies. I quickly scan the bookshelves of the Annapolis house, and there it sits with the predictable prominence of the Bible. I read the passage to Jane wherein Scarlett O'Hara ponders the wisdom of Mammy, who has been maligning Yankee women for speaking their minds.

The mothers of all her girl friends impressed on their daughters the necessity of being helpless, clinging, doe-eyed creatures. Really, it took a lot of sense to cultivate and hold such a pose. Perhaps she had been too brash. Occasionally she had argued with Ashley and frankly aired her opinions. Perhaps this and her healthy enjoyment of walking and riding had turned him from her to frail Melanie.

There was no one to tell Scarlett that her own personality, frighteningly vital though it was, was more attractive than any masquerade she might adopt. Had she been told, she would have been pleased, but unbelieving. And the civilization of which she was a part would have been unbelieving too, for at no time, before or since, had so low a premium been placed on feminine naturalness.

Jane's face lights up. "Right!" she says, her eyes sparking. "My mother was raised in that tradition. I watched her live that way. I am on the edge of it myself."

Jane Turner decided some time ago that she was going to remain Ted Turner's wife. Perhaps she weighed the trade-off and found it acceptable in her terms. Perhaps the amount of love exchanged—and love is definitely exchanged in this relationship—was sufficient, and the amount of abuse, which ranges from verbal to physical, was not considered excessive. What one will endure depends on what one is used to, first of all. And like a snowflake, the system of exchange in any relationship is always unique.

How Jane arrived at her decision is less important than that it was made. It certainly bespoke courage on Jane's part. And she probably could not have succeeded without a heritage of old-fashioned Southern womanhood, which happens to include a lion's share of strength. For in the midst of their calculated frailty, their fainting spells and doe-eyed helplessness, their self-imposed submergence of personality and identity, Southern women managed enormous plantations, quietly had their babies in candle-lit back bedrooms, nursed the sick, sewed and cooked, bandaged the wounded, and saw to it that their blustering, drunken husbands were gently tucked in their beds.

Liberation may be de rigueur, but who is to say the women of the Old South didn't prolong an ancient tradition of the strong, subservient female that was well suited to survival in that era? When it comes to the marital relationship, Ted Turner is the anachronism; Jane is responding to him with reflex, in kind.

Perhaps, as Judy Nye Hallisey suggests, Ted would be married to someone. But he would have to scrounge to find a wife as suited and devoted to her herculean task as Jane. Of all the people in Ted Turner's embroiled world—executives, managers, children, financial experts, players, coaches, sailing crews—the role of wife is by far the most demanding.

Enduring relationships are based on need, and the Turners' is no exception. Jane leaped to Ted's defense when she was cornered the day after the party at Bailey's Beach by her hostess of the infamous evening. "I have a terrific influence on Ted," Jane says. "It may not seem so because I stay in the background. I don't like to put myself on display. But it would hurt Ted if I was down. I'm a stabilizing influence. He needs me to be in a good mood. If I'm down, he's down."

Ted can't stand many moments of life without companionship. A governess would never suffice. For all his strut, swagger, and cheek, his out-front dalliances and runaway egotism, Turner's little-boy side cries out for affection and nurturing—and support.

As Ted has become more and more a public figure, Jane has become increasingly concerned over her family's exposure. She says it is a sacrifice for her to be put in the public eye. "He feeds on it, but I don't," she says. "One of the Australian sailors came down to Atlanta and went to a ball game with Ted. He said it was like being with Caesar in the Coliseum." And when multi-million-dollar figures are announced in connection with Ted's corporate acquisitions, Jane becomes frantic over the safety of the children. The windows in the Turners' previous home in Atlanta were nailed shut. In the Marietta house, the system of locks and closures is enough to discourage the most determined housebreaker.

But the press hasn't exactly beaten a path to her door, a situation that elicits contradictory feelings from her. Not once during the summer did a candid photograph of Ted and her appear in the newspapers. Jane should know. She compiled complete scrapbooks.

"As a rule, I am pushed back by the press," Jane says. "Of all the pictures that were taken at the Atlanta airport when we arrived home after Ted won the Cup, they used a picture of Ted with some strange girl. Mayor Maynard Jackson pulled me up on the rostrum with him. That was nice.

"In Newport the same thing happened. The press didn't want me in the scene. I suppose it's not too flattering—too colorful—to be pictured with your wife. It spoils the image the press wants, I guess. But LaBelle Lance was with Bert." When she is denied her recognition as Mrs. R. E. Turner she becomes angry.

It might spoil the image Ted wants, too. Many a time after a race in Newport Ted let Jane stand awkwardly alone amid the crowd of press and well-wishers on the dock while he strutted and exchanged banter with strangers.

Jane understands that Ted couldn't tolerate a wife who competed with him, and says as much. At parties she often leaves Ted at the door and heads for a neutral corner to avoid the embarrassing, introductory afterthought, "Oh yes, and this is Jane. . . ." She balances his frequent long absences with the spin-off of fascinating people he attracts to their life. She shrugs off the women who pursue him as casual inevitabilities that don't invade their reality. "Ted is crazy about me," she avows. "Plus he's the father of my children.

"I've learned so much in the last ten years," Jane says. "I've found out I'm a fighter. I'm going to win. I may look passive, but I don't just sit back." With the children growing older and becoming less dependent, Jane has in fact begun to crack the homebody mold. She has been modeling occasionally for an Atlanta boutique, and she talks with enthusiasm about the group therapy course she is taking to strengthen her self-image.

One evening when Ted and I arrived at his home in Marietta, he pulled open the refrigerator, stared into it a while, then gave Jane a lecture about its lack of food. The next morning our departure was delayed a few minutes by a pair of socks tumbling in the clothes drier. When Ted began a short lecture on sock management, tossing in the food shortage for general emphasis, Jane blew up, saying she didn't tell him how to run the office. "Maybe I should. I certainly would never have traded Sosa and Lacey for Mike Marshall."

Turner winced. "I didn't make the trade," he mumbled. "I was sailing 5.5s in Norway."

But such occurrences are rare. Jane knows as well as anyone that those who would attack Ted Turner had best carefully pick their moment, and then be wearing their fastest guns. Because even a small stakes game of backgammon or a casual argument

191

can quickly become a competitive battle, and with Ted Turner the competition is always without barred holds. Most people just aren't ready for that.

"He's put me in a role," Jane says. "I have to accept it to be with him. Silence is my best weapon. If I say something he'll just turn it around—he's a great debater. So I'm often silent. It's difficult, but I'd say I'm happy. I just sit back. I enjoy the show."

Defending

AT LEAST FIFTY PEOPLE had been invited aboard Baron Marcel Bich's 139-foot, steel, three-masted gaff-topsail schooner *Shenandoah* to watch Ted Turner and crew on *Courageous* mount the twenty-third defense of the America's Cup in 126 years. The challenger was *Australia,* a sleek vessel owned by a syndicate headed by Alan Bond, representing the Sun City Yacht Club of Western Australia. Her skipper was Noel Robins.

Australia won the right to challenge by beating *Gretel II* (of the Royal Sydney Yacht Squadron, Australia) and *Sverige* (Royal Gothenburg Yacht Club, Sweden), which had previously beaten Bich's *France* (Yacht Club d'Hyères).

On *Shenandoah,* the able-bodied and willing among us were assigned to deck gangs at each mast. We had barely cleared the dock before Bich's requests were coming to us in French over strategically placed loudspeakers. We removed the stops from the huge, gaff-rigged sails of heavy Dacron. The boss of each crew threw three turns of thick halyard around an electric winch drum, and as one the big sails rose like the side windows on a Lincoln Continental. We flaked an endless amount of halyard on the deck in ovals with a six-foot span. Then the crews sprung to the sheets to trim the sails, four or five of us hauling rhythmically with teeth gritted, muscles straining, and hands tingling from friction as we coaxed the huge sail in, inch by grudging inch. No sooner had we made fast than the white-haired, barrel-chested Bich, resplendent in gray slacks, blue blazer, open-necked white shirt, and dashing cap, issued his next order from the polished brass of his windowed wheel house on the afterdeck.

At each station, a topsail was broken out, a small, pesky, but effective sail that hoists to the topmast and sheets to the ends of the gaff, filling the triangular space formed by those two spars. The topsails were hauled and sheeted by hand with a great deal of grunting and laughing among the Frenchmen, who told us the skipper often put up a bottle of wine for the first sail set properly. The crews joined forces to secure the downhauls, such was the strain.

When at last we had a chance to look up and flex our hands to work out the kinks from this unaccustomed effort, we were making nine knots toward the starting line in the 15-knot sou'westerly breeze. If we were already feeling cheered and wonderfully exhilarated by a rare chance to work before the mast on such a noble vessel, the sight on all sides heightened the excitement.

The passage by water from Newport to the sea must rank among the world's most beautiful harbor entrances. It is two and a half miles long, and wide enough for six or eight destroyers to steam comfortably side by side. To the west is the rocky shoreline of Jamestown (Conanicut Island), which rises to steep, impressive cliffs frosted with green fields. To the east are the stately mansions of what at one time was Newport's "400." Many of them have been reduced to restaurants, schools, or historic sites. Even the old Auchincloss farm where Jackie Onassis romped as a girl has recently been divided. But to the transient seaman their grandeur remains. Their green lawns and fields still slope to the water's edge. Cattle still graze, horses still roam.

This body of moderately trafficked water now supported an enormous fleet of infinite variety. As many as 200 boats were bouncing and churning their way out the passage, creating a choppy disturbance that came from all directions at once. The vessels ranged from often frighteningly unseaworthy outboard skiffs to the multimillion-dollar floating palaces of syndicate members. This motley fleet of spectator craft rose and fell in the confused chop with all the randomness of bumper-to-bumper turnpike traffic that has suddenly encountered a few miles of badly potholed dirt road. It was a bigger crowd than the arrival of the tall ships had attracted, and boats were still coming out of Newport and other harbors further up Narragansett Bay to join the parade.

Once outside, past the Brenton Reef light tower, the fleet was divided efficiently in two by little Coast Guard crash boats with blue lights flashing on their cabin tops that stormed around like border collies at work on a herd of sheep. The division was "them" and "us." "Us" had been granted special numbered flags; "them" had not. It was succinct of the New York Yacht Club to designate the flags with the single word "privilege."

There were twenty-five of "us" who were swept by the collies to the left, toward the starting line. The others numbered at least five or six hundred—it was impossible to make an accurate count. But when "them" were in position roughly two miles downwind of the starting line behind a cordon of Coast Guard and Navy escort vessels that included some of the largest Coast Guard cutters afloat, this huge and unfortunate spectator fleet spreading out along the horizon looked like the rooftops of a small city under a yellow-gray pollution cloud of its own making. From its distant, low-to-the-water vantage point, even through the strongest of field glasses, the 12-meters would look like ants on a tablecloth.

Overhead, 19 light planes and helicopters flew in a tight circle centered on the starting line, where the two twelves had now raised mainsails and were cruising back and forth in casual disdain of each other like a couple of toughs from different neighborhoods before a fist fight. And the Goodyear blimp, on leave from the National Football League, motored majestically like an airborne whale in slow motion, putting the ultimate media seal of approval on the proceedings.

At water level, the press was observing from a sixty-foot, chunky-looking party fishing boat built on twin catamaran hulls. Painted red and called *Hellcat,* she was hated passionately by her passengers. The frequent reports on her performance were ominous, and a source of constant amusement to those who didn't have to ride on her. She leaked everywhere, including at the wheel-house windows, which passed spray as though they were wire screen. It was said that *Hellcat* could make a two-foot seaway feel like a four-foot chop. The jolt of seas hitting the flat platform between the hulls was enough to loosen teeth.

We doused *Shenandoah*'s sails and were invited below to sample the delicious buffet lunch that had been set out in the elegant main salon of the vessel. The walls were white, paneled, and decorated with moldings like a proper turn-of-the-century town house. The plush wall-to-wall carpet ("bulkhead-to-bulkhead" would seem an inappropriate term for such a room) was on the dark side of royal blue. Sideboard, tables, and chairs were nautical antiques in cherry, walnut, and maple. Some of the chairs were cushioned in a soft fabric the color of the carpet. Dividing the forward wall of the salon was a decorative section of mast measuring two feet across, passing through the salon. It was handsomely staved with varnished oak for effect. The real masts were farther forward and aft.

We selected from three rich pâtés, six large cheeses, three varieties of freshly sliced cold meat, two hot dishes, two huge bowls of tossed salad, and a wealth of garnishes. The wines were red and white varietals. The timing was perfect. No sooner had we finished lunch than the thud of a cannon fired on the committee boat let us know that in ten minutes the first race of the 1977 America's Cup would begin.

If recent history was any indicator, the next thirty minutes would provide the only anxious period in the America's Cup series. At this point the two contenders have never sailed so much as a foot against one another. Despite what the Cup sages say, regardless of the most learned predictions, no one *really* knows how they will do. Good coaches can predict the score of a track meet to within a few points. Other contests are not that difficult to prejudge, given an insider's position, and allowing for good and bad days and injuries. But the only way to tell a fast 12-meter from a faster 12-meter is to put the two head to head on the same ocean on the same day.

Strange as it may seem, given America's total dominance in this contest, once more the tension mounted. Finally, after nearly two years of preparation and three months of serious competitive sailing, the moment of reckoning was at hand.

Ted Turner was as meek as a kitten on the starting line. With six minutes left, Robins on *Australia* tried to engage Turner in one of those tail-chasing, circling maneuvers typical of match-racing starts. The idea is to get behind your opponent, dog his every move, keep him where you want him, and grab a favored position on the line at the last second. Turner would have none of it. He brought *Courageous*'s bow around into the wind and sat luffing.

At four minutes, Turner put a loose cover on Robins, duplicating his moves. Then as time ran out, Turner tacked for the line, letting Robins go nearly to the weather end before he, too, had to tack. It was a dull start. The boats crossed within a few seconds of one another. *Courageous* was perhaps three or four seconds ahead, with *Australia* holding an advantageous position three boat-lengths to windward.

We waited, and we watched, trying to assess from our good vantage point in *Shenandoah*'s comfortable rigging which boat was closer to the wind and faster. Without a perfect position astern, it is impossible to read the angles. Ten minutes passed. It looked like *Courageous* was pulling out, and pointing higher. Eighteen minutes passed. Activity on *Courageous*'s deck. A new jib was being readied. *Courageous* tacked at 18:30, changing jibs with such finesse that the slow-eyed never saw it. As the boats converged, *Australia* showed activity. We looked at the mast heights, the only sure indicator of relative positions. *Courageous*'s mast appeared shorter. She would cross *Australia*. *Australia*'s tack confirmed it. *Australia* slowed in her tack, and *Courageous*'s momentum carried her directly to weather of the challenger, by two boat-lengths.

The first mark ended the suspense. *Courageous* led by more than a minute. On *Shenandoah,* Bruno Bich, son of Baron, passed out cigars and Bic lighters bearing the French colors and letters A.F.C.A.: Association Française de la Cup Americas. A few took cigars. Everyone took a lighter. The 50 guests reacted like children. For a few minutes, fifty people on this magnificent sailing yacht in the middle of the America's Cup race course—with its teak bathrooms containing bidets, and toilets that flushed like those in New York City apartments—stood around looking at each other with silly grins, flicking their Bics.

When *Courageous,* under tow after the race, passed Fort Adams and turned into the harbor at Newport, Turner called Mickey Spillane on the radio. "Take me in," he told Mickey, "along the waterfront."

Led by two of the Coast Guard collies, *Rage,* with *Courageous* lashed alongside, passed close by the docks of Newport so Ted Turner could acknowledge the plaudits of those who had gathered by the hundreds to cheer him. He flashed big smiles and gave them great doffs of his cap. At Bannister's Wharf, where the biggest crowd had gathered, he cocked his head to one side, shrugged his shoulders and extended his arms with the elbows bent and the palms of his hands toward the heavens. It was his very best humble-kid-from-Georgia signifier, and he cut it as if he had been practicing all week in front of a mirror.

Ted Hood and Lee Loomis leaped on board with congratulations. Beer was opened. Gary Jobson was trying not to look too pleased. "They aren't slow," he said. "They aren't fast either."

The scene outside Bannister's Wharf was reminiscent of that outside a stage door after a rock concert. The crowd was less violent and pushy, but it had the same intense fervor. No one grabbed for Turner's hat, or gave him the full, matinee-idol rush, but several people were observed grinning with some embarrassment after reaching to touch him unobtrusively.

As the white-trellised gates to the wharf opened and TV lights blazed, murmurs passed through the crowd: "There he is. . . . Here he comes." Then a little aisle opened just big enough for Turner to pass through. Race by race the crowd was to increase until it filled the wide, hundred-yard lane lined with shops and restaurants that leads to Thames Street.

Post-race press conferences were held at the America's Cup Press Center, situated in the suffocating confines of the National Guard Armory, a ten-minute walk down Thames Street from Bannister's Wharf. It was a well-conceived set-up, with banks of proper lights, a platform for four TV cameras, and 50 folding chairs beneath a raised dais on which long tables and microphones had been placed. There was even a keg of beer flowing in one corner of the large room.

Bill Ficker had been selected to moderate the press conferences. Ficker, a former America's Cup winner who is readily identifiable by his shaved and glistening pate, and known for his measured, immaculately disciplined behavior, was a good choice for the job. But the legendary cool of this West Coast architect would be tested.

At the first press conference, Ficker gave the floor to the Australians, Robins and Bond, who were encouraged by the scantiness of the winning margin (under two minutes) and said that but for an unwise selection of jibs, they might have done better.

Turner was subdued on the platform, almost sober. Loomis, beside him, looked ill at ease, and tough as usual. Bill Kutik remarked in his *Newport Daily News* column the next day, "Am I the only one who thinks Loomis looks just like those bullet-headed characters in Herblock cartoons representing the military-industrial complex?" When after a time no questions had been directed at Loomis, Ficker diplomatically asked him for a statement. Loomis said he was proud of Turner. He said winning was a matter of "tuning your weapon," and complimented *Courageous*'s crew on having done that.

Turner also made a statement. He thanked people in general: "The crew is superb, I'm so proud, I, I, I, there's too much emphasis on the skippers, we have 11 people out there plus Lee Loomis, Ted Hood, Robbie Doyle, who built the sails. . . . Last time in *Mariner* we lost by ten minutes. This summer has been great. We always were close enough to hear the gun, even when we lost."

In answer to a question about the jibs he used, Turner said he used the five-ounce, the seven-ounce, and the nine-ounce. When asked to elucidate, he said, "Well, we used the five-ounce when it was light, the seven when the wind got a little heavier, and the nine when it blew hardest. Now even the guys from Cleveland, Ohio, should understand that."

The press loved it. It was the first Cup in recent history that had produced a newsworthy skipper. It quickly became evident that each day's sailing was to be a long and dreary prelude to a zippy press conference. From his position at the table, Turner looked out over a bedraggled corps of reporters, weary from their trying day aboard that tortuous craft so aptly named *Hellcat,* and soothed them with his tongue. Their smiles of gratitude beamed back at him. It was like shooting fish in a barrel.

After the second day's victory, Turner settled in behind his mike, tapped it to see if it was live, and before Ficker called the proceedings to order, Turner warmed 'em up: "Hey, excuse me, but does anyone have a hunk of chewin' tobacco or a cigar? I'm havin' a nicotine fit up here." Reporters nearly broke their arms digging for smokes, a half-dozen of which flew through the air and landed on the table.

When it was his turn to speak, Turner got into one of his bored, drawling rambles: "I just thank God that the wind blew, that it was a nice day. . . ." When asked if he was prepared to race the following day, Turner said, "As much as we'd like to watch the Brown-Yale game on television, I imagine lots of people would be upset if we called a lay day for that reason."

After his third victory a reporter trying desperately to find out something significant about the mysterious doings on the water asked Turner what the result would be if the two skippers and crews simply switched boats. Turner said that was a stupid question. "We're used to our boat, our sails, our rig. Noel is used to his. It's like asking Noel Robins or me what would happen if we switched wives. Noel is used to his wife, and he likes her better than mine. And I like mine better than his." While the press was chuckling over this, Turner added quietly to no one in particular—not quite out of microphone range—"She ain't much, but she's all I got." He smiled broadly into the whirring cameras as he joined the general laughter coming from the floor.

The last race was a repeat of the first. Knowing he had boat speed, Turner played the conservative, letting Robins start ahead and to weather to avoid a foul. As the wind increased, both boats changed jibs in the first ten minutes of the race. Then Turner tacked to the left. Robins delayed, preferring the side of the course he was sailing. When the two boats crossed, *Courageous* had it, and while twenty-two more miles had to be sailed to make it official, that was that.

At the finish, Turner leaped out of the cockpit and jumped for joy as the biggest spectator fleet of all leaned hard on every horn available.

Courageous immediately got her sails down and was taken under tow. She quickly became the object of every boat in the fleet that could make her towing speed of nine knots. From every direction they came, all with the singular intention of slipping in as close as possible to the seductive folds of her wake. A thousand whirling bronze screws thrashed the sea into steep, intermingling lines of wash powerful enough to beam-end casually even a vessel of moderate size that became careless. Boats of all sizes and shapes—ferries swarming with people, Coast Guard cutters, fast runabouts, sailing auxiliaries, palatial yachts—grappled for position alongside and behind *Courageous* like a pack of race cars dueling for the lead.

The Coast Guard prudently decided that their intervention would cause havoc, if not disaster. They sped alongside the 12-meter, sirens blaring, blue lights flashing, hoping for the best.

To be amid the scene was to be stunned. It was an armada gone mad, water-borne jubilation approaching hysteria. If *Courageous* had made straight for Brenton Reef, the ecstatic fleet might have followed like lemmings. Perhaps 400 vessels cavorted at speed, rolling and surging and crashing along, bows slapping spray 40 feet in either direction, the throb of powerful engines a discordant earth rumble, the cheers and blowing of horns continuous.

Overhead, small planes seemed to relive wartime dogfights

as they vied for camera angles. The blimp descended like a dark cloud, her dangling mooring lines curving sensuously toward *Courageous*'s swaying mast tip. Coast Guard fire boats pumped towering plumes of water, filling the air with mist. Rising and falling on the swells as she plunged through the disturbed water as fast as she could go, *Courageous* was a wanton, naked beauty in a lascivious dance before a whole flotilla of lust-crazed Turks.

Turner's arms were thrown skyward, his fists clenched. His cigar was clamped in his teeth like a bullet. His cap was rakishly angled. So postured, he turned this way and that, seeming to conduct the frenzy. He would embrace crew members, then take a slug from the case of beer that had been put aboard by the tender, then posture again, the winner and folk hero in his element. When boats in the fleet with attractive women aboard got close enough, Turner would grab his shirt at the hem and pull it up, exposing his bare chest, and yell at them. It was one of the *Courageous* crew's patented gestures of the summer: "Show me your tits!" A few did.

At Fort Adams *Rage* slowed to take *Courageous* alongside, and to wait for *Australia* before parading into the harbor. The spectator fleet had gone ahead, with as many vessels as physically possible clustering off Bannister's Wharf at the northeast end of the harbor. Barely three feet separated one vessel from another. Twenty-footers were sandwiched between sixty- and eighty-footers. The high bows of motor yachts loomed over the low sterns of ocean racers. Passengers held fenders on all four sides of every boat, and only the most adroit backing and filling by skippers kept the situation miraculously collision-free.

Every dock and pier along the waterfront was jammed with people. Every rooftop had been turned into bleachers. Everything that could float had been cast into the harbor and was manned.

As *Courageous* and *Australia* approached along the waterfront led by the two fire boats, the place exploded like a Rose Bowl crowd exulting over a winning score in the last seconds of a game. But the spectacle in this unlikely waterfront stadium was even more striking. Cannon were fired. Horns blew in a cacophony of screeching. Fishermen at the docks paused in their labors to drink a beer and watch. Cameras went off like machine guns. Spray filled the air. Laughing and crying, people embraced. Off to the south, a colorful hot-air balloon rose and drifted past on the breeze. Not since the political marches and rallies of the sixties had I seen such a spontaneous public display of energy.

Courageous docked. Already well fortified with beer during the hour-long tow in, the crew popped champagne and began more celebration. The ceremonial dunking of the crew began, along with the ceremonial struggles between crew members that somehow reaffirm individual honor, self-respect, and competitiveness. The groupies of the summer and wives and girlfriends showed up in time to join husbands and lovers in baptismal rites in the foul waters at dockside. All but Jane Turner. Ted was self-consciously hollering for her as two girls looking like finalists in a wet T-shirt contest clung to his side. Jane was at the head of the dock telling an older woman she didn't like the water and that it would ruin her hair-do. With those other girls down there making over the crew, the older woman later remarked, it might have made more sense if Jane had gone in for the wet look.

Lee Loomis, bearing champagne, was one of the first to board *Courageous* as she docked, and the last to end up in the water. Loomis's popularity with the *Courageous* crew had been dwindling all summer. He and their skipper were at odds, after all. And a number of events toward the end, like the evening he was observed gleefully pinning a "Beat the Mouth" button to a "Go Courageous" poster hanging in the dining room at Conley Hall, did nothing to improve his stock. The crew had discussed what they should do with Loomis after it was all over. Of the reasonable alternatives suggested—putting a pie contract out on him, drowning him, or ignoring him—they settled on the most passive. So Loomis wasn't thrown in. Several people, and Dick Enersen's movie camera (ah, sweet revenge), saw him jump.

The crowd outside the gates of Bannister's Wharf waiting for Turner to appear had reached maximum proportion for the space available. A wall of people stretched from the gates to Thames Street in the gathering dusk. But they would have to wait. Turner, already three beers over the line in spite of his refreshing swim, had adjourned to quarters over the wharf offices to change out of his wet clothes. The wet T-shirt winners were still with him. Clutching a bottle of Aquavit that the Swedish crew had thoughtfully provided, our hero was standing before a full-length mirror in his wet clothes, admiring the wet, puckered female bodies still in close flanking positions, but mostly admiring himself. "You," he said, lifting the Aquavit bottle in tribute to his mirrored image and speaking in his most heartfelt, cheerful tones, "are the fucking greatest!"

He then regarded the girls. "To the victor," he announced, "go the spoils," and he made a token effort to remove their clothes.

The throng that accompanied Turner and Jobson to the armory for the final press conference stopped traffic on Thames Street. With Jane finally beside him, Turner staggered this last mile with a little help from his friends, the Newport police, his wife, and the bottle of Aquavit. Several times he hollered for Gary to stay close. Gary shrugged and borrowed the Aquavit. "Look at this," he said, marveling at the crowd jamming the street. "What the hell, Ted Turner for President."

Unofficially, the final press conference began on the men's room floor of the Rhode Island National Guard Armory in Newport, where our hero stopped to rest. He was brought around by his tactician and sidekick, Gary Jobson, and pointed toward his place at the table. Jobson, not Loomis, sat beside him. But Turner was still standing. The applause when he entered was thunderous, and he stood basking in it like a shark on the mirror surface of a sun-baked sea. His cap was pulled down over one eye. Under it his hair was in disarray. His cigar was at ease at arm's-length by his side. As the applause roared around his head, Turner stood motionless, having fixed the cheering throng with a look of arrogance and self-satisfaction so consummate, so sublime, so frightening that it made the famous and heretofore archetypal image in that category—the profile photograph of Franklin Delano Roosevelt with the sharply angled cigarette holder clenched in his bared teeth—look like a study in humility. Then he and Jobson were lost in a cloud of blue smoke as they lit cigars, while the Australians, stage right, scored heavily with a rousing chorus of "Dixie."

Turner set his bottle of Aquavit on the table with a heavy thud, and started in on that irresistible microphone when he was half in his seat. Ficker shut him off. "It's your boat but it's my press conference," said the stern alumnus of the exclusive club Turner had just joined. As Ficker called things to order and gave the floor to Alan Bond, Turner leaned back in his chair, tilted his head, and studied this new threat to his existence through narrowed eyes. As Bond began to speak, Turner reached for his bottle. It wasn't there. Slowly, he slid off his chair and disappeared under the table. Bond paused. The press waited. Up he came, like a diver from the deep, the smiling face first, indicating success, then the two fists, each clutching a bottle of Aquavit, which he clumped on the table with obvious satisfaction. Ficker, under the glare of the TV lights, forced a smile. Bond chuckled, shook his head. The press had quiet hysterics.

The scene recalled the late James Thurber's short story ("The Greatest Man in the World") about a tobacco-chewing garage mechanic from Iowa who flew around the world non-stop, then eschewed the ethics of heroism and insulted even the President. Thurber had high government officials solve the problem by shoving the badly behaved aviator out a ninth-story window. In the armory, certain New York Yacht Club members had to be entertaining similar notions.

Bond continued as Turner lifted a bottle and took a hit W.C. Fields would have been proud of. Then he reached behind Ficker with a long arm, and massaged the back of Bond's neck as he finished. As Ficker thanked Bond, Turner regarded Ficker with the delight of an infant discovering a new toy in his playpen. He reached up and gave Ficker's shining head an affectionate and lingering rub. Ficker looked like he had been shot. He tried his best to retract his head into his chest cavity, like a turtle. But to his everlasting credit he grinned his way out of it, and hastily handed Turner the floor.

Turner's eyes were slits. He had about two minutes of consciousness left. "I never loved sailing against good friends any more than the Aussies," he said, struggling over the words. "I love 'em. They are the best of the best. The best . . . of the best. That's important. . . ." He paused. His head swayed on its mounts. Gary nudged him. Turner looked down at the note Gary had written.

"And I want to thank George Hinman and the New York Yacht Club for the opportunity. We worked hard, we busted our behinds. . . . I love everybody in the room. I like Ficker, too. . . ." Gary nudged him again.

"And I want to thank Bob McCullough, Commodore McCullough, and the crew of *Courageous,* my crew—"

The crew of *Courageous* poured onto the stage with a cheer, grabbed their skipper, and carried him off like a rag doll. The timing was perfect.

"We, too," Ficker said with relief, "would like to thank the crew of *Courageous.*"

Having been with him almost every day, all day, for more than four months, having been combatant, father confessor, reader of press clippings and articles, conscience, whipping boy, fellow political conspirator and street fighter, croquet opponent, tactical advisor, and guiding light, Gary Jobson had gotten to know Ted Turner perhaps better than anyone ever has. Yet even he was awed by the final gush of ego Turner produced.

"His major concern at the start of the second race against *Australia,*" Jobson says, "was the diminished size of the spectator fleet. He kept wondering where they all were and bemoaning his inability to draw a crowd. After the last race, when we were coming into that amazing throng of people and boats, I turned to Turner and told him, 'Here's your crowd, man, here's your crowd.'

"I was getting some publicity toward the end, and it caused Ted to play mind games. During that second race I told him to tack. He said no. I really knew we should tack, so I was pushing. We had those kinds of disagreements all along. It's normal. But that day he said either I could do it his way or he would get someone else who would. I told him to feel free, but in the meantime, we should tack.

"It got pretty heavy at the end, yet at the same time he was talking about me steering a 12-meter at some point, and how I had to get ready for that, and that he would nominate me for membership in the New York Yacht Club" (which Turner did: Jobson is now a member).

What really got to Jobson was Turner's insistence, in the aftermath, that the wind slants *Courageous* had worked to advantage all summer were nothing more than good luck. The fact that *Courageous* had been on the correct side of wind shifts with amazing consistency contributed greatly to her success—even the guys from Cleveland knew that. About halfway through the summer, the press began to give Jobson, as tactician, the credit he deserved.

No one, least of all Jobson, would dispute that varying degrees of luck are present in the winning of sailboat races. But as Jobson told the press when they asked, he had spent a lot of time sailing in tricky places like Barnegat Bay and the Hudson River, and he had become adept at understanding wind signs (ripples, slicks, the sailing angles of other boats, flags, smoke, and other indicators) and reading them with success. Now Turner was easing Lady Luck and the Good Lord in, and Jobson out.

A month after the Cup was history I was riding home from the office with Turner in Atlanta when I asked him why he thought he won the Cup. "Why did we win?" he mused, savoring the reminder. Then he sang it: "Why . . . did we win?" in low, resonant tones like an operatic baritone beginning a ballad. "I'll tell you why we won," he said. "Because one, I had the most experience sailing big boats. Two, I was the best organizer and leader. Three, I didn't make a lot of changes. I just concentrated on sailing. And Doyle made us great sails."

When I asked him about their uncanny ability to pick shifts, he laughed. "Seventy-five percent of the time whichever way we went was right," Turner said. "We tacked in headers and sailed in lifts, I don't know, someone in heaven, whoever controls the wind, must have said, 'I like Turner.' Maybe the god of the winds is an amateur, too. 'Our uncanny ability to pick shifts.' It wasn't uncanny. Wherever we were was right, especially when we were behind and *had* to tack for tactical reasons."

In Annapolis, Jobson was suffering a case of the post-partum blues with complications. The complications were starting a new job (sailing coach at the U.S. Naval Academy), moving into a brand new house in which a faulty installation had caused the clothes washer on the second floor to overflow, and sounds in the night of stealthy footsteps and creaking doors as a phantom thief named Turner tried to make off with his ego.

At midnight Jobson sat in the dark in front of a lone pressed-wood log flickering with chemical colorations in the fireplace, drinking one in a series of rum and Cokes. The lights were out to hide the godawful mess made when a washing machine on the second floor overflows. Half the sheet-rocked ceiling was down, revealing electric wiring and heat ducts. Soggy carpet was rolled aside. Gary's wife Janice had escaped the mess by falling asleep on the sofa.

"You know," Jobson said sleepily, "I give Ted a lot of credit for his ability to analyze situations. He told everybody what they had to do to win. He told Hood he had to have Doyle on board, that he had to reduce the fullness of *Independence*'s bow, and practice in the ocean, not the bay, with a settled crew. He told North his chances would be better if he sold him sails so they could talk over the faults they showed. And he told Noel Robins that without a locking trim tab on the keel *Australia* wouldn't be able to maneuver with us. And he was right in each case.

"But this thing about wind shifts. . . . I can't believe it." Jobson fixed two more drinks.

"Several times here was the situation. I would say tack. Ted: 'No.' Tack! 'No.' Tack, God damn it! Okay, we would tack, and suddenly our lead would be doubled. How can he say it was luck?!"

At three in the morning, several rum and Cokes later, we were taking some air, walking around the complex of condominium row houses in the crisp fall evening. We had rehashed a lot of the summer, but Gary kept coming back to Turner's audacity, his outrageous, blatant attempt at theft. Jobson had played by the rules. He had hung up his guns, and perhaps he mistakenly figured that for him, just one or two holds might be barred, maybe in the interest of closeness, or even good fellowship, or brotherhood, or whatever it is that makes even a dedicated outlaw decide not to squeeze the trigger. "Hey," Gary said, stopping to climb a few rungs on a neighborhood jungle gym, "tell me something: did the summer happen? Was I there? Did I do anything?"

Then Let's Keep Dancing

IN SEPTEMBER, TURNER STOPPED in New York and went a few rounds with Dick Cavett. Turner and Cavett make an unlikely pair, and Turner's opening moves did nothing to nourish compatibility. When Turner arrived at the studio, Cavett was taping another show. So Turner cruised around looking things over, puffing on his cigar, tapping ashes here and there, striking poses, and remarking to Cavett's production people that Dick sure had come down a peg to be working in this kind of set-up. Preoccupied though he was, Cavett got the vibes.

When Turner went on, Cavett made an unfortunate thrust right off the bat, introducing Turner by his most despised nickname, "Mouth of the South." Then he took the stance of a prosecuting attorney, setting up a direction for the show based on hastily researched sensationalism. Turner responded as a surly witness. For his first question, Cavett asked Turner if he was a millionaire. Turner bobbed and weaved. Dead end. Cavett said Turner seemed well behaved. Turner shrugged.

Baseball was next. Turner said he approved of the game as a nonviolent sport. Cavett said he had seen batters rushing the mound to punch pitchers. Cavett said he once saw a woman killed by a foul ball in Wrigley Field. Turner shrugged. Dead end.

Cavett asked how Turner had gotten on with the Newport establishment, hinting it had been stormy. Turner flared. "Have you talked to anyone in the Newport establishment about me?"

"What?" Cavett said, being distracted, playing to his camera. "I was killing a fly. Ah, weren't you canned from the Black Pearl? Let's not leave viewers with a false impression. You are a colorful, boisterous, sometimes inebriated playboy type. Maybe it's an act, or it's created by the press, but that is your image. You wouldn't deny that, would you?"

"I have heard you are a little twinkle-toed TV announcer. Would you deny that?"

Commercial.

The trial continued. Cavett wanted to know why Turner was suspended from baseball.

"For a remark I made at a cocktail party."

"So you *do* make cocktail party remarks."

"Don't you?"

"You're so sensitive!"

"I *am*!"

Cavett asked if Turner had fired a certain Braves employee when Turner bought the team.

"Yes."

"Wasn't he a midget?"

"Yes. He's the only midget I've fired in my 20 years in business."

"Didn't you have a good line about that?"

"I said I set him on a desk so I could look him in the eye. But it wasn't my line. If so, I'd have your job and you'd have mine."

Cavett in close-up to camera: "Yes, but you have a long way to go."

The show was never aired.

Back home in Atlanta, Turner kept on flailing. His office, in the weeks following the America's Cup, should have been designated a hard-hat area.

The management of his empire hadn't been a full-time priority item for many months, and the overflowing desk, the constant phone calls from as many well-wishers as businessmen, the numerous, ongoing negotiations and confrontations over player acquisitions, trades, and salaries, the hassles with various league offices, the decisions over television schedules, all the plots and intrigues, coupled with the inevitable boss's prerogative to think that the business has gone to hell while he was away, were causing Turner to pull at his hair. He had traded a whole waterfront full of cheering fans for an office full of old faces and old problems, and it was enough to make a man very nasty.

Even for a fellow who owns two TV stations, two professional sports teams, a cable-satellite business, two radio stations, an outdoor billboard company, and a small fleet of racing boats, winning the America's Cup was an undeniably momentous peak. The comprehensiveness of the project, the toll it exacts mentally and physically, and in time, effort, and money, had to produce a let-down even for Ted Turner. Dedicated as he might be to the plateau theory, on Monday morning as he looked to jump, the tops of the neighboring plateaus were all puzzlingly below the level on which he was poised.

As Terry McGuirk said, "It was one of those times you shut your office door and hoped like hell he wouldn't call."

At a morning meeting of key people, Turner responded to a carefully conceived and well-researched idea for a new venture with an emotional display that in children is called a tantrum.

He screamed and banged his fist on the table. He harangued, derogated, disparaged, threatened, defamed, and intimidated his top managers and advisors. His frenzied behavior caused some concern among them. "We should have known," one of those present said. "The idea wasn't revolutionary enough. Ted doesn't want modestly profitable deals. He wants fliers. . . ."

In his office, Turner growled at a visitor for crunching a piece of hard candy. He took phone calls on a loudspeaker unit while he did paperwork and made notes. One caller, a Hawks official who drawled on about a problem, was rudely shut off in mid-sentence. Another, an old friend from Savannah who apologetically said he was probably the last to call to congratulate Ted on winning the Cup, was told, "I certainly hope so." When Turner discovered the dates for the SORC hadn't been added to his desk calendar, he berated his secretary, dwelling on her general lack of intelligence and efficiency to an embarrassing degree.

He stimulated the firing of Hawks general manager Mike Storen. Then long-suffering Braves manager Dave Bristol was fired by the Braves board of directors. Bristol packed his bags and left in relative peace. Storen, a more volatile fellow ("He's a radio like Turner," a Hawks official says. "They were like two radios trying to talk with each other."), left with volleys and flourishes, making a surprise appearance at the press conference called to announce his firing, telling the press he had been treated unfairly. He said Turner kept changing his mind on player deals he had approved. Storen then went to court with allegations of contract violation.

When Turner bought a piece of Atlanta's stumbling basketball team, the Hawks, in January, 1977 (he paid $500,000 cash and picked up a million-dollar note), he played it low-key. He told a corps of sportswriters used to hearing big promises, "All I can guarantee is the team will play here one more year. Better to have a bad team than no team at all."

After the altercation with Storen, a sportswriter shook his

head and told Turner that in five years of covering the Hawks it had been an unending series of crises. Turner told him there has only been one newspaper job more depressing than his: "The French correspondents who retreated from Moscow with Napoleon's army. They left with 200,000 of the finest, bravest, handsomest young men in France. Less than 10,000 crossed the Polish border six weeks later. Ninety-five percent were killed or captured. Can you imagine the Paris papers every morning? Six weeks of horror: 30,000 men froze to death last night; four thousand cut to ribbons by Russian cavalry. I told him it would be harder to get the Hawks turned around than to get Hitler elected premier of Israel." Turner was laughing.

He has often cheered up the Braves sportswriters as well. "There's too much emphasis on winning," he has told them, after somehow convincing himself at least for the moment he believes that. "Either the team wins or it's a disaster. It's not a disaster if we don't win. It's a game. The song says, 'if they don't win it's a shame.' It's a shame, not a disaster."

Maybe Turner does believe that. Or like a man vowing his next drink will be his last, his intentions are good. But while he is adept at soothing the savage beasts, inside he is consumed.

His employees have been wonderfully forgiving. The consensus is that Turner just wasn't used to the anticlimax, that his ire was understandable. It would take him a while to become re-acclimated to the battle. Until then, keep a low profile. Given the solidarity of his work force, such forgiveness is predictable. In 1977 one of the seven account executives at WTCG quit to go elsewhere; his was the first sales job to turn over in six years.

A man who does business with WTCG is annoyed by the way Turner handles his people. He tells a story of the memo Turner sent all Braves personnel commenting on their bad attitude and giving them notice that he would be watching them closely for a week. A staff meeting was scheduled for the end of the week, with promises that heads might roll. Turner called the meeting a day early, appearing before the assembled throng with a baseball bat in hand. He waited for silence, then recited "The Star Spangled Banner" in its entirety. His lecture began: as long as the flag continued to fly over Fulton County Stadium, everything would be all right. He pounded the end of the bat on the table and dismissed the group.

After spending a few days with Turner in Atlanta, Gary Jobson wondered how he kept it all running, especially with his off-the-wall approach to business. "I don't think *he* knows. When I was there one of his top guys came in to present an idea he had obviously worked on a long time. Turner never looked up at him. He asked him what he wanted to talk about and kept working. The guy said his piece, Turner grunted a few times, interrupted him once or twice to take calls or say something to his secretary, then told the guy no. The guy just shrugged, packed his stuff, and left the office."

The table of organization Turner uses funnels all important decisions to him. There is no second or third in command. Twelve different people all report directly to Turner, a system which can provide excitement. If it hadn't been for someone in the company who had nothing official to do with the Hawks checking into a scheduling problem, the team would have had one game scheduled with no place to play it.

"To be successful working for Ted you have to be 50 percent psychologist," one of the twelve says. "You really have to be able to gauge his mood before you talk with him. You have to know the signals or you won't get anywhere." The psychological know-how must include the broaching of ideas, a delicate business over which definite jealousy emanates from the top.

Some of Turner's people are not so tolerant of their boss. "He's hard to live with sometimes," one employee says. "He runs people down, calls them stupid, or talks about them in a derogatory manner. Sometimes he lacks appreciation for people who are here day after day making it possible for him to go sailing."

Chances are his employees would be a lot *less* tolerant if Turner spent a normal amount of time at his desk. Absence, in this case, may make the heart grow fonder and, as financial vice president Will Sanders says, the company more stable. "He stirs up so much turmoil that if he didn't stay away for extended periods the whole place might collapse. During the Cup summer, for instance, he spent only ten days here. That was fine. I told him once when he was worrying about money that if he would agree to take a one-year world cruise, he would be a rich man when he returned. He is swinging away all the time. He does business wherever he meets people. He'll meet a guy on an airplane. Then he'll call: how come we don't do this or that? Once in a while the dust has to settle. Occasionally you need smooth water to tidy up the ship."

As Turner's interests come and go, so do people connected with those interests. His sailing crews are excepted from this cycle. So is Jane Turner. Otherwise, people as such don't have much of a place in Turner's scene. Turner's interaction with people, even those who might be considered "old friends," is sporadic, and often based on what they can contribute to whatever master plan is afoot. Or on how doggedly available they have been to him within the terms of an extreme double standard. Those folks might get an occasional bone. As for the rest, Turner frankly prefers the company of strangers, as one might suspect of a hard-charging plateau jumper who is busy pickin' 'em over.

Turner's old friend Peter Dames understands this, but it doesn't bother him. The billboard operation has been playing second fiddle since the TV stations came along. A mighty important second fiddle. Without the billboard company's cash flow, the initial TV losses could never have been sustained. But second fiddle, nonetheless. To Turner, the billboard company is old hat, and not at all glamorous, which pleases Dames just fine. It means he sees Turner once or twice a year on business. The rest of the time he has a piece of the action and runs the company as if it were his own, which in turn pleases Turner.

The Turners and I had met Dames and his children at Little League football games, an important, well-attended Saturday morning ritual in the Southeast. Both Turner and Dames had sons in the conflict.

This particular Saturday was Turner's thirty-ninth birthday. In the morning before football, Turner had to drive 20 minutes from his home to a small pond where a duo from *People* Magazine had been laboring to assemble a Minifish sailboat that was now tied to a rickety dock. Turner eyed the set-up with annoyance, announcing they had eight minutes to perpetrate their photographic crimes before he had to leave to watch his son play football. But he dutifully put on a Braves cap and crouched in the tiny boat. He took the basketball, baseball, and bat he was handed and tried unsuccessfully not to look too foolish while being photographed. The lady reporter crouched on the dock in her jodhpur boots and asked wooden questions, while in the middle of the pond a waddle of ducks quacked without restraint. But what the hell. *People* was billing him as one of the 25 most interesting people of the year. And as the 98-pound, leather-faced old lady who led a well-known all-cowgirl college drill team out in west Texas used to shout through her loud hailer on 100-degree days when her high-kicking lovelies were dropping like flies, "Remember girls, beauty knows no pain."

At the football game, Ted prowled the sidelines, chatting with the other dads while not totally sharing their gung-ho attitudes. When his son, a guard, jumped offside twice in one series of downs, he waxed philosophical. When his son's team lost, and to a man came off the field in tears, he registered healthy amusement aside, and did a good job comforting Saturday's non-hero. He chatted with neighbors, then stopped at the refreshment stand run by mothers and sisters of players for a sausage patty sandwiched in a fresh biscuit. Jane took the kids home. Ted left for an appointment in the afternoon.

Dames and I climbed into his silver 1962 Mercedes 190-SL convertible, put the top down, and drove off to have a few beers at a Saturday afternoon singles madhouse called "Friday's."

Friday's is a sub-cultural phenomenon in a city where the singles vote is almost as important as the black vote. On this balmy fall afternoon, upwards of 400 people—most of them under 30—were jammed three-deep at a hundred feet of U-shaped bar and waiting in clusters for tables. Ten bartenders were full out. The booze was flowing like water, trying its best to keep up with the lines and hustles being exchanged among the customers. One might have thought bad weather had driven the fun-loving multitudes inside. But the make, not the weather, was the priority for these nattily attired hopefuls, and Friday's was the arena. "If you can't pick up a girl in here," Dames said, "then you can't pick up a girl."

Dames spotted two he knew at the bar. We shouldered our way into the front lines and ordered drinks. Turner's name was mentioned.

"Have I met him!" exclaimed the blonde, who worked for an Atlanta advertising agency, rolling her eyes and laughing. "Listen—the first time I ever met him was at this business cocktail party. He grabbed my tits." She obviously hadn't been insulted by the experience.

Dames told a story about the aftermath of a lavish company party. Late one evening Turner and one of his executives had poured themselves into the motel elevator and leaned against the back wall for support. Two couples got into the car with them, and faced forward as people do in elevators. "The next thing the guy with him knew," Dames recounted, "Ted had run his hand up the back of one woman's legs and was patting her ass. He figured that's it, we're finished. But the woman never so much as flinched. If I had done that, it would have been jail, or at least a punch in the mouth."

It was difficult to imagine that the Ted Turner I had seen at home the previous evening could be such a raffish fellow. Enjoying a relatively rare evening *en famille,* Turner was the veritable picture of a middle-class family man. Jane cooked dinner, which we ate in the TV den, a small, cozy room with a floor-to-ceiling wall of sailing trophies. Then the three youngest children joined us to watch *The World at War,* a 24-part series Turner purchased for Channel 17. Turner sat on the big leather couch with a child tucked under each arm, sharing their leftover Halloween candy and joking about how the advertisements for an Atlanta Dodge dealer were reaching prospective buyers in Anchorage, Alaska.

Saturday night, the Atlanta Hawks were playing the New York Nets, so Turner and I met at the Omni at 5:30. He wanted to see Mike Gearon, his new general manager. Gearon wasn't in, so we played backgammon in his office.

Skip Caray, who announces Hawks games, poked his head in to see Gearon. Turner told him he didn't want to be critical, but he thought Caray had been rough on the Hawks during the previous broadcast.

Caray: "If you're saying it was a horseshit broadcast, then I agree with you. I was really off. I had a bad night. You're right." Caray shrugged.

"I also thought you could be a little friendlier about reading the movie spots," Turner said.

"Hey," Caray said, smiling, "you should see what I have to read. You want to see it? It's pretty hard to get excited about a Dirk Bogarde film festival." Turner laughed. During the conversation with Caray, he had continued to roll the dice and make his moves on the board.

When Gearon came in, the game continued. Gearon is a tall,

handsome man in his late forties who did well in the real estate development business. In his soft turtlenecks, tweed jackets, and gold-rimmed Ray Bans, he could be mistaken for one of several actors.

Gearon went from avid fan to general manager quickly and reluctantly. He and Turner knew each other as businessmen, and Turner saw Gearon at every home game only a few seats removed from his own front row place on the floor. When Mike Storen's tenure was terminating in the fall of 1977, Turner called Gearon and asked him to join the Hawks board of directors. Gearon declined, having recently extracted himself from the daily business grind. Turner pressed him. Gearon said no thanks. Turner asked Gearon if the Hawks were really in a bind would he do it. Gearon the fan said he guessed he would. Turner told him the Hawks were really in a bind.

"Those first two weeks," Gearon recalls, "were a nightmare."

Turner rolled double sixes and took a moment to gloat over the backgammon board while talking to Gearon about a player the Hawks were dealing for. Reports indicated the player had been a troublemaker. Turner winced. Gearon said the source of the trouble was the player's advocacy of black power. Turner looked relieved. "If that's the problem, then there *is* no problem," Turner said.

"I'm going to apply to the Ford Foundation for a grant," Turner said later. "Because if there was ever a worthy cause, we are it. We're bringing blacks and whites together by the best possible means: by the example of brotherhood on our teams.

"In the next generation we have to set the standards for integration. Carter, and our mayor, Maynard Jackson, have been great at that. There's a lot of good things that have happened, and I just want to be a part of it.

"It's going to take another generation, but it's happening. People in leadership positions, like the President and myself, have to bend over backwards to set a good example. People do things because they see the people they respect doing them, not because of the law. There is legal, then physical integration—then philosophical integration, and that's the real thing.

"I'm cool, I really am. I've gone from giving the thing lip service to having black friends. That will probably keep me out of a few clubs. Look at Bill Lucas. He and I talk black together. Lucas is the only black general manager in baseball. He was named one of the top 100 blacks by *Ebony* Magazine.

"And I was named the Urban League's Employer of the Year!"

Gearon says the main thing Turner did for the Hawks was to improve communications. "Under the old system," Gearon says, "nobody talked to anybody. Then Ted gave player selection back to the coach, Hubie Brown. Hubie decides who he wants, we set economic parameters, then I get on the phone. Ted wants to know what's going on at all times.

"He handled the press pretty well, too. Ted is the only guy I know who could go over to the *Atlanta Constitution* and rave at them for an hour and a half and not get burned out of town."

Will Sanders, his wife, and Jane met us for dinner at the Omni. The Turner kids were in town for the game. Jinny, the youngest, eight years old, precocious, and gorgeous, gingerly approached our table and interrupted Ted and Will. Ted was short with her. She hung in, handed him a small birthday package. Ted retreated.

"For me?" Jinny nodded. He opened it just enough to peek inside. "Cheese?" She nodded. "Thank you, honey, that's real nice." She handed him a larger package. "Would these be the crackers?" She nodded. "Yep." He didn't open them. "Great Jinny, now how about if you take these and run down and put them in the car for me, okay? Great." Turner quickly resumed his conversation with Will.

Before the game started Ted went to meet Oscar Robinson,

one of the all-time great NBA stars. "He wanted to talk about sailing," Ted reported when he joined us at courtside. Bob Hope, who was doubling his public relations duties to include the Hawks, came by to report attendance in excess of 6000. Turner was pleased. "It took 26 home games last year to reach the attendance we hit this year in seven. But that don't mean we're getting rich." The Hawks had in fact gotten off to a surprising start, winning seven of their first twelve. They were getting great play from the league's smallest man, Charlie Criss. Turner was worried Criss would bang up his head on opponents' knees, but meanwhile he was providing great floor leadership.

Tom MacMillen had also been traded to the Hawks. He would be suited up for the first time tonight. Turner was exclaiming over MacMillen, and a few fans behind him got into the conversation. "Yeah, he's a quarter-million-dollar-a-year man," Turner said. "We pay half, and the Knicks, because they got more money than we do, they pay the other half. We need a Federal subsidy for some of these guys." The fans were enjoying the show, and so was Turner.

At half time he was presented an appalling beige cake in the shape of half a basketball. Frosting hands with almond fingernails clutched at it. The applause from the crowd was heartfelt.

The 1978 Hawks, much to everyone's surprise, made the playoffs with a .500 record. They lost to the Washington Bullets in the opening round (the Bullets went on to defeat the powerful Philadelphia 76ers and the Seattle Supersonics and win the title), but the accomplishment was sufficient for Hubie Brown to be voted NBA Coach of the Year. The difficult odds Brown struggled against included Turner's decision to cut the payroll sharply, making it the smallest in the NBA, thus limiting the talent Brown could obtain.

Turner is learning about professional sports. He is getting smarter. As Dave Bristol suggested, Turner is paying players a lot of money after they produce, not before. One of Turner's complaints about Bristol was that the ol' boy from North Carolina was old-fashioned, not able to handle today's high-powered athletes. But Bristol had some points. When Andy Messersmith, Gary Matthews, and Willie Montanez elected to miss the team outing in Newport, Turner was hurt that three of his big guns, three of his hard-won players had given him the bird. "He learned you don't buy loyalty," a Braves official said. "It hurt him, but it was great for the future."

And in January, when the all-star game was played at the Omni, as promised, basketball commissioner Larry O'Brien roasted Turner with a hoax telegram from Bowie Kuhn that he read aloud at a pre-game dinner. "You neglected to invite me. . . . My fond hope is that one day you'll devote your entire energies to basketball." Turner just smiled.

One afternoon in Atlanta I was walking through the parking lot at WTCG-TV in the shadow of the 1093-foot transmitting tower—one of the highest free-standing towers in the country—when I passed a magnificent-looking fellow leaving the building. He was at least 6′ 5″, and must have carried 275 pounds of muscle on his huge frame. He wore cowboy boots and a western-cut blue suit. His white shirt was open three buttons, revealing gold chains sparkling against his hairy chest. His hair was platinum against a rugged, tanned face, and brushed straight back in styled waves. He could have been a TV evangelist, a country-and-western singer, a pro football player.

"He's one of my star wrestlers," Turner said when I got to his office. "He wants to be a bigger star. He's doing it, too. He wrestled the other night in Madison Square Garden and people were paying the scalpers 100 dollars a ticket to see him.

"He made 200,000 dollars last year. He works hard. Those guys wrestle 230 nights a year. I've got to keep that in mind when my ballplayers start telling me it's rough playing 162 games.

"His name is Dusty Rhodes, calls himself 'The American Dream.' I said, 'Rhodes, I am the American Dream.' He said 'no, *I* am.' I said 'no, *I* am.' " Turner laughed with delight.

The scope of the old dream is revealed in such a debate. The infinite faces of the American Dream have made it a myth powerful enough to sustain these many years, to be endlessly redefined according to our devious rationales, to be molded like putty in the hands of sly copywriters, to raise collective havoc with our frail sensibilities.

Ed Turner pursued it and found emptiness. Then Ted picked up the ball and ran, having been born and conditioned to the tradition. He has run with abandon, with a recklessness and hell-bent daring that has cowed the competition. He has accomplished what his father could not. As the Cup defense came to a close, it was Turner's devout hope that he would make the covers of *Sports Illustrated, Time,* and *Newsweek.* He made *SI* and the corner flap of *Time*'s cover. He made *People*'s top 25. He was voted Yachtsman of the Year for an unprecedented third time. He was presented with the key to the city of Atlanta. And *Newsweek*'s Pete Axthelm told him he had never met anyone who was so good at so many things, a quote Turner repeated to everyone at least twice for two weeks, and which inspired him to compare himself to Franklin W. Dixon's Hardy boys.

"Did you ever read those books? That's my deal. Ted Turner Buys a Baseball Team. Ted Turner Wins the America's Cup. Ted Turner in Star Wars With His Satellite. Ted Turner Sails Across the Atlantic. . . ."

No one can argue that Ted Turner's life hasn't been at least superficially eventful. Yet one day in late August when it looked like the Cup was wrapped up and Turner was losing his concentration, getting itchy, he said with some real panic, "Hey, what are we gonna do next? Putting a ball team together and then winning the World Series won't be enough to keep me going. . . ."

And he took a minute to review the situation. "In college there was no reason that I should end up winning the America's Cup more than any of the other good sailors. But I went out and made it to the top. I went into the real world and went to work. I worked 18 hours a day. I moved with speed. I plotted, schemed, and planned, and did crazy things. . . . When you're little you have to do crazy things, you can't just copy the big guys. To succeed you have to be innovative.

"I really wonder whether or not too much emphasis is placed on success. I think it's overrated. The average person realizes that it's hardly worth making the effort to get to the top. They take it easy and have a good time, play softball. To get to the Olympics as a swimmer you have to swim eight hours a day for 15 years. Then what have you got? Prune skin from too many pools. You have no chance to date, to get to know people. It's crazy."

In the background, the old Peggy Lee song is playing: "Is That All There Is?" ("If that's all there is, my friend, then let's keep dancing. . . .")

Turner has already begun. Recently he concluded the purchase of a 5200-acre plantation in South Carolina. The price was around two million dollars. He digs the pictures out of his Gucci briefcase and shows them with enthusiasm: the tree-lined approach to the large, white plantation house, the numerous out-buildings, the fields and ponds. He speaks of buying a few horses, spending three or four days a week there, organizing his business so more responsibility is delegated, maintaining more of an overview and less day-to-day interest in details. His voice brightens as he talks. "The first time I was down there for a couple days I saw 40 or 50 wild turkeys, 60 deer, and at least that many alligators, some of them nine feet long! It's a great place." He imagines the good times. Hunting. Fishing. Sailing. Maybe he'll plant some rice. He jokes about releasing 500 naked women and hunting them down with his friends.

When Ted's mother heard about the purchase she developed a severe case of hives.

Peter Dames shook his head. "I can't imagine it. If you get into that kind of scene you have to play the role. You can't have Jimmy Brown hanging around in old stained pants. Ed Turner knew how to do it. He was a great host. The labels on his whiskey said 'Bottled Especially for R. E. Turner, Jr.' Ted is a lousy host. He just isn't bothered with entertaining people."

Some who know Ted can't imagine him slowing up enough to enjoy such a place. Those who know him better are chilled by the ill-fated footsteps he seems to be retracing, by what might be a compulsion to ride into the same box canyon that claimed his father. Jane feels he is past that crisis. "I used to worry," she says, "about him ending up like his father. But he's more stable now than when I first met him."

Meanwhile, Turner will keep dancing. The satellite business rolls on. Don Anderson predicted WTCG will be in two million cable homes by the end of 1978. And the station itself is gaining strength. WTCG now owns three mobile production units, which have been employed steadily by the three networks. In 1977, WTCG beefed up its sports schedule to include 77 Braves games, 26 Hawks games, 8 NBA games of the week, the NBA playoffs, 10 college basketball games plus play-offs, 26 Atlanta Flames hockey games, plus the Stanley Cup finals, 6 Atlanta Falcons pre-season football games, and 5 North American Soccer League games.

After losing 100 games in 1977, the announcement that 100 Braves games would be televised in 1978 had to be a vote of confidence for the team's new young manager Bobby Cox, formerly a Yankee coach. With the help of ham radio operators, publicist Bob Hope had planned a spectacular start for the new season by issuing alien spacecraft an invitation to make their first landings on earth in the stadium on opening night. The only immediate problem was Chief Nocahoma, who quit over a salary dispute, rejecting counter offers of an Indian princess and a color TV for his teepee in the process. (The chief later capitulated. He was on hand as the season opened.) While the Braves were thumping the Red Sox in exhibition, 5–3, Hope was still looking for someone to throw out the first ball. "Bert Lance participated in the first-ball ceremony last year," Hope said, "starting a bad year for both him and the Braves."

Turner's sailing schedule was as ambitious as ever. While there were no new plateaus immediately available, with competition getting tougher and the ocean always ready to provide a rigorous test, satisfaction in this area is almost always guaranteed. At least it is never dull. First there was another southern circuit (*Tenacious* was second in class, sixth overall), then Turner journeyed westward to defend his Congressional Cup crown. He finished poorly. Back east, he got a second in class in the Bermuda Race. And he was pondering another boat, something in the 48- to 55-foot range that he would race in the 1979 southern circuit in hopes of being selected to the three-boat United States team in the annual Admiral's Cup event sailed off Cowes, England.

To that end, Turner entertained three of the hottest designers in the world aboard *Tenacious* after one of the 1978 circuit races. "Doug Peterson, Bruce Farr, and Ron Holland all showed up at the same time to see Ted," Gary Jobson said. Jobson had recovered from the post-Cup blues, and was back in the cockpit with Turner. Jobson was feeling good. He had two book contracts lined up, he was up to his neck in lectures and sailing seminars, he had embarked on an Olympic effort in Finn dinghies, and he and Turner were working hand in glove.

"It was a great scene," Jobson said. "Turner had on white pants, with his shirt unbuttoned, his big cigar, and he was strolling around the boat with these guys trailing after him."

Tucked into position in Turner's mind right behind the 1979 Admiral's Cup was, of course, the next Cup defense in 1980. Negotiations to secure *Courageous* for himself were progressing nicely.

The folk-hero business was still cooking, to be sure. The very definition of folk hero tends to change as a culture evolves. But certain folk-hero criteria remain constant. Candidates must have made it big. They must be well-known, public people. And they must capture our imaginations, either by the way they have made it, or by their style. They must be one of the folk, either in fact or at heart. Because we must identify with them, and cheer them on.

As a wealthy media manipulator and spectacularly successful businessman whose reputation as a fast-living, hard-playing, boozing, womanizing son of a gun who loves kids, good sportsmanship, and the flag, and puts the work ethic on a pedestal, he certainly represents a lot of those things Americans hold most dear.

Whether Turner could pass the more rigorous, academic demands of the "hero" part of "folk hero" is debatable. But fortunately the folk hero is more of a street kid. Less is expected of him in the more lofty areas. Perhaps given the current state of the union, Turner is sufficient: honest enough, family man enough, popular enough, crusader enough, crazy enough, funny enough, folksy enough, and enough of a hero to be the one.

Turner's forthright claim to the role would help, as an advertisement for oneself often does. But the full title is yet to be bestowed.